PROJECT AIR FORCE

T0294852

Access Granted

Political Challenges to the U.S. Overseas Military Presence, 1945–2014

Stacie L. Pettyjohn, Jennifer Kavanagh

Prepared for the United States Air Force
Approved for public release; distribution unlimited

For more information on this publication, visit www.rand.org/t/RR1339

Library of Congress Cataloging-in-Publication Data is available for this publication.
ISBN: 978-0-8330-9459-9

Published by the RAND Corporation, Santa Monica, Calif.
© Copyright 2016 RAND Corporation
RAND® is a registered trademark.

Cover: U.S. Air Force photo by Osakabe Yasuo.

Limited Print and Electronic Distribution Rights

This document and trademark(s) contained herein are protected by law. This representation of RAND intellectual property is provided for noncommercial use only. Unauthorized posting of this publication online is prohibited. Permission is given to duplicate this document for personal use only, as long as it is unaltered and complete. Permission is required from RAND to reproduce, or reuse in another form, any of its research documents for commercial use. For information on reprint and linking permissions, please visit www.rand.org/pubs/permissions.

The RAND Corporation is a research organization that develops solutions to public policy challenges to help make communities throughout the world safer and more secure, healthier and more prosperous. RAND is nonprofit, nonpartisan, and committed to the public interest.

RAND's publications do not necessarily reflect the opinions of its research clients and sponsors.

Support RAND
Make a tax-deductible charitable contribution at
www.rand.org/giving/contribute

www.rand.org

Preface

American policymakers and defense analysts have long worried that host nations will restrict or rescind U.S. basing rights, thereby impeding the ability of the United States to execute military operations. A number of recent studies have claimed that access problems are growing increasingly severe and that the United States may not be able to sustain its global base network. In response to this apparent trend, the Department of Defense has made a concerted effort over the past decade to adapt its overseas military presence. Rather than rely almost entirely on large, fixed garrisons, it is now placing a much greater emphasis on the temporary or periodic use of facilities in partner nations. Yet it is unclear whether this change will make access more reliable.

The RAND Corporation has a long history of examining the U.S. global defense posture—its network of forces and facilities overseas. A number of recent studies have focused on different aspects of the U.S. posture, including the following:

- Lynn E. Davis, Stacie L. Pettyjohn, Melanie W. Sisson, Stephen M. Worman, and Michael J. McNerney, *U.S. Overseas Military Presence: What Are the Strategic Choices?* MG-1211-AF, 2012.
- Stacie L. Pettyjohn, *U.S. Global Defense Posture, 1783–2011,* MG-1244-AF, 2012.
- Jennifer Moroney, Patrick Mills, David T. Orletsky, and David E. Thaler, *Working with Allies and Partners: A Cost-Based Analysis of U.S. Air Force Bases in Europe,* TR-1241-AF, 2012.

- Stacie Pettyjohn and Alan Vick, *The Posture Triangle: A New Framework for U.S. Air Force Global Presence,* Santa Monica, Calif.: RAND Corporation, RR-402-AF, 2013.
- Patrick Mills, Adam R. Grissom, Jennifer Kavanagh, Leila Mahnad, and Stephen M. Worman, *A Cost Analysis of the U.S. Air Force Overseas Posture: Informing Strategic Choices,* RR-150-AF, 2013.
- Lostumbo, Michael, Michael J. McNerney, Eric Peltz, Derek Eaton, David R. Frelinger, Victoria A. Greenfield, John Halliday, Patrick Mills, Bruce R. Nardulli, Stacie L. Pettyjohn, Jerry M. Sollinger, and Stephen M. Worman, *Overseas Basing of U.S. Military Forces: An Assessment of Relative Costs and Strategic Benefits,* RR-201-OSD, 2013
- Alan J. Vick, *Air Base Attacks and Defensive Counters: Historical Lessons and Future Challenges,* RR-968, 2015.

This report builds on RAND's earlier posture work by focusing on the issue of political access. It seeks to unpack the access issue and systematically explore the entire spectrum of political access problems that the United States has confronted since 1945. It offers a framework for understanding threats to access and then conducts qualitative and quantitative assessments in an effort to better understand the severity of access problems and how they have changed over time. This report should be relevant for policymakers who are responsible for building and sustaining relationships with host nations but should also be of interest to scholars who have studied the political effects of U.S. overseas bases and to analysts of U.S. foreign and defense policy.

This report integrates findings from a fiscal year (FY) 2011 RAND Project AIR FORCE study commissioned by the U.S. Air Force Vice Chief of Staff and an FY 2013 study commissioned by the U.S. Air Force Director of Operational Planning. The FY 2011 study results were originally published in Stacie Pettyjohn and Alan Vick, *The Posture Triangle: A New Framework for U.S. Air Force Global Presence,* RR-402-AF, 2013. This report was completed using concept formulation support from the Strategy and Doctrine Program within RAND Project AIR FORCE.

RAND Project AIR FORCE

RAND Project AIR FORCE (PAF), a division of the RAND Corporation, is the U.S. Air Force's federally funded research and development center for studies and analyses. PAF provides the Air Force with independent analyses of policy alternatives affecting the development, employment, combat readiness, and support of current and future air, space, and cyber forces. Research is conducted in four programs: Force Modernization and Employment; Manpower, Personnel, and Training; Resource Management; and Strategy and Doctrine. The research reported here was prepared under contract FA7014-06-C-0001.

Additional information about PAF is available on our website: http://www.rand.org/paf/

Contents

Figures

Tables

Summary

Does the United States face an "access problem"? According to many policymakers, academics, and analysts, the United States faces a variety of external and internal political challenges to its use of overseas military facilities. For instance, since the late 1990s, the U.S. Department of Defense has expressed concerns about anti-access strategies, which aim to impede the deployment of expeditionary forces by attacking the forward bases U.S. forces depend on to project power, among other potential targets. Potential opponents may also try to undermine the political foundations of U.S. access. By wielding military, diplomatic, and economic levers, an adversary could try to compel allies and partners to close U.S. bases or deny the United States permission to use them during a contingency, effectively neutralizing most of the U.S. military's capabilities without firing a shot. Importantly, though, coercive anti-access threats are only one part of the access problem. Local opposition often emerges organically within nations that permit U.S. forces on their soil, and at times, these internal access threats can force the host nation to restrict or rescind U.S. access.

This report aims to fill a gap in the existing literature on political access problems by carrying out a comprehensive and empirical analysis of the challenges the United States confronted between 1945 and 2014. In doing so, it seeks to answer the following questions: What access problems has the United States faced? How severe were they? How did these access problems change over time? And most important, how can the United States, in general, and the U.S. Air Force, in particular, counter these political threats to access? These questions remain vitally important to U.S. national security because the United States depends on access to overseas bases to project military power around the globe. It is therefore important that the United States distinguish between nations that it can rely on to host a peacetime presence and those that are likely to allow U.S. forces to operate from their territory for particular missions. This research employed both qualitative and quantitative methodologies to consider the separate but related problems of peacetime and contingency access risk.

Findings

Political challenges to access have occurred regularly, but the threat has often been overstated. Although there are very real and nontrivial internal and external threats to U.S. access overseas, there is a tendency to inflate the scope and magnitude of these challenges. This misconception about access problems is due in part to the lack of longitudinal data on this issue. Our research shows that peacetime access challenges have declined since their peak during the latter part of the Cold War. Furthermore, 90 percent of the formal U.S. requests for contingency access have been approved. Nevertheless, U.S. policymakers should not assume that access to foreign bases is ever assured. Changes in the international system—in particular, declining U.S. power, the absence of a unifying global threat, the strengthening norm of sovereignty, the increasing influence of public opinion, and the proliferation of information and communications technologies—are likely to make it more difficult for the United States to gain and maintain access to foreign bases during peacetime and for contingencies in the future. Furthermore, a high rate of success on formal access requests can be misleading: It does not take into account the times the United States may not bother to make a formal request, assuming the request will be denied.

The United States faces two distinct access problems, but some partners are likely to be more or less reliable during peacetime *and* contingencies. Peacetime and contingency access decisions are driven by fundamentally different dynamics. The former are rooted in broader and more stable (although not immutable) factors, such as a host nation's domestic political institutions and its access relationship with the United States; the latter are heavily influenced by context-specific factors. Consequently, the United States may have very secure peacetime access in a nation that denies U.S. forces contingency access because of the particular circumstances. Nevertheless, certain partners tend to be more or less reliable in peacetime and during contingencies. In particular, enduring partner nations—countries in which there is strong elite support for the relationship with the United States—are the least likely to evict or restrict U.S. peacetime basing rights and the most likely to allow U.S. forces to operate from their bases during a crisis. In contrast, transactional partners—nations motivated primarily by compensation—are the most likely to limit or rescind U.S. peacetime basing rights and the least likely to permit U.S. forces to use their bases during a contingency.

The presence of large permanent bases does *not* increase the likelihood of securing contingency access. In fact, unstable peacetime access can actually reduce the probability that the United States will ask for permission to use a facility during a crisis. Having a permanent military presence in a nation during peacetime does not guarantee or even increase the probability of being granted permission to use bases during a contingency.

Certain types of operations—especially limited punitive strikes and major combat operations—are associated with access problems. It should come as no surprise that it is easier to obtain access for noncontroversial military operations, such as humanitarian assistance and disaster relief, than for those that involve the use of force. What is somewhat surprising is the fact that limited strikes have encountered more access problems than major combat operations. Host nations have more often denied access for the former type of operation but only restricted access for the latter. This outcome seems to be driven by the fact that concerns about retaliation were often greater with limited strikes.

Contingency access permissions are dynamic and may change throughout the course of an operation. Because of the tendency for countries to revisit contingency access decisions, the United

States should not take a positive response for granted or assume that a negative or qualified response is absolute. Countries that provided U.S. forces with restricted access seem most liable to modify that position, although they can grant U.S. forces more latitude or can become more restrictive. Consequently, U.S. officials must endeavor to maintain and expand U.S. access permissions throughout the duration of an operation.

Access permission is more likely when the host nation has its own reasons for supporting a U.S. operation or when the mission can be credibly presented as legitimate. Nations often permit the United States to use their bases even if doing so is not directly in their interest. Access was more likely to be granted if a government could defend its decision to support a U.S. operation to domestic and international audiences, which largely depended on whether the operation was seen as legitimate. Legitimacy can stem from any number of sources, including responses to overt aggression, an explicit or implicit United Nations Security Council (UNSC) resolution authorizing the use of force, or endorsement by a regional international organization.

Access denial was more likely when there was domestic opposition to an operation or when the host nation feared that it would be subject to reprisals. In nearly all cases, these two factors have influenced states' decisions to refuse or restrict contingency access. While domestic opposition is fundamentally an internal threat to access, third parties can help generate or exacerbate both of these obstacles to access.

Recommendations:

Following from these findings, the United States should take the following actions:

Maintain access in enduring partner nations and, whenever possible, avoid transactional partners. The type of access relationship influences the reliability of both peacetime and contingency access, with enduring partners being the most and transactional partners the least dependable. Consequently, the United States should seek to retain bases in enduring partner nations that continue to be useful for future challenges and to minimize the number of bases it has in transactional partner nations. Since 2001, the United States has increasingly forged transactional basing agreements; if this practice expands, access problems are also likely to grow.

Be cognizant of host-nation sensitivities. Although this advice seems obvious, it bears repeating. U.S. officials and forces need to shed any lingering sense of entitlement and recognize that, whether their presence is temporary or permanent, they are visitors in another sovereign nation that has every right to place limits on their activities. Far too often, American officials react with shock and outrage when another country challenges U.S. basing rights or denies U.S. forces access for an operation. An attitude change is not likely to resolve access problems that emerge in high-risk countries (i.e., authoritarian or democratizing transactional partners) but can help to mitigate the irritants and issues that inevitably arise. Most importantly, deferring to the host nation's wishes and expecting it to have a say on U.S. military activities can help strengthen relationships with enduring and mutual defense partners, minimizing any internal threats to access that might emerge. It would also help to undercut the claims of third parties that seek to delegitimize the U.S. military presence overseas by claiming that it is imperialistic.

Be aware of a potential host nation's red lines and plan around them. The contingency access analyses reveal that many nations traditionally have been willing to provide certain types of access but not others. U.S. military planners should be aware of past access decisions and carefully consider this context before requesting access. U.S. officials thinking about asking for something unprecedented should reflect on a nation's interests and constraints to determine whether approval is likely.

If an operation is not in response to overt aggression, the United States should try to enhance perceptions of its legitimacy by securing the explicit or implicit support of international organizations. The United States can improve the likelihood of securing and maintaining contingency access by getting international buy-in in the form of an explicit or implicit UNSC mandate or the authorization of a regional international organization. Working through institutions can improve the probability of securing access by enhancing the legitimacy of an operation and by reassuring host nations that the United States will consult with them and act with restraint.

To reduce the susceptibility of host nations to domestic critics and third-party bullying, ensure that these nations are not isolated. In general, the case studies show that nations prefer to avoid being the only country providing access to U.S. forces. Granting such access can be the focal point for condemnation at home and abroad and, potentially, make the nation a target for retaliation. Therefore, in general, nations seem more comfortable providing access to U.S. forces if there is a formal or informal coalition supporting the operation. The former, particularly with endorsement from the UNSC or a regional international organization, typically offers more legitimacy than the latter.

To improve political resiliency, the United States should seek access to multiple countries for any given scenario. In the end, contingency access is very idiosyncratic and remains difficult to predict. Consequently, it is prudent for the United States to hedge against access denials by asking multiple nations that have bases that could be used to support the same operation for access. This reduces the leverage that any one state has in this situation and improves the probability that at least one country will respond positively.

Final Thoughts

Incidents such as Turkey's refusal to allow U.S. ground forces on its territory for the 2003 invasion of Iraq and Kyrgyzstan's decision to expel U.S. forces from Manas Air Base appear to have had an oversized influence on the thinking about access problems. Prominent recent examples have led observers to conclude that the U.S. overseas military presence is politically unsustainable. Yet it is important to put these events in a broader context. Peacetime access challenges have significantly declined since the end of the Cold War. Although access challenges continue to occur regularly, the United States has maintained a global network of overseas bases for more than 60 years, which is unprecedented in modern times. This network has steadily shrunk from its peak in the late 1950s, but downsizing decisions have often been voluntary. Moreover, many countries welcome the presence of U.S. forces because of the security that they offer or because they boost the local economy. Equally important, when the United States has formally asked for access to foreign territory for a particular operation, access has been fully granted an astonishing 90 percent of the time. Like peacetime access challenges, contingency access denials and restrictions have become less common since the end of the Cold War.

In sum, history demonstrates that these threats to access have been overstated. Between 1945 and 2014, both peacetime and contingency access problems have been persistent but largely manageable. This conclusion should not create complacency, because access to foreign bases can never be assured.

Moreover, a number of trends suggest that access could become a larger problem in the future. The impressive U.S. track record to date is largely due to the Cold War, American hegemony, and the herculean efforts of American policymakers to build and sustain relationships. Today, there is no longer any single, overriding, and unambiguous global threat akin to the Soviet Union during the Cold War, which makes securing access more difficult. Additionally, there is often a mismatch between the U.S. desire for flexible basing agreements that can be used for a variety of global operations and the desires of host nations, which are focused on specific and geographically discrete challenges. If American power continues to decline, obtaining and preserving access is likely to become even more challenging because the United States may be seen as a less capable and therefore less desirable security partner and because American policymakers will have fewer carrots to offer to incentivize cooperation. Finally, new information and communication technologies make it even more difficult for the United States and a supportive host government to conceal a U.S. military presence or contain antibase movements. All these factors suggest that access will remain a recurring and perhaps even a growing problem in the coming years.

While it is important not to exaggerate the risks to access, the United States must also be mindful that access is never guaranteed and that changes in the international system are likely to complicate efforts to secure and maintain access in the future. Therefore, U.S. policymakers must be aware of these risks and must also continue to endeavor to create a sustainable posture into the future.

Acknowledgments

The authors would like to thank the following RAND colleagues for their valuable feedback on this research: Dick Anderegg, Adam Grissom, Ted Harshberger, Jacob Heim, Andrew Hoehn, David Orletsky, Scott Savitz, and Stephen Worman. In particular, we are indebted to Alan Vick and Paula Thornhill for their guidance and support of this project. We also thank Evan Montgomery for his helpful comments on early drafts. The Air Force Historical Studies Office and the Pacific Air Forces Historian's Office provided invaluable assistance with the archival research. Additionally, we would like to thank Ambassador Lincoln Bloomfield, Lt Gen David Deptula (Ret.), Gen T. Michael Moseley (Ret.), and William Quandt for sharing their experiences with us. We benefited greatly from the comments and insights of the reviewers, Alexander Cooley and Stephen Larrabee. We are grateful to Erin York for the excellent research assistance she provided to this project and to Sunny Bhatt for formatting the draft. Finally, thanks to Phyllis Gilmore for her skillful edit of the manuscript.

CHAPTER ONE

Understanding Political Access Problems

Does the United States face an "access problem"? In recent years, there has been a growing focus on external and internal political threats to U.S. access to overseas military bases. On the one hand, for nearly two decades, the U.S. Department of Defense (DoD) has voiced concerns about growing anti-access threats.[1] Anti-access and area-denial strategies avoid symmetrically challenging U.S. forces in favor of asymmetric tactics that exploit U.S. vulnerabilities—particularly the U.S. military's dependence on overseas bases to project power. While there is considerable research on the military capabilities being fielded to hold U.S. forward bases and forces at risk, opponents may also try to undermine the political foundations of U.S. access.[2] By wielding mili-

[1] DoD, *Report of the Quadrennial Defense Review*, Washington, D.C., May 1997, Section 2; DoD, *Quadrennial Defense Review Report*, Washington, D.C., September 30, 2001, pp. 25, 31; DoD, *Quadrennial Defense Review Report*, Washington, D.C., February 6, 2006, pp. 30, 47; DoD, *Sustaining U.S. Global Leadership: Priorities for 21st Century Defense*, Washington, D.C., January 2012, pp. 4–5.

[2] John Stillion and David T. Orletsky, *Airbase Vulnerability to Conventional Cruise-Missile and Ballistic-Missile Attacks: Technology, Scenarios, and U.S. Air Force Responses*, Santa Monica, Calif.: RAND Corporation, MR-1028-AF, 1999; Roger Cliff, Mark Burles, Michael S. Chase, Derek Eaton, and Kevin L. Pollpeter, *Entering the Dragon's Lair: Chinese Antiaccess Strategies and Their Implications for the United States*, Santa Monica, Calif: RAND Corporation, MG-524-AF2007; Christopher Bowie, *The Anti-Access Threat and Theater Air Bases*, Washington, D.C.: Center for Strategic and Budgetary Assessments, 2002; Andrew Krepinevich, Barry Watts, and Robert Work, *Meeting the Anti-Access and Area Denial Challenge*, Washington, D.C.: Center for Strategic and Budgetary Assessments, 2003; Evan Braden Montgomery, "Contested Primacy in the Western Pacific: China's Rise and the Future of U.S. Power Projection," *International Security*, Vol. 38, No. 4, Spring 2014,

tary, diplomatic, and economic levers, an adversary could try to compel allies and partners to expel U.S. forces or deny them permission to use bases during a contingency, effectively neutralizing most of the U.S. military's capabilities without firing a shot.

On the other hand, coercive anti-access threats are only one part of a broader "access problem" that the United States faces. Local opposition to U.S. basing rights often emerges organically within nations that host U.S. forces and can, at times, force a country to restrict or rescind U.S. access.[3] This should not be surprising; the presence of foreign forces within another country is often controversial. Moreover, changes in the international system—in particular, the strengthening norm of sovereignty, the increasing influence of public opinion, and the diffusion of information and communications technologies—have made it even more difficult for the United States to station its forces in other countries.[4] Some have even gone so far as to characterize access denials as a form of "soft balancing"—the use of nonmilitary tools to "delay, frustrate, and undermine" the United States.[5] As a result of

---

pp. 115–149; Alan J. Vick, *Air Base Attacks and Defensive Counters: Historical Lessons and Future Challenges*, Santa Monica, Calif: RAND Corporation, RR-968-AF, 2015, pp. 19–37; Eric Heginbotham, Michael Nixon, Forrest E. Morgan, Jacob Heim, Jeff Hagen, Sheng Li, Jeffrey Engstrom, Martin C. Libicki, Paul DeLuca, David A. Shlapak, David R. Frelinger, Burgess Laird, Kyle Brady, and Lyle J. Morris, *The U.S.-China Military Scorecard: Forces, Geography, and the Evolving Balance of Power, 1996–2017*, Santa Monica, Calif.: RAND Corporation, RR-392-AF, 2015.

[3] Alexander Cooley, *Base Politics: Democratic Change and the U.S. Military Overseas*, Ithaca, N.Y.: Cornell University Press, 2008; Alexander Cooley and Hendrik Spruyt, *Contracting States: Sovereign Transfers in International Relations*, Princeton, N.J.: Princeton University Press, 2009; Andrew Yeo, *Activists, Alliances, and Anti-U.S. Base Protests*, Cambridge, UK: Cambridge University Press, 2011; Kent E. Calder, *Embattled Garrisons: Comparative Base Politics and American Globalism*, Princeton, N.J.: Princeton University Press, 2007; Stacie L. Pettyjohn and Alan J. Vick, *The Posture Triangle: A New Framework for U.S. Air Force Presence*, Santa Monica, Calif.: RAND Corporation, RR-402-AF, 2013, Chapter Four.

[4] Alexander Cooley and Daniel Nexon, "'The Empire Will Compensate You': The Structural Dynamics of the U.S. Overseas Basing Network," *Perspectives on Politics*, Vol. 11, No. 4, December 2013, pp. 1040–1042; Pettyjohn and Vick, 2013, pp. 38–43.

[5] Robert A. Pape, "Soft Balancing Against the United States," *International Security*, Vol. 30, No. 1, Summer 2005, pp. 10, 36; Stephen M. Walt, *Taming American Power: The Global Response to U.S. Primacy*, New York: W.W. Norton and Company, 2005, pp. 126–131.

these growing internal political challenges, U.S. overseas bases have been characterized as "embattled garrisons."[6]

Access can mean many different things, but for our purposes, we define it as the permission to use another country's territory or airspace for military operations. Before World War II, the United States had a limited military presence abroad, and most of its overseas bases were located on U.S. territories or dependencies in the Philippines, Panama, Hawaii, Guam, Wake Island, Puerto Rico, and American Samoa.[7] Given the imperial character and limited size of the U.S. overseas military presence, access was not an issue. This dramatically changed with the outbreak of the World War II in Europe as the United States began to seek rights to air bases within the Western Hemisphere to defend against a possible Nazi invasion. Later, as U.S. military officials planned for the postwar era, they concluded that the United States needed a large network of air and naval bases to head off future threats far from the U.S. homeland. Consequently, access to foreign military bases became a critical and enduring concern for DoD.[8]

In a departure from prewar U.S. practices, most postwar U.S. basing rights were obtained through voluntary arrangements with other nations.[9] While these agreements varied significantly in form, substance, and scope, they all codified fundamentally the same bargain: The host nation circumscribed its authority by allowing U.S. forces to be stationed on its soil in return for security or compensation. Initially, these accords overwhelmingly favored the United States.

[6] Calder, 2007.

[7] Stacie L. Pettyjohn, *U.S. Global Defense Posture 1783–2011,* Santa Monica, Calif.: RAND Corporation, MG-1244-AF, 2012, pp. 28–33.

[8] Melvyn P. Leffler, "The American Conception of National Security and the Beginnings of the Cold War, 1945–48," *American Historical Review,* Vol. 89, No. 2, April 1984, pp. 350–353; Melvyn P. Leffler, *A Preponderance of Power: National Security, the Truman Administration, and the Cold War,* Palo Alto, Calif.: Stanford University Press, 1993, pp. 56–63; Pettyjohn, 2012, Chapters Eight–Ten.

[9] Exceptions include Okinawa prior to 1972; the Panama Canal Zone; Guantanamo Bay, Cuba; and occupations in the aftermath of wars (Christopher Sandars, *America's Overseas Garrisons; The Leasehold Empire,* Oxford: Oxford University Press, 2000, pp. 126–138, 161–166).

Because host nations ultimately retained their sovereignty, however, they had the right to renegotiate the terms of the agreement, which they quickly exercised to tilt the balance back in their favor.[10] Some nations went even further and demanded that the United States remove its forces and bases from their territories. Because of host-nation opposition, budgetary pressures, and advances in technology, the U.S. overseas military presence has steadily contracted since its apex in the late 1950s.[11] Nevertheless, the United States still maintains a global network of permanent overseas garrisons, as well as "warm" bases and partner-nation facilities that it has the right to use occasionally.[12]

In general, the United States needs access to foreign soil for three reasons: to maintain ties with close allies and critical regions; to generate and sustain operational effects; and to support global military activities.[13] We refer to these types of locations as *strategic anchors, forward operating locations*, and *support links*. First, *strategic anchors* are the permanent bases that tie the United States to key partners and vital regions and that simplify the peacetime missions of deterrence, assurance, and regional stability. Second, because of the limited range and endurance of many U.S. military platforms, *forward operating locations* are typically needed to carry out military operations effectively far from the continental United States, but these installations are often more austere and temporary than strategic anchors. Finally DoD needs *support links*—which include communications facilities, satellite ground stations, and en route infrastructure—to have global reach. In

---

[10] Cooley and Spruyt, 2009, p. 101.

[11] James R. Blaker, *The United States Overseas Basing: An Anatomy of the Dilemma*, New York: Praeger, 1990, pp. 30–37. For the number of major USAF air bases overseas over time, see Pettyjohn and Vick, 2013, p. 67.

[12] DoD refers to these three types of facilities as *main operating bases, forward operating sites,* and *cooperative security locations*. For a list of recent list of U.S. bases, see Michael Lostumbo, Michael J. McNerney, Eric Peltz, Derek Eaton, David R. Frelinger, Victoria A. Greenfield, John Halliday, Patrick Mills, Bruce R. Nardulli, Stacie L. Pettyjohn, Jerry M. Sollinger, and Stephen M. Worman., *Overseas Basing of U.S. Military Forces: An Assessment of Relative Costs and Strategic Benefits*, Santa Monica, Calif.: RAND Corporation, RR-201-OSD, 2013, pp. 20–35.

[13] Pettyjohn and Vick, 2013, pp. 11–16.

short, access to foreign territory is a critical enabler of U.S. global military hegemony.[14]

Existing studies on access challenges disproportionately focus on the U.S. Air Force (USAF) and argue that it is uniquely dependent on foreign bases and therefore is uniquely vulnerable to political access problems.[15] In contrast, the U.S. Navy (USN) has supposedly eliminated its need for "coaling stations" by relying on nuclear power and developing the means to resupply ships at sea. According to this view, political access problems underscore the need for sea power, especially aircraft carriers.[16] Yet USN ships are not as access-insensitive as their proponents contend. All the services rely—to varying degrees—on access to foreign territory to conduct sustained operations far from the United States. For example, the maritime surveillance aircraft that protect carrier strike groups from submarines operate from land bases. Moreover, USN ships and submarines armed with vertical launch missiles must return to a calm port to reload after expending their munitions.[17] Base access, therefore, is needed during protracted operations because many USN ships are payload constrained.[18] Ground forces, by definition, operate on the land and consequently require access to

---

[14] Barry Posen, "Command of the Commons: The Military Foundations of U.S. Hegemony," *International Security*, Vol. 28, No. 1, Summer 2003, pp. 16–17; Michael C. Desch, "Bases for the Future: Military Interests in the Post–Cold War Third World," *Security Studies*, Vol. 2, No. 2, Winter 1992, p. 202.

[15] Adam B. Siegel, *Basing and Other Constraints on Land-Based Aviation Contributions to U.S. Contingency Operations*, Arlington, Va.: Center for Naval Analyses, March 1995, p. 1; Owen R. Cote, Jr., *The Future of Naval Aviation*, Cambridge, Mass.: Massachusetts Institute of Technology, February 2006; Owen R. Cote, Jr., "Assuring Access and Projecting Power: The Navy in the New Security Environment," paper, Cambridge, Mass.: Massachusetts Institute of Technology, April 2001.

[16] Cote, 2006, pp. 18–19.

[17] Jan Van Tol, with Mark Gunzinger, Andrew Krepinevich, and Jim Thomas, *AirSea Battle: A Point-of-Departure Operational Concept*, Washington, D.C.: Center for Strategic and Budgetary Assessments, 2010, p. 78

[18] U.S. attack submarines typically carry the smallest payloads, around 12 missiles, while the modified *Ohio*–class guided-missile submarines (SSGNs) carry the largest payloads, up 154 Tomahawk missiles. Aegis cruisers have 122 vertical launching system (VLS) cells, while destroyers have 96 (Van Tol, 2010, p. 46).

foreign territory for overseas garrisons and forward operating bases. In short, access is an important issue for all the services, but the term is often used imprecisely, which hinders an understanding of the challenges the United States faces.

The existing literature conflates two separate issues: peacetime challenges to U.S. bases and problems securing permission to use another nation's bases or territory for a specific operation.[19] The former (peacetime access) involves the reliability of steady-state rights to foreign military facilities, while the latter (contingency access) involves obtaining the consent of another nation to operate from (or use the forces stationed on) its territory for a particular mission (see Table 1.1).[20] This is problematic because peacetime and contingency access are analytically and empirically distinct phenomena. To date, the bulk of the existing literature has focused on the former and neglected the latter. Moreover, the relationship between these two factors is not well understood. It is often assumed that peacetime and contingency access problems have the same root causes and that obtaining and maintaining peacetime access is necessary for securing access to bases during a contingency. But neither of these propositions has been examined systematically.

Even a cursory historical survey reveals that, although these two types of access can move in lockstep, they often do not (see Figure 1.1). For example, all U.S. North Atlantic Treaty Organization (NATO) allies—with the exception of Portugal—famously refused to allow the United States to use air bases in their countries to resupply Israel during the 1973 Yom Kippur War. In this incident, the United States had difficulty obtaining contingency access, but its peacetime basing

---

[19] Siegal, 1995; Bowie, 2002; David A. Shlapak, John Stillion, Olga Oliker, and Tanya Charlick-Paley, *A Global Access Strategy for the U.S. Air Force*, Santa Monica, Calif.: RAND Corporation, MR-1216-AF, 2002; Yeo, 2011; and Calder, 2007. Cooley, 2008, differentiates analytically between permanent bases and use rights, but his study overwhelming focuses on the former rather than the latter.

[20] Pettyjohn and Vick, 2013, p. 37. Peacetime access includes permanent U.S. garrisons, such as the ones in Germany and South Korea, but also covers facilities to which U.S. forces deploy only intermittently, such as those in Romania and Oman. Peacetime access overlaps with DoD's enduring locations, which consist of main operating bases, forward operating sites, and cooperative security locations.

Table 1.1
Two Types of Access

Type of Access	Definition	Example
Peacetime	Steady-state rights to use bases in another country's territory for routine operations	• Ramstein Air Base (1952–2014) • Yokosuka Naval Base (1945–2014) • Prince Sultan Air Base (1996–2003) • Thumrait Air Base Oman (1980–2014)
Contingency	Permission to use another country's territory, airspace, or U.S. forces stationed in its territory for a nonroutine mission	• Use of Ramstein Air Base to support Operation Enduring Freedom (2001–2014) • Restricted use of Prince Sultan Air Base for nonlethal operations during Operation Iraqi Freedom (2003) • Use of Thumrait Air Base for Operation Desert Fox (1998)

Figure 1.1
The Linkage Between Peacetime and Contingency Access

Peacetime access

	Yes	No
Contingency access — Yes	Germany and UK Operations Desert Storm and Iraqi Freedom	France and Hungary Operation Allied Force
Contingency access — No	Turkey Operation Iraqi Freedom	Austria and Switzerland Operation Blue Bat

RAND RR1339-1.1

rights in Europe remained secure.[21] Of course, host nations frequently do allow the United States to use their bases for specific operations.

[21] This incident contributed to a debate within NATO about using NATO bases and assets for out-of-area operations. See John Chipman, "Allies in the Mediterranean: Legacy of Fragmentation," in John Chipman, ed., *NATO's Southern Allies: Internal and External Challenges*, New York: Routledge, 1988, pp. 62–63; Geir Lundestad, *The United States and Western Europe Since 1945*, Oxford: Oxford University Press, 2003, pp. 142–167; Richard F. Grim-

USAF bombers have operated from bases in the United Kingdom (UK) during both the 1991 and 2003 wars against Iraq. Similarly, the United States deployed some of its forces based in Germany and used German air bases to support operations in both gulf wars.

Conversely, U.S. forces have also carried out specific operations from countries in which the United States had no peacetime basing rights. During NATO's air war over Kosovo, for instance, U.S. air forces used Hungarian and French airfields even though the United States did not have bases in either country.[22] At other times, however, nations in which the United States has no peacetime access may deny permission to use their airspace or territory for a contingency. Returning to the Kosovo example, the U.S. Army's Task Force Hawk ultimately deployed to Albania because Macedonia prohibited offensive operations from its territory. In this instance, the United States did not have a peacetime military presence in either Balkan nation.[23] Similarly, during the 1958 U.S. intervention in Lebanon, Austria and Switzerland refused to allow U.S. aircraft to fly through their airspace en route to the Levant. In short, the United States has to confront two connected but separate access problems. These issues must be considered individually to ascertain whether they have similar or different causes and to determine how the United States can mitigate these problems.

This report systematically explores the entire spectrum of political access problems United States confronted from 1945 to 2014 to address the following questions: What access problems has the United States faced? How severe have they been? How have access problems changed over time? And most important, how can the United States counter these political threats to access?

---

mett, *U.S. Military Installations in NATO's Southern Region*, Washington, D.C.: U.S. Government Printing Office, 1986, pp. 1–2.

[22] U.S. General Accounting Office (GAO), *Kosovo Air Operations: Combat Aircraft Basing Plans Are Needed in Advance of Future Conflicts*, Washington, D.C., May 2001, p. 6.

[23] Bruce Nardulli, Walter L. Perry, Bruce R. Pirni, John Gordon, and John G. McGinn, *Disjointed War: Military Operations in Kosovo*, Santa Monica, Calif.: RAND Corporation, MR-1406-A, 2002, pp. 61–66.

To answer these questions, this report builds on several years of research and employs multiple methodologies. The first approach involved compiling and analyzing data on peacetime access challenges and formal contingency access requests over time. By collecting longitudinal data on peacetime and contingency access, we were able to conduct the most comprehensive assessment of access issues to date. The second approach used qualitative methods, in particular, case studies, to explore in greater detail why different access outcomes occurred and other factors that cannot be captured in the quantitative analysis. Together, these two methodologies provided both breadth and depth and increased our confidence in the generalizability and accuracy of our findings.

In short, we found that the United States faces two separate access problems: challenges to its peacetime basing rights and difficulties securing contingency access permissions. Peacetime and contingency access are linked, but not in the way that many assume. Access to large permanent bases during peacetime does *not* increase the probability that the United States will be granted permission to use a facility during a crisis. Instead, only enduring partners—nations having an elite security consensus in support of the U.S. presence—offer more-reliable access during peacetime *and* in contingencies. Since World War II, the United States has regularly encountered access problems; at times, these threats have been severe. But, in general, the access threat has been overstated. Peacetime access challenges have declined from their peak during the latter decades of the Cold War; between 1945 and 2013 the overwhelming majority (90 percent) of formal U.S. requests for contingency access were granted. Nevertheless, U.S. policymakers should not assume that access to foreign bases and territory is ever assured. Changes in the international system—in particular, declining American power, the absence of a unifying global threat, the strengthening norm of sovereignty, the increasing influence of public opinion, and the proliferation of information and communications technologies— are likely to make it more difficult for the United States to gain and maintain access to foreign bases during peacetime and contingencies in the future. Furthermore, a high rate of success on formal access requests can be misleading; it does not take into account the times the

United States may not make a formal request, assuming its request will be denied.

   This report will proceed in seven chapters. Chapter Two explores the various political factors that threaten U.S. access to foreign bases and territory. Chapter Three examines threats to peacetime access, establishes which countries are reliable host nations, and explores how peacetime access threats have changed over time. Chapter Four considers the issue of contingency access and identifies factors that are statistically associated with access permissions and denials. Chapter Five highlights the qualitative factors that impact access outcomes in the case studies. Chapter Six considers some integrated insights from the qualitative and quantitative analysis. Chapter Seven offers findings and recommendations for how the United States can create a resilient posture by mitigating political threats to access. Appendix A lists peacetime access challenges. Appendix B details the results from the statistical analysis of contingency access. Finally, Appendix C contains the contingency access codebook.

CHAPTER TWO

Internal and External Threats to Access

With the exception of a few halcyon years following the outbreak of the Korean War, U.S. access to foreign bases has faced persistent political threats. Opposition to U.S. basing rights and contingency access has arisen within host nations and from outside sources. A local population challenging a U.S. military presence or U.S. forces' right to operate from its nation's territory poses an *internal* access threat. Conversely, a third party pressuring a host nation to deny, restrict, or rescind U.S. basing rights presents an *external* access threat. Although internal or external access threats may be present separately, the two are often connected because outside actors frequently try to exploit indigenous antibase sentiment.

Internal Threats

Internal threats to access have been present throughout nearly the entire history of the U.S. "leasehold empire."[1] The brief exception was in the early 1950s. This honeymoon period was due to a unique and fleeting set of circumstances, in particular, the inability of U.S. allies and partners to meet the seemingly imminent threat the Soviet Union posed on their own because of the devastation they had suffered during World War II. Consequently, many states authorized the establishment of U.S. military bases in their countries to contain communism, and

---

[1] Sandars, 2000.

their publics generally supported this action.[2] Yet by the mid-1950s, as these nations rebounded economically, dissatisfaction with the U.S. military's presence grew.[3] As a result, host nations increasingly reopened basing negotiations to "specify, delineate, and restrict" U.S. rights and began to express reservations about U.S. forces conducting operations from their territories.[4] Around the same time, decolonization was gaining momentum, which created problems for U.S. bases in former European dependencies, such as Libya and Morocco. These newly independent nations questioned the need for a U.S. military presence, which had been established without their consent and which local populations saw as continuation of imperial domination.[5] Since the mid-1950s, it has become common for local movements within countries to challenge the presence of U.S. forces.

In general, antibase movements are motivated by either ideology, local grievances, or both. Someone may be philosophically opposed to a U.S. military presence for any number of reasons, including a commitment to nonviolence, an opposition to nuclear weapons or imperialism, or a belief in Marxism or nationalism.[6] On the Japanese island of Okinawa, for example, many residents want U.S. military bases closed because the horrific memory of the Battle of Okinawa transformed them into "absolute pacifists."[7]

---

[2]   Lundestad, 2003, pp. 27– 34.

[3]   Frank Nash, "United States Overseas Military Bases: A Report to the President," December 1957, declassified December 13, 1996, pp. 5–6; Alvin J. Cottrell and Thomas H. Moorer, *U.S. Overseas Bases: Problems of Projecting American Military Power Abroad*, Washington, D.C.: Center for Strategic and International Studies, Georgetown University, 1977, pp. 8– 9. By the 1970s, the idea of containing the Soviet Union had lost its relevance in many places (Grimmett, 1986, p. 11).

[4]   Cooley and Spruyt, 2009, p. 119.

[5]   George F. Lemmer, *USAF Overseas Bases 1957–1961*, Washington, D.C.: USAF Historical Division Liaison Office, April 1963, p. 26.

[6]   Calder, 2007, p. 84, identifies three types of antibase movements: pragmatic, ideological, and nationalist. We consider *nationalist* to be a subset of *ideological*.

[7]   Miyume Tanji, *Myth, Protest and Struggle in Okinawa*, New York: Routledge, 2006, p. 41.

Throughout the Cold War, leftist organizations were often at the forefront of antibase movements around the globe.[8] Yet the single largest ideological challenge to U.S. bases has come from the strengthening norm of sovereignty and the concomitant rise in nationalism, which has made a foreign military presence less acceptable.[9] During the Cold War, for instance, French President Charles de Gaulle sought to reinvigorate national pride and restore France's great power status by promoting its sovereignty and grandeur. As a result, de Gaulle refused to allow U.S. nuclear weapons to be stationed on French territory unless Paris had at least partial control of the nuclear stockpile.[10] Because of this prohibition, U.S. Air Forces in Europe (USAFE) relocated its three nuclear-capable tactical fighter wings from France to Germany and the UK in 1959 and 1960.[11] This did not mollify de Gaulle, however, who informed U.S. President Lyndon Johnson that "France intends to recover, in her territory, the full exercise of her sovereignty, now impaired by the permanent presence of allied military elements" in a March 7, 1966, letter.[12] Johnson duly complied with de Gaulle's demand, and the last U.S. forces departed France by April 1967.[13]

---

[8] Calder, 2007, p. 84.

[9] Even by 1958, host-nation sensitivity about sovereignty was already an issue. See Nash, 1957, pp. 68–69.

[10] Patrick Facon, "U.S. Forces in France, 1945–1948," in Simon W. Duke and Wolfgang Krieger, eds., *U.S. Military Forces in Europe: the Early Years, 1945–1970*, Boulder, Colo.: Westview Press, 1993, pp. 246–247; Anni P. Baker, *American Soldiers Overseas: The Global Military Presence*, Westport, Conn.: Praeger, 2004, p. 72.

[11] Lawrence R. Benson, *USAF Aircraft Basing in Europe, North Africa, and the Middle East, 1945–1980*, Ramstein Air Base, Germany: Office of History, Headquarters U.S. Air Forces in Europe, 1981, declassified July 20, 2011, p. 38. The United States offered France a deal in which U.S. forces would have custody of the nuclear weapons, while French forces would secure the storage sites, but this was refused (Lemmer, 1963, pp. 21–22).

[12] Quoted in Simon Duke, *United States Military Forces and Installations in Europe*, Oxford, UK: Oxford University Press, 1989, p. 150.

[13] According to Foreign Minister Maurice Couve de Murville, France worried that an "infinitely more powerful partner" could sway the French government "to orient its policy in a direction quite different from the one it would have spontaneously chosen" (quoted in Diana Johnstone and Ben Cramer, "The Burdens and the Glory: U.S. Bases in Europe," in Joseph

At times, nationalism has also inhibited the United States from freely using its overseas bases. During the 1967 Arab-Israeli War, for example, riots in Libya posed a threat to Wheelus Air Base. The Libyan public supported the Arab belligerents and suspected that, in contravention of their wishes, the United States was using Wheelus to aid Israel. Consequently, U.S. forces evacuated all U.S. military dependents from Libya to ensure their safety.[14] As the Libya example suggests, nationalist outrage is likely to be particularly acute if a host nation believes that the United States is ignoring its preferences. During a 1975 operation to free a hijacked U.S. merchant vessel—the *Mayaguez*—President Gerald Ford ordered U.S. troops to execute the rescue operation from bases in Thailand, even though the Thai Prime minister had expressly forbidden their use. U.S. forces succeeded in recovering the *Mayaguez* and its crew, but U.S. disregard for Thai sovereignty had long-term repercussions. As a result of popular indignation at the blatant U.S. disregard for its wishes, Thailand refused to renew U.S. basing rights, leading to the expulsion of all U.S. forces in 1975.[15]

Even when a foreign government is willing to invite U.S. forces into its territory, the general public often objects because an outside military presence is viewed as a sign of subordination. After the first Gulf War, many Saudis resented the U.S. military presence that remained in their nation to enforce the no-fly zone against Iraq. For some Saudis, U.S. forces reminded them of Western domination, while others believed that the presence of non-Muslim U.S. forces desecrated the Islamic holy sites of Mecca and Medina.[16] Consequently, the Saudi government, which valued the U.S. forces as a safeguard against a

Gerson and Bruce Birchard, eds., *The Sun Never Sets: Confronting the Network of Foreign U.S. Military Bases*, Boston: South End Press, 1991, p. 220).

[14] Daniel L. Haulman, *United States Air Force and Humanitarian Airlift Operations, 1947–1994*, Maxwell Air Force Base, Ala.: Air Force Historical Research Agency, 1998, p. 301

[15] R. Sean Randolph, *The United States and Thailand: Alliance Dynamics, 1950–1985*, Berkley, Calif.: Institute of East Asian States, University of California, 1986, pp. 179–192.

[16] Alfred B. Prados, *Middle East Attitudes Toward the United States*, Washington, D.C.: Congressional Research Service, December 31, 2011, p. 9.

resurgent Iraq, tried to conceal the U.S. presence by relocating it to a remote region and prohibiting U.S. troops from leaving the base.[17]

One of the most common issues that arouses nationalist opposition is criminal jurisdiction, in particular, whether U.S. military personnel are tried under the host nation or the U.S. military's system of justice. Therefore, the terms of a status of forces agreement (SOFA)—a treaty that delineates the rights of U.S. forces in a foreign country and how domestic laws are applied—are often seen as a benchmark for measuring whether the U.S.-host nation relationship is equitable or whether the host nation is a junior member.[18] Regardless of the SOFA, if a U.S. service member commits a crime and is not tried in local courts, the host nation's public often views this as a terrible injustice. For example, disapproval of the United States soared in South Korea after a 2002 accident in which a U.S. armored vehicle ran over and killed two young Korean girls. According to the terms of the agreement, because the U.S. servicemen were on duty at the time of the accident, they fell under U.S. military jurisdiction. Yet the South Korean government and public insisted that the Americans be tried within the South Korean legal system.[19] When the U.S. military courts cleared the two U.S. soldiers of any wrongdoing, there were widespread protests in South Korea against verdict and, more generally, against the U.S. military presence.

In addition to ideological opposition, pragmatic issues related to a U.S. military presence often strain relations with neighboring communities. Civilian populations proximate to a U.S. military base often take exception to the pollution, noise, crime, hazards, and unsavory businesses that accompany military bases, which are collectively known

---

[17] Calder, 2007, p. 156; Rebecca Grant, "The Short Strange Life of PSAB," *Air Force Magazine,* July 2012.

[18] For more on SOFAs, see R. Chuck Mason, *Status of Forces Agreement (SOFA): What Is It, and How Has It Been Utilized?* Washington, D.C.: Congressional Research Service, March 15, 2012.

[19] Cooley, 2008, pp. 125–126.

as "not in my backyard" (NIMBY) concerns.[20] Frequently, antibase protest movements begin at the local level in response to these types of issues. One of the more-contentious NIMBY issues is land use policy.[21] Many military bases require large, contiguous tracts of land that are increasingly scarce and therefore increasingly valuable.[22] For years, there has been pressure on the United States to relocate Yongsan Garrison outside the center of Seoul to a less-populated region and thus free a prime piece of real estate. Yet when the United States and the Republic of Korea (ROK) finally agreed to move Yongsan in April 2003, communities around Pyeongtaek, the location of the new garrison, opposed the plan because it necessitated expropriating land around the existing U.S. Army base—Camp Humphreys.[23]

Other NIMBY objections center around the fact that military bases often disrupt a region's ecosystem and damage the environment.[24] When the United States announced that it was enlarging its Army garrison at Vicenza, Italy, in 2006, a local antibase movement—No Dal Molin—tried to scuttle the plan on the grounds that the extension would cause overcrowding and environmental degradation. The protests also focused on the fact that the new facilities would be built near the historic town center, sullying a United Nations (UN) Educational, Scientific and Cultural Organization World Heritage site.[25] Although

---

[20] Yeo, 2011, p. 19; Mark L. Gillem, *America Town: Building the Outposts of Empire*, Minneapolis: University of Minnesota Press, 2007, pp. 34–70.

[21] Nash, 1957, pp. 74–77.

[22] For more on how DoD has exported immoderate U.S. land-use practices overseas, see Gillem, 2007; Mark L. Gillem, "Homeward Bound: Assessing the Geopolitical Ramifications of Sprawl," in L. Rodrigues and S. Glebov, eds., *Military Bases: Historical Perspectives, Contemporary Challenges*, Washington, D.C.: IOS Press, 2009.

[23] Andrew Yeo, "Local-National Dynamics and Framing in South Korean Anti-Base Movements," *Kasarinlan: Philippine Journal of Third World Studies*, Vol. 21, No. 2, 2006, p. 43; Yeo, 2011, pp. 131–135.

[24] Joseph Gerson, "The Sun Never Sets," in Gerson and Birchard, 1991, pp. 19–21.

[25] Yeo, 2011, pp. 102–106; Paul A. Iverson, "No Peace or Justice: America's Plans to Expand a US Military Base in Vicenza, Italy," *No DalMolin*, March 20, 2007.

No Dal Molin organized a demonstration that attracted nearly 100,000 protestors, it ultimately failed to stop the base expansion.[26]

As the previously mentioned Army accident in South Korea illustrates, a military presence also creates hazards and increases the likelihood of mishaps that can seriously injure or even kill civilians. Throughout much of the Cold War, DoD held the annual Return of Forces to Germany (Reforger) exercise to practice the rapid deployment of more than 100,000 U.S. troops to Europe. This enormous maneuver warfare exercise was notorious for wreaking havoc in Germany as heavy armored vehicles and tanks rode roughshod through the countryside, damaging yards, farmland, and motorways.[27] In addition to the destruction of private property, five German civilians were killed during the exercise in 1988.[28]

In short, many ideological and pragmatic factors may strain relations between U.S. forces and a host nation, but this tension often remains fairly contained. Figure 2.1 depicts different types of antibase opposition and how they may evolve from narrowly focused movements into larger national or transnational campaigns.

Nevertheless, a grassroots movement focused solely on NIMBY issues is likely to remain limited unless it broadens its focus by framing the issue in a way that resonates with a wider audience. Catalysts, such as high-profile crimes or accidents, present opportunities for creating new and more-inclusive frames by raising the profile of U.S. transgressions and attracting the attention of the general public.[29] By evoking national pride, sovereignty, or peace, antibase activists may be able to rouse a larger number of people and galvanize them to take action against the U.S. presence. For example, beginning in 1988, residents living near the Kooni Firing Range in South Korea lobbied to close down the U.S. training facility. Yet it was not until 2000, when a USAF

---

[26] Yeo, 2011, pp. 105–116.

[27] GAO, *Military Damage Claims in Germany: A Growing Burden*, Washington, D.C.: October 9, 1980.

[28] Yarrow Cleaves, "U.S. Military Presence in Germany," in Gerson and Birchard, 1991, p. 237.

[29] For more on catalysts, see Calder, 2007, pp. 86–88.

Figure 2.1
Types of Antibase Movements

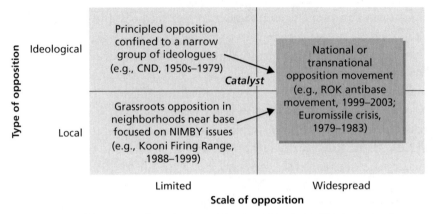

NOTE: Adapted from a typology developed by Yeo, 2011, p. 18. This is obviously an abstraction; most antibase movements contain a mixture of ideological and NIMBY motivations.
RAND RR1339-2.1

A-10 errantly dropped six bombs on the village of Maehyangri, that a broader coalition rallied around this issue. While the accident fortunately resulted in no deaths, it underscored the dangers associated with the U.S. military presence and led to demonstrations that included protestors physically occupying the training range. After a number of concessions intended to defuse opposition, which included prohibiting the use of live ammunition, the United States opted to close the Kooni Range in 2004.[30]

Alternatively, ideological opposition may form the nucleus of an antibase movement. In Panama, for example, nationalists protested against absolute U.S. control over the canal area by planting Panamanian flags throughout the zone in the late 1950s.[31] Around the same time, antinuclear activists formed the Campaign for Nuclear Disarmament (CND) in the UK, calling for abolition of nuclear weapons and the removal of U.S. strategic forces from British territory. During the

---

[30] Yeo, 2011, p. 130; Andrew Yeo, "Anti-Base Movements in South Korea: Comparative Perspective on the Asia-Pacific," *The Asia-Pacific Journal: Japan Focus*, June 14, 2010b.

[31] Baker, 2004, pp. 100–101.

1960s and 1970s, CND targeted naval bases in Scotland used to support U.S. and UK ballistic missile submarines.[32] While CND persisted as an organization, its public support dwindled until NATO announced the dual-track decision in 1979. In response to the deployment of mobile, medium-range SS-20 missiles in Eastern Europe, NATO declared that it would pursue arms control talks with the Soviet Union but that, if an agreement was not reached by 1983, the United States would deploy 572 intermediate-range nuclear armed ballistic and cruise missiles to Western Europe.[33] This announcement precipitated widespread anti-nuclear protests throughout Western Europe, the so called Euromissile crisis. In October 1981 in Bonn, 300,000 people demonstrated against the planned deployment of U.S. missiles. The following year, protestors began to block the gates of more than 50 bases in West Germany. Similarly, British women established encampments around Royal Air Force (RAF) Greenham Common in an effort to impede the deployment and operation of U.S. ground-launched cruise missiles.[34] Residents of the Italian city of Comiso initially had misgivings about the construction of a cruise missile base in their town because they were concerned about land expropriation, Mafia infiltration, and the rising cost of living. By 1982, local base opponents had been joined by the international peace movement, which staged a demonstration attended by more than 60,000 protestors.[35]

Successful antibase mobilization, therefore, partially depends on forging a broad coalition that encompasses both local and ideological base opponents. Nevertheless, while the formation of a more-inclusive coalition puts more pressure on the United States and the host-nation

---

[32] Campaign for Nuclear Disarmament, "The History of CND," web page, undated.

[33] The United States planned to deploy 108 medium-range Pershing II land-based ballistic missiles and 464 ground-launched cruise missiles (BGM-109G), which were land-based variants of the USN's Tomahawk cruise missiles. Baker, 2004, p. 86.

[34] "The Women's Peace Camp," BBC, November 10, 1999.

[35] Laura Simich, "The Corruption of a Community's Economic and Political Life: The Cruise Missile Base in Comiso," in Gerson and Birchard, 1991, pp. 81–84; Lawrence S. Wittner, *The Struggle Against the Bomb,* Vol. 3, Palo Alto, Calif.: Stanford University Press, 2003, pp. 160–162.

government, that alone does not guarantee success. Many other factors influence the outcome, including the host-nation government's position toward the United States and how the United States chooses to respond to the opposition movement.[36] Moreover, expansion can also sow the seeds of a movement's demise because competing interests can divide and undermine the cohesion of an antibase movement.

In sum, the United States faces diverse internal challenges to its overseas bases. While these challenges have been present since the 1950s, new technologies make it even more difficult for the United States and a supportive host government to conceal a U.S. military presence or contain opposition movements. Advancements in communications technologies facilitate the shift toward national or transnational movements as satellite television, computers, and mobile phones enable individuals to share information, images, and videos in near real time. These technologies are powerful tools that empower activists by enabling the documentation and dissemination of local grievances, connecting them to other likeminded individuals and groups, and sharing best practices and mobilization strategies. Consequently, antibase organizations around the globe can coordinate their activities and work together to achieve common objectives.[37]

External Threats

Internal challenges clearly pose a serious threat to the U.S. global network of bases and access rights, but they are not the only political challenge that the United States must confront. In addition to challenges to a U.S. military presence that emerge organically within host nations, third parties may try to limit U.S. access to foreign bases by pressuring or persuading other countries to deny U.S. basing rights. Politi-

---

[36] In particular, Yeo, 2011, pp. 21–27, argues that it is the strength of the security consensus among host-nation elites that determines whether antibase movements succeed.

[37] For more on transnational antibase networks, see Andrew Yeo, "Not in Anyone's Backyard: The Emergence and Identity of a Transnational Anti-Base Network," *International Studies Quarterly*, Vol. 53, 2009.

cal anti-access strategies aim to limit U.S. freedom of action and the U.S. military's ability to operate effectively by undermining a nation's willingness to host U.S. forces through a combination of propaganda, threats, selective incentives, and domestic subversion. We identified at least four distinct ways a state may attempt to discourage another nation from hosting U.S. forces: bullying, bribing, delegitimizing, and inciting (see Figure 2.2).

Bullying

Bullying involves threatening to punish nations that provide access to their territory or airspace to U.S. forces. Punishments often include an implicit or explicit threat to use force against a host nation unless it withdraws U.S. access rights. Intimidation may be even more likely to succeed at scuttling ongoing negotiations before an agreement has been reached. For instance, in 1952, the Soviet Union successfully compelled the Danish government to reject an agreement to station U.S. air forces in Denmark. In an official communication on October 2, the Soviet government asserted that "military bases at the dis-

Figure 2.2
External Anti-Access Threats

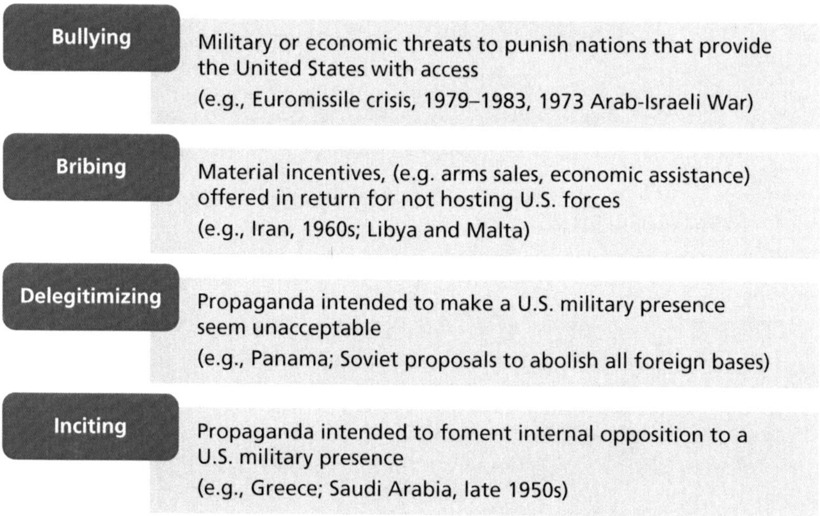

Bullying	Military or economic threats to punish nations that provide the United States with access (e.g., Euromissile crisis, 1979–1983, 1973 Arab-Israeli War)
Bribing	Material incentives, (e.g. arms sales, economic assistance) offered in return for not hosting U.S. forces (e.g., Iran, 1960s; Libya and Malta)
Delegitimizing	Propaganda intended to make a U.S. military presence seem unacceptable (e.g., Panama; Soviet proposals to abolish all foreign bases)
Inciting	Propaganda intended to foment internal opposition to a U.S. military presence (e.g., Greece; Saudi Arabia, late 1950s)

RAND *RR1339-2.2*

posal of foreign armed forces" are "regarded as a threat against the safety of the Soviet Union and the other Baltic countries." Moreover, the Soviets cautioned "that the responsibility for the consequences of such a policy will rest upon the Danish government."[38] As a result of these threats, Denmark refused to allow the United States to establish air bases in its country.

Bullying has also affected agreements that were already in place. For example, on August 1, 1958, the Soviet Union sent a note to Israeli Prime Minister David Ben-Gurion objecting to the fact that U.S. and UK aircraft were using Israeli airspace to support the British intervention in Jordan.[39] Although the Israeli government later denied that Soviet pressure influenced its decision, Ben-Gurion demanded on August 3, 1958, that U.S. and UK aircraft immediately cease transiting through Israeli airspace. After the ominous Soviet note, Ben-Gurion reportedly decided that "he could no longer submit the Israeli people to the risks involved in the overflights."[40] Israel's ambassador to the United States, Abba Eban, affirmed that Ben-Gurion "was deeply concerned over the malevolent power of the Soviet Union which could destroy Israel in five minutes."[41] Lacking a formal security guarantee from the United States, it appears that the Israeli government determined that the risk of provoking the Soviet Union was too great.[42] After learning that Israel

---

[38] Quoted in Jonathan N. Brown, "Immovable Positions: Public Acknowledgment and Bargaining in Military Basing Negotiations," *Security Studies*, Vol. 23, No. 2, 2014a, pp. 281–282.

[39] Oma Almog, *Britain, Israel and the United States, 1955–1958: Beyond Suez*, London: Frank Cass Publishers, 2003, p. 188.

[40] "Memorandum of a Conversation, Washington, August, 3, 1948, 3 pm," *Foreign Relations of the United States* [FRUS] *1958–1960*, Vol. XI: *Lebanon and Jordan*, Washington, D.C.: Government Printing Office, 1992, p. 426.

[41] "Memorandum of a Conversation, Washington, August, 3, 1948, 3 pm," *FRUS 1958–1960*, Vol. XI, 1992, p. 427.

[42] Ben Gurion's decision was also influenced by domestic Israeli politics. In particular, many of the leftist parties within the government, which had an anti-American bent, demanded that Israel revoke the overflight permissions that had been granted to U.S. and UK aircraft (Avi Shlaim, "Israel, the Great Powers and the Middle East Crisis of 1958," *Journal of Imperial and Commonwealth History*, Vol. 2, No. 2, May 1999).

had rescinded U.S. overflight permissions, U.S. Secretary of State John Foster Dulles summoned Ambassador Eban and sharply rebuked the Israelis for capitulating to the Soviet demands. Ben-Gurion and Eban hoped to use the crisis to obtain more U.S. support and an explicit security guarantee, but Dulles firmly insisted that the "Eisenhower doctrine made clear that the US would come to the support of Israel should it be attacked by a Communist power."[43] Realizing that Israel's future relationship with the United States was in jeopardy, Ben-Gurion reversed his earlier decision on August 5 and allowed the resumption of U.S. overflights for a limited time.[44]

Similarly, after the U-2 reconnaissance aircraft piloted by Gary Powers was shot down over the Soviet Union in May 1960, Soviet Premier Nikita Khrushchev promised to deliver a "shattering blow" with nuclear missiles against any country that U.S. aircraft used to violate Soviet airspace.[45] Soviet Foreign Minister Andrey Gromyko confirmed that "[i]f such provocative acts continue, then . . . we shall strike at the bases from which the aggressors carry out their flights.[46] This was unfortunate timing because the United States was in the midst of contentious negotiations to renew its basing rights in Japan, one of the countries where the Central Intelligence Agency based its secretive strategic reconnaissance aircraft. Moreover, while the majority of Japanese had consistently opposed the post-occupation U.S. military presence, Japanese public support for U.S. bases had dwindled to a low of 8 percent by 1958.[47] In this context, Soviet threats were extremely effective and prompted "near panic about the consequences of retain-

---

[43] "Memorandum of a Conversation, Washington, August, 3, 1948, 3 pm," *FRUS 1958–1960*, Vol. XI, 1992, p. 427.

[44] Almog, 2003, pp. 194–195. Israel also restricted U.S. aircraft to nighttime flights (George S. Dragnich, *The Lebanon Operation of 1958: A Study of the Crisis Role of the Sixth Fleet*, Arlington, Va.: Center for Naval Analyses, September 1970, p. 68).

[45] Quoted in Michael Schaller, *Altered States: The United States and Japan Since the Occupation*, New York: Oxford University Press, 1997, p. 149.

[46] "Questions and Answers," Moscow, TASS Radioteletype, May 11, 1960, tr. in Daily Report, Foreign Radio Broadcasts, FBIS-FRB-60-093, May 12, 1960.

[47] Cooley, 2008, pp. 181–183.

ing American Air and naval bases on Japanese soil."[48] Consequently, on July 8, 1960, the government of Japan asked the United States to remove its U-2s, which were stationed at Naval Air Station Atsugi. The United States complied by dismantling the spy planes and shipping them home.[49]

Later, during the early 1980s Euromissile crisis, the Soviets tried to intimidate NATO allies in an effort to block the deployment of U.S. intermediate-range nuclear missiles to Western Europe. Soviet propaganda reminded U.S. European allies that retaliatory strikes would "be delivered not only at the United States launching cities, but at headquarters, communications centers and arsenals, many of which, as is known are situated directly in the densely populated regions of countries of Western Europe."[50] At another time, the Soviets cautioned that if "a global conflict" began "the Western European countries where Pershing II intermediate-range missiles are deployed will become 'nuclear targets' for Soviet nuclear missiles, and thus become a 'danger' to West Europe."[51] Another Soviet outlet hyperbolically claimed that "Europe, the cradle of détente, has already begun to be called, 'Euroshima,' recalling the tragic fate of Hiroshima."[52] In this instance, however, Soviet bullying did not produce the desired effect; U.S. allies ultimately accepted the deployment of Pershing IIs and ground-launched cruise missiles.

In addition to military coercion, states may threaten economic sanctions against nations that host U.S. forces. During the 1973 Arab-Israeli War, for instance, the Organization of the Petroleum Exporting

---

[48] Schaller, 1997, p. 149.

[49] Gregory W. Pedlow and Donald E. Welzenbach, *The Central Intelligence Agency and Overhead Reconnaissance: The U-2 and Oxcart Programs*, Washington, D.C.: Central Intelligence Agency, 199, pp. 181–182.

[50] "Further Report on Possible USSR Retaliation," Moscow World Services, November, 30, 1982, tr. in Daily Report, Soviet Union, FBIS-SOV-82-231, December 1, 1982.

[51] "Soviet Responses to Strengthening West European Defense Noted," Beijing Renmin Ribao, September 13, 1979, tr. in Daily Report, People's Republic of China, FBIS-CHI-79-187, September 25, 1979.

[52] "Opposition to Euromissile Deployment Very Serious," Moscow Novoye Vremya, April 10, 1981, tr. in Daily Report, Soviet Union, FBIS-SOV-81-074, April 17, 1981.

Countries used the threat of an oil embargo to discourage U.S. European allies from allowing the United States to use their air bases to support an airlift to Israel. Even before the war began, Saudi Arabia had signaled that it might employ the "oil weapon" unless the United States adopted a more pro-Arab stance, which in turn produced widespread concern about an energy crisis in Western Europe and Japan.[53] During the war, when the United States publicly announced on October 14 that it was commencing an airlift to resupply Israel, it abandoned any pretense of neutrality by publicly aligning itself with one of the belligerents. Consequently, three days later, the Arab oil ministers announced that they were cutting oil production 5 percent from the September level and that they would subsequently cut production by an additional 5 percent every month until they had achieved their objectives. At the same time, they promised to continue to supply friendly states with oil at prewar levels.[54] In response to the announcement that the United States would provide Israel with a $2.2 billion military aid package, the Arab nations entirely cut off the supply of oil to the United States and other nations that backed Israel.[55]

In reality, the production cuts had a greater effect than the oil embargo, but together, these measures were extremely successful at driving a wedge between the United States and its European allies.[56] Under great pressure from the United States, only Portugal eventually permitted the Military Airlift Command to use an air base on the

---

[53] Daniel Yergin, *The Prize: The Epic Quest for Oil, Money and Power*, New York: Free Press, 1991, pp. 595, 598.

[54] Yergin, 1991, p. 607.

[55] Yergin, 1991, p. 608.

[56] This stands in contrast to the oil embargo the Arab states put in place against the United States and the UK during the 1967 war. The primary difference between 1967 and 1973 was that, in the former instance, the United States remained the supplier of last resort, while, by 1973, the Arab oil-producing states in general, and Saudi Arabia in particular, had supplanted the United States. As a result, the 1967 embargo was not only ineffective but self-defeating because the Arab states sacrificed revenue and markets, while the United States increased production to offset the effects of the ban (Yergin, 2001, p. 594; Rachel Bronson, *Thicker Than Oil: America's Uneasy Partnership with Saudi Arabia*, New York: Oxford University Press, 2006, pp. 99–101).

Azores for the airlift.[57] Other European allies, which were extremely dependent on Middle Eastern oil, tried to disassociate themselves from the United States and its support for Israel. Secretary of State Henry Kissinger disparagingly observed that the European states "seemed to have no specific aim except to seek the goodwill of the oil producers."[58] The denial of European air bases ultimately did not prevent the USAF from delivering arms and munitions to Israel, but it did complicate the operation.

Bribing

While many of the political anti-access tactics involve some form of coercion, a third party may also offer carrots to try to incentivize states to deny U.S. forces access. Essentially, a state may try to bribe another nation to encourage it to abrogate existing U.S. basing rights or deny U.S. forces the right to enter its country in the first place.

Throughout the Cold War, both the United States and Soviet Union used aid and arms sales as tools to pry less committed states from the adversary's camp.[59] The U.S.-Soviet competition over Morocco in the 1950s is an example of this. After the Kingdom of Morocco secured its independence, relations with the Untied States soured as Morocco considered whether it would uphold the U.S. basing agreement that had been negotiated by the French. By 1959, King Mohammed V faced mounting pressure to expel U.S. forces, even though his country, which was in the midst of a financial crisis, desperately needed U.S. financial aid.[60] The situation was further complicated when the Soviet Union offered Morocco a generous interest-free loan. Fearful that, if the Soviet Union supplanted the United States as Morocco's primary benefactor, U.S. forces would lose access to Strategic Air Command air

---

[57] President Richard Nixon reportedly sent a message to the Portuguese Prime Minister threatening to withdraw the U.S. security commitment unless access to Lajes Field was granted (interview with William B. Quandt, Washington, D.C., May 29, 2013).

[58] Henry Kissinger, *Years of Upheaval*, Boston: Little, Brown and Company, 1982, p. 537.

[59] Robert E. Harkavy, *Bases Abroad: The Global Foreign Military Presence*, New York: Oxford University Press, 1989, p. 365.

[60] Nash, 1957, p. 105.

bases and a vital communications station at Port Lyautey, the United States quickly granted a Moroccan request for military assistance.[61] Despite these efforts, the Moroccan government demanded in December 1959 that the United States vacate its air bases by 1963.[62] It is unclear whether the Soviet loan offer influenced the Moroccan government's decision to terminate U.S. basing rights, but this sort of ambiguity is not uncommon. In general, it is often difficult to determine the effects of political anti-access tactics on outcomes. Nevertheless, it is possible to establish that the Soviets attempted to undermine the U.S. relationship with Morocco by offering bribes.

Other states have also employed bribes to deny their opponents basing rights. For example, former Libyan president Muamar Qaddafi provided Malta with considerable financial support in exchange for not permitting the United States or NATO to use its airfields or harbors.[63] More recently, Russian payoffs complicated U.S. efforts to retain access to an air base in Kyrgyzstan that was critical for operations in Afghanistan. In February 2009, Kyrgyz President Kurmanbek Bakiyev announced that he was revoking U.S. basing rights and accepting a Russian aid package consisting of $2 billion worth of incentives and emergency assistance. Ultimately, Bakiyev shrewdly played the Russians and the Americans off each other to his advantage. After taking an initial $300 million payment from Russia, Bakiyev violated

---

[61] "Memorandum of the Substance of Discussion at the Department of State—Joint Chiefs of Staff Meeting, Pentagon, Washington, November 21, 1958, 11:30 am," *FRUS 1958–1960*, Vol. XIII: *Arab-Israeli Dispute; United Arab Republic; North Africa,* Washington, D.C.: U.S. Government Printing Office, 1992, pp. 772–776; "Memorandum of Discussion at the 417th Meeting of the National Security Council, Washington, August 18, 1959," *FRUS 1958–1960*, Vol. XIII, pp. 785–788; "Memorandum from the Acting Secretary of State to the President Washington September 22, 1959" *FRUS 1958–1960*, Vol. XIII, pp. 789–791; "Memorandum from the Acting Secretary of State to the President, Washington, March 4, 1960," *FRUS 1958–1960*, Vol. XIII, pp. 801–802.

[62] Lemmer, 1963, pp. 27–29.

[63] Harkavy, 1989, p. 368; Paul Lewis, "In Malta, Ties to the West at Issue Again," *New York Times,* May 11, 1987.

his understanding with Moscow by renegotiating U.S. basing rights in return for significantly higher annual rental payments.[64]

Delegitimizing

States may also try to undermine support for U.S. basing rights through information campaigns that attempt to make a U.S. military presence seem less acceptable. Propaganda can target a specific U.S. military presence or might attack the general notion that foreign forces should be based on another country's soil. Both tactics attempt to weaken the moral legitimacy of a U.S. military presence overseas. The first approach may raise questions about the stated rationale of U.S. bases in a particular country and suggest that there are hidden and usually more nefarious motives at play. The second approach is more ambitious because it tries to shift global norms by persuading the international community that foreign bases are an unnatural extension of imperialism that violate a state's sovereignty.

The Soviet Union used both tactics extensively during the Cold War with varying degrees of success. In the early 1950s, Soviet media outlets portrayed U.S. forces in France, the UK, and Italy as "occupation troops" who acted with impunity because "the laws of these countries have no bearing on them."[65] U.S. forces were also accused of committing crimes, such as looting and imperiously expropriating the best land to build its airfields. At other times, the Soviet Union attacked the notion that the U.S. forces were stationed overseas for defensive purposes, claiming that this was a "false pretext . . . against a nonexistent 'communist threat.'"[66] Soviet propaganda maintained that "one of the best proofs of the aggressive policy of the United States is its

---

[64] Alexander Cooley, "Manas Hysteria: Why the United States Can't Keep Buying Off Kyrgyz Leaders to Keep Its Vital Air Base Open," *Foreign Policy*, April 12, 2010; Alexander Cooley, *Great Games Local Rules: The New Great Power Contest in Central Asia*, Oxford, UK: Oxford University Press, 2012, pp. 123–127.

[65] "U.S. Military Subjugates W. Europeans," Moscow Soviet Home Service, December 11, 1951, tr. in Daily Report, Foreign Radio Broadcasts, FBIS-FRB-51-245, December 12, 1951.

[66] "NATO Bases in Europe Threaten Peace, Liquidation Demands," Moscow Krasnaya Avezda, March 31, 1974, tr. in Daily Report, Soviet Union, FBIS-SOV74-066, April 4, 1974.

formation of a widespread network of naval and air bases throughout the world."[67] At the Berlin Conference in January and February 1954, Soviet Foreign Minister Vyacheslav Molotov again leveled the charge that "American military bases" have "nothing to do with the purposes of defence."[68]

Claiming that U.S. bases were part of a secret and aggressive U.S. plan continued throughout the Cold War. In the 1980s, for example, Soviet radio programs accused the United States of having a hidden agenda in Panama. Instead of enhancing the security of the Western Hemisphere, these programs charged that "the real U.S. interest" was "to ensure its permanence in Panama and that everything else was just pretexts and accusations to hide imperialist interests in our country."[69] Soviet outlets also frequently noted that U.S. bases in Panama were a "convenient stronghold," which the United States used "for military-political actions aimed at suppressing national liberation movements in the region" and as a "bridgehead for undertaking aggression against other states."[70]

The Soviet Union also sought generally to make foreign bases seem unacceptable. During the 1950s, when many states had just recently secured independence, the Soviet Union frequently charged that U.S. bases were a new form of imperialism that sovereign states should not accept. For instance, after U.S. forces returned to Wheelus Air Base in Libya in the late 1940s, Soviet-sponsored radio broadcasts claimed that

---

[67] V. M. Molotov, "World-Wide U.S. Bases Threaten Peace," Moscow, Soviet Home Service, March 20, 1949, tr. in Daily Report, Foreign Radio Broadcasts, FBIS-FRB-49-053, March 21, 1949.

[68] "Results of the Berlin Conference: Statement by V. M. Molotov, Minister of Foreign Affairs to the U.S.S.R.," New Supplement, No. 6, March 16, 1954. Instead, U.S. bases "facilitate[e] the engineering of another war." Molotov also expressed the hope that, with the end of the Korean War, there would be a "general relaxation of international tension, including a reduction of armaments and prohibition of foreign military bases on the territories of other countries."

[69] Quoted in Howard M. Hensel, "Soviet Media Perspectives on the Crisis in Panama, 1987–1990: A Case Study of the Application of Propaganda Techniques," in Howard M. Hensel, Nelson Michaud, eds., Global Media Perspectives on the Crisis in Panama, Burlington, Vt.: Ashgate, 2011, p. 84.

[70] Quoted in Hensel, 2011, p. 84.

the United States had placed "fresh bonds of slavery on the people of Libya."[71] At the 8th UN General Assembly meeting, the Soviet delegation went so far as to submit a proposal calling for the "the liquidation of military bases on foreign territory." According to the Soviets, foreign bases increased the probability of another world war and undermined a state's independence. The Soviets singled out the United States as the greatest offender, with bases in 49 countries that "cover the globe like a menacing net."[72] Communist propaganda disparaged countries and leaders who permitted U.S. forces on their soil, accusing leaders of compromising their nations' rights and acting as the "obedient executor of all the requests of the U.S. ruling circles."[73] After permitting the establishment of a large number of USAF air bases, Great Britain was dismissed as little more than a "vassal state of America."[74] Similarly, all the European countries that hosted U.S. bases were criticized for meekly accepting "a foreign yoke" and surrendering their independence.[75]

This type of rhetoric continued even in the latter years of the Cold War. When the Carter administration decided to seek access to additional bases in the Middle East, the Soviets tried to scuttle the initiative by claiming that an "American military presence in this region constitutes a threat to the independence of states in the region and is contrary to the interests of peace and security."[76] When possible, Soviet propaganda exposed access negotiations that might be under way and targeted leaders who appeared most amenable to supporting the United

---

[71] "American Bases in Libya Are Illegal," Moscow, March 2, 1948, tr. in Daily Report, Foreign Radio Broadcasts, FBIS-FRB-48-259, March 3, 1948.

[72] "U.S. Bases Abroad Vulnerable to Attack," Moscow, Soviet Home Service, October 14, 1953, tr. in Daily Report, Foreign Radio Broadcasts, FBIS-FRB-53-202, October 15, 1953.

[73] "Arab States Oppose Plan for War Bases," Moscow Soviet Near Eastern Service, September 17, 1951, tr. in Daily Report, Foreign Radio Broadcasts, FBIS-FRB-51-186, September 18, 1951, p. bb3.

[74] "Report on Conditions in Europe Given," July 10, 1950, tr. in Daily Report, Foreign Radio Broadcasts, FBIS-FRB-5-132, July 10, 1950.

[75] "U.S. Policy Built on Foreign Bases," Moscow Soviet European Service, July 9, 1957, tr. in Daily Report, Foreign Radio Broadcasts, FBIS-FRB-57-132, July 10, 1957.

[76] "Paper Questions U.S. Plans for Island Near Oman," Moscow, March 28, 1977, tr. in Daily Report, Soviet Union, FBIS-SOV-77-060, March 29, 1977.

States, such as Sultan Qaboos of Oman, who was denounced as a "tool in the hands of the imperialists."[77]

In general, it is very difficult to assess how successful Soviet efforts to delegitimize U.S. bases were, particularly when used alone. What can be established is that U.S. officials believed that Soviet propaganda adversely affected U.S. access. In particular, Soviet efforts to encourage other nations to adopt a neutral or nonaligned foreign policy, which meant no foreign bases on their territories, were seen as a serious threat to U.S. bases in the developing world.[78]

More recently, Russian leader Vladimir Putin has aggressively used the media to challenge the United States and to "reinven[t] reality."[79] In Kyrgyzstan, for instance, Russian-controlled media regularly published unflattering stories about the U.S. air base at Manas, including accusations that the United States used the base as a hub for drug trafficking and as a location to conduct illegal surveillance on China and Russia.[80] The Russian-language media also focused on a 2006 incident when a U.S. serviceman shot and killed a local fuel truck driver at the base's gate. While the United States claimed that the driver had been armed, the media played up suspicions that this was an act of wanton violence and that the United States had tried to cover up the event by removing the accused from Kyrgyzstan. Later stories highlighted what proved to be an additional U.S. misstep—the offer of $2,000 to the fuel truck driver's family, which was seen as a deliberate insult.[81] This propaganda damaged the U.S. image in Kyrgyzstan and helped to fuel the resentment against the U.S. base that resulted in its closure in 2014.

---

[77] "Paper Questions . . . ," 1977.

[78] Nash, 1957, p. 26.

[79] For more on Russian information warfare, see Peter Pomerantsev, "Russia and the Menace of Unreality," *The Atlantic,* September 9, 2014, and Jill Dougherty, "How the Media Became One of Putin's Most Powerful Weapons," *The Atlantic,* April 21, 2015.

[80] David Satter, *The Last Gasp of Empire: Russia's Attempts to Control the Media in the Former Soviet Republics,* Washington, D.C.: Center for International Media Assistance, National Endowment for Democracy, January 8, 2014, pp. 22–24; Dmitry Solovyov, "U.S. Spies on China from Kyrgyz Base: Russian TV," Reuters, April 5, 2009.

[81] Cooley, 2012, p.122; Scott Horton, "The Mess at Manas," *Harper's Magazine,* February, 4, 2009.

Inciting

Another political anti-access strategy entails fomenting opposition to a U.S. military presence within host nations or strengthening existing antibase movements. A nation may directly funnel money, resources, or know-how to groups resisting a U.S. military presence. Yet, far more often, states incite indirectly through propaganda that highlights the downsides of U.S. bases; advertising and often exaggerating the degree of local opposition to U.S. forces; and, more generally, spreading disinformation that is intended to incense local sensibilities.

Soviet broadcasts, for example, frequently reported on crimes committed by U.S. servicemen stationed overseas and implied that U.S. troops were rarely punished for their offensives. For instance, in a 1964 broadcast, Soviet propaganda charged U.S. troops in the Philippines of acting "like a master in the islands" and of killing 39 Filipinos that year alone. The broadcast also highlighted the fact that U.S. military personnel who commit crimes "cannot be held responsible by the Philippine authorities" and demanded that "the Manila authorities to do their utmost to have the root of the trouble removed and . . . dismantle its bases."[82] Similarly, in Japan, the official Soviet news agency, TASS, characterized U.S. bases as "a hotbed of criminality." It then accused "American troops stationed in the Pentagon's bases in Japan" of committing "a multitude of offenses and serious disturbances of the peace." Despite this fact, the Soviets claimed that "not a single one of the serviceman apprehended at the scene of the crime has yet been handed over to the Japanese legal authorities." Instead, they were turned over to the U.S. military justice system, and "after a certain period of time the offenders are freed."[83]

At other times, a third party may try to strengthen existing opposition movements by highlighting and even exaggerating their activities and level of support. TASS, for instance, reported in 1985 that there was a "mammoth meeting" in Greece where protestors

---

[82] "Filipinos Demand Dismantling of U.S. Bases," Moscow, December 29, 1964, tr. in Daily Report, Foreign Radio Broadcasts, FBIS-FRB-65-002, January 5, 1965.

[83] "Japanese CP Calls for Abolition of U.S. Bases in Japan," Moscow Domestic Service, May 12, 1975, tr. in Daily Report, Soviet Union, FBIS-SOV-75-093, May 13, 1975.

shouted slogans, including "Down with American bases" and "No to Reagan's star wars plans," "Yes to Nuclear-free Balkans."[84] Similarly, in 1974, TASS reported that there was "a powerful wave of protest" in India against the Anglo-American plan to build a base on the island of Diego Garcia.[85] Today, some suspect that the Chinese government is encouraging opposition to U.S. bases on the Japanese island of Okinawa by spreading anti-American propaganda and by bankrolling anti-American political candidates and antibase social movements.[86]

Additionally, third parties may try to turn the population of a host nation against a U.S. military presence by spreading disinformation that casts U.S. forces or their activities in a negative light. For example, during the 1973 Arab-Israeli war, the official Soviet news agency reported that the United States had ignored the wishes of many of its European allies and was shipping U.S. military equipment from their nations to Israel and was using European ports and airspace to support the resupply of Israel.[87] Similarly, at a critical moment in the 1978 U.S.-Spain base negotiations, U.S. officials believed that the Soviet Union began a disinformation campaign to try to scuttle the talks. Leftist magazines in Spain reported that the United States had an official policy of penetrating and manipulating host-nation governments and terrorist organizations to stimulate anticommunist sentiment. These reports, however, were based on forged documents. U.S. officials concluded that the stories were intended to "result in maximum embarrassment" and "to discredit the U.S. in Spain at a time

---

[84] "Greeks March in Protest of U.S. bases," Moscow TASS, July 16, 1985, tr. in Daily Report, Soviet Union, FBIS-SOV-85-137, July 17, 1985.

[85] "Indian Popular Protests Against Diego Garcia Base Reported," *Moscow TASS*, February 23, 1974tr. in Daily Report, Soviet Union, FBIS-SOV-74-040, February 27, 1974.

[86] Makiko Segawa, "Japan Conservatives See China's Hand in Okinawa Anti-Base Movement," Shingetsu News Agency, January 21, 2011.

[87] "U.S. Arms Delivers to Israel Continue, FRG Objects," Moscow TASS, October 25, 1973, tr. in Daily Report, White Book, FBIS-FRB-73-207, October 26, 1973.

when possible entry into NATO and future U.S. base rights are being considered by the Spanish government."[88]

Mixed Strategies

While these four political anti-access strategies are analytically distinct, they often go hand in hand in practice. For example, in the early 1960s, the Soviet Union employed a dual-pronged approach in an effort to compel the Shah of Iran to close sensitive U.S. intelligence facilities and adopt a neutral foreign policy. First, the Soviets targeted the shah with a barrage of propaganda that denounced the Iranian leader for "turning the country into an appendage of the U.S. Defense Department," which could be used "in all sorts of adventures and for sedition."[89] After putting the shah on the defensive, the Soviet Union then indicated that, if he broke with the United States, he would not only "escape this pressure" but could also "expect economic and even some military assistance from the [Soviet Union]."[90] In this instance, this strategy of inciting and bribing failed to produce the desired outcome.

During the Vietnam War, the Chinese government bullied the government of Japan and tried to incite opposition to the U.S. military presence. It did so by first threatening to retaliate against Japan if U.S. forces bombed China because "the U.S. is out of our reach. We are not able to return the blow. However, it is not impossible for us to reach

---

[88] Zbigniew Brzezinski,""National Security Adviser Provides President Jimmy Carter with Information on the Following World Events: An Update on Soviet Disinformation Propaganda Directed at Discrediting U.S.-Spanish Relations; Status of Brazilian-U.S. Relations; Reports of Rhodesian Raids into Mozambique; Investigation into Cuban Corruption in Angola," memorandum, September 25, 1978, U.S. Declassified Documents Online, July 16, 2016, Declassified on January 31, 2005, DDRS-300095-i1-3.

[89] "Iranian Shah Tool of U.S. Imperialists," Moscow Soviet Near Eastern Service, June 5, 1960, tr. in Daily Report, Foreign Radio Broadcasts, FBIS-FRB-60-109, June 6, 1960.

[90] "Memorandum from the Vice Chairman of the Policy Planning Council (Morgan) to the President's Special Assistant for National Security Affairs (Bundy)," March 27, 1961," FRUS 1961–1963, Vol. XVII: Near East, Washington, D.C.: U.S. Government Printing Office, p. 544.

Japan."[91] While these threats tried to directly encourage the Japanese government to rein in the United States, they also indirectly placed pressure on the government by inflaming the antiwar movement. China's statements galvanized Japan's peace movement and were cited as evidence that there was a real risk that Japan would be pulled into the U.S. conflict in Southeast Asia. Between 1965 and 1970, nearly 18 million Japanese protested against the Vietnam War; this, in turn, significantly weakened support for the alliance with the United States.[92]

Similarly, Egyptian President Gamal Abdel Nasser sought to delegitimize, bully, and incite unrest in Arab states that hosted U.S. forces. Nasser was the lead proponent of the ideology of Arab nationalism—the notion that Arab states should be independent of foreign influences and unified. Accordingly, Arab nationalists regarded foreign military bases as an anathema.[93] Using Cairo Radio and other outlets, Nasser launched an incessant and vitriolic propaganda campaign against the pro-Western Arab regimes that maintained close relations with the United States.

Two of Nasser's favorite targets were the pro-Western monarchies that governed Libya and Saudi Arabia. In 1958, when Nasser was near the apex of his influence, U.S. officials noted the effectiveness of these attacks: "[T]he Western-supported conservative governments of the Middle East have seen their influence and authority slip away."[94] As a result of this pressure, Saudi Arabian Crown Prince Faisal was "moving toward closer relations with the [United Arab Republic]" because he believed it was "the best means of preserving the Saudi dynasty." Despite this gradual shift, U.S. intelligence officials concluded that

---

[91] Quoted in Schaller, 1997, p. 194.

[92] Schaller, 1997, pp. 194–195.

[93] Michael Barnett, *Dialogues in Arab Politics: Negotiations in Regional Order*, New York: Columbia University Press, 1998, pp. 66–68; "Special National Intelligence Estimate: Arab Nationalism as a Factor in the Middle East Situation, August 12, 1958," *FRUS 1958–1960*, Vol. XII: *Near East Region; Iraq; Iran; Arabian Peninsula*, Washington, D.C.: U.S. Government Printing Office, 1992, p. 515.

[94] "Special National Intelligence Estimate: Arab Nationalism as a Factor in the Middle East Situation, August 12, 1958," *FRUS 1958–1960*, Vol. XII, 1992, p. 506.

"the likelihood of political upheaval in Saudi Arabia is considerable."[95] By 1961, U.S. officials observed that "the Saudis have been keenly conscious of their vulnerability to Arab nationalist attacks for being host to foreign military forces," and Arab nationalists continued to pressure the Saudi kingdom "to terminate United States operational facilities at Dhahran."[96] Eventually, the Saudi government determined that it could not withstand the Arab nationalist onslaught and that continuing to permit U.S. forces to use Dhahran airfield put the future of the regime at risk. As a result, in 1962, the Saudi government announced it was going to allow the United States lease to Dhahran to expire because it "was too politically costly for the kingdom to maintain."[97]

Nasser also employed similar tactics to great effect against King Idris of Libya. During a speech on February 22, 1964, Nasser attacked the idea of foreign military bases in general, claiming that they were a "derogation of sovereignty and a threat to the independence and integrity of . . . Arab states."[98] Consequently, Nasser proclaimed that "no country can claim independence unless the military bases on its territories are liquidated." In the same speech, Nasser also raised the specter that foreign bases could be used against Arabs to support Israel and falsely claimed that this had occurred during the 1956 Suez war.[99] Within days of Nasser's speech, Idris announced that Libya would not renew U.S. basing rights after the current agreement expired in 1970. But Nasser was not content with this promise, so the Egyptian president continued to pressure Libya to immediately abrogate U.S. basing rights. The 1967 Arab-Israeli War provided Nasser with an opportu-

---

[95] "Special National Intelligence Estimate: Arab Nationalism as a Factor in the Middle East Situation, August 12, 1958," *FRUS 1958–1960*, Vol. XII, 1992, p. 507.

[96] "Memorandum from the Department of State Executive Secretary (Battle) to the President's Special Assistant (Dungan), March 21, 1961," *FRUS 1961–1962*, Vol. XVII, Washington, D.C.: U.S. Government Printing Office, 1994, pp. 517–518.

[97] Bronson, 2008, p. 79.

[98] Quoted in William J. Burns, *Economic Aid and American Policy Toward Egypt, 1955–1981*, Albany, N.Y.: State University of New York Press, 1985, p. 154.

[99] Quoted in Ronald Bruce St. John, *Libya and the United States, Two Centuries of Strife*, Philadelphia, Pa.: University of Pennsylvania Press, 2002, p. 80.

nity to undermine Idris's rule, which he seized by claiming that U.S. jets based in Libya were secretly assisting Israel. As a result of this disinformation, riots erupted in Tripoli, forcing the United States to evacuate American civilians.[100] Although Idris was able to weather the 1967 unrest, his regime did not have long to survive. In 1969, Muammar Qaddafi deposed Idris and immediately expelled U.S. forces from Wheelus Air Base.[101]

Today, Chinese military strategists have discussed waging a diplomatic struggle as a part of their broader counterintervention or anti-access strategy.[102] These writers have identified the U.S. dependence on its allies for basing and support as a critical weakness that can be exploited. Consequently, China is using "diplomatic, informational, military and economic instruments for countercontainment in peacetime and counterintervention in a crisis."[103] In the event of a conflict with the United States, Chinese strategies plan to divide Washington from the Asian allies on whose support the United States relies to conduct military operations. In particular, Chinese political anti-access strategies have focused on sidelining Japan during a conflict over Taiwan.[104] For instance, a professor at China's National Defense University claimed "that China could make Japan remain neutral."[105] Chinese writings on this topic tend to emphasize bullying strategies that employ the threat to retaliate against nations that allow U.S. forces to use bases on their territory. Yet, given China's growing economic clout, it possible that Beijing could also offer bribes and brandish economic sanctions against noncooperative states.

[100] Douglas Little, *American Orientalism: The United States and the Middle East Since 1945,* Chapel Hill, N.C.: University of North Carolina Press, 2008, p. 211.

[101] Alison Pargeter, *Libya the Rise and Fall of Qaddafi,* New Haven, Conn: Yale University Press, 2012, pp. 44–46, 71.

[102] Cliff et al., 2007, pp. 77–79.

[103] David J. Berteau, Michael J. Green, et al., *U.S. Force Posture Strategy in the Asia Pacific Region: An Independent Assessment,* Washington, D.C.: Center for Strategic and International Studies, August 2012, p. 20.

[104] Cliff et al., 2007, p. 78.

[105] Quoted in Cliff et al., 2007, p. 79.

Conclusion

The United States faces two separate but related political threats to its overseas bases in peacetime and during contingencies. Internal threats have been a persistent problem since the United States established its large network of foreign military bases after World War II. In an effort to mitigate domestic opposition to a U.S. military presence, DoD began nearly a decade ago to move toward a new model of overseas presence that centers around periodic rotations of U.S. forces to scalable facilities or partner-nation installations. This is an attempt to be more circumspect of host-nation sovereignty and to reduce some of the frictions associated with a permanent large-scale base. Yet it is not clear whether these steps will be sufficient to neutralize internal threats to access.

In addition to dealing with internal access threats, DoD also must come to terms with the fact that external access threats are not a relic of the Cold War but a growing cause for concern, particularly in the Asia-Pacific region. The United States will need to shore up its relationships with allies to ensure that these tactics do not deprive the United States of needed support. To deal effectively with these internal and external threats to access, the United States needs to identify which nations offer reliable access in peacetime and during contingencies and prioritize efforts in these nations. The next three chapters take steps in that direction.

CHAPTER THREE

Peacetime Access Challenges

This chapter explores in greater detail the risks to the U.S. peacetime presence overseas, which often stem from internal access threats. Some might think that peacetime access is not necessary today, given the relatively benign security environment and DoD's capacity to project power rapidly anywhere in the world from the United States. According to this perspective, the U.S. military only needs temporary access to foreign facilities during a crisis. Yet this view overlooks the enduring importance of peacetime access, which includes large permanent bases (such as those located in Japan and Germany) and the partner-nation facilities to which U.S. forces regularly deploy (such as those located in Oman and Australia). There are four major reasons that steady-state basing rights remain important.

First, missions critical to national security—such as deterring aggression, assuring allies and partners, and ensuring the freedom of the commons—are carried out during peacetime. Forward-based U.S. forces serve as important symbols of the U.S. commitment to a partner nation and to a broader region, strengthening deterrence and assurance and enhancing stability.[1]

Second, after more than a decade of fighting in Iraq and Afghanistan, the United States is in the process of defining the future shape and focus of its peacetime defense posture. DoD has announced that it will rebalance its forces from Western Europe to East Asia but is simultaneously seeking to respond to instability in the Middle East

---

[1] Pettyjohn and Vick, 2013, pp. 13–14.

and a revanchist Russia in Eastern Europe. As the United States considers modifying its network of bases, it needs to be mindful of which nations are likely to be reliable hosts and where U.S. basing rights are likely to be at risk. Given that bases tend to endure beyond their original purpose, it is essential that DoD take a long-term perspective as its revises its defense posture. This is particularly important today as defense budgets shrink. DoD does not want to squander its limited resources by constructing new bases or improving the infrastructure at existing facilities if its access is likely to be restricted or revoked.

Third, basing rights can cast a shadow over the relationship between the United States and a host nation and become a distraction, one that harms an otherwise strong bilateral partnership.

Finally, basing controversies, especially evictions, can harm the U.S. reputation and undermine its credibility in the international community. Other states, particularly potential adversaries but also allies and partners, may doubt the sustainability of the U.S. military presence and therefore its ability to fulfill its extended deterrent commitments. In sum, while contingency access to foreign bases is often necessary, dependable peacetime access for steady-state missions is also critical.

This chapter seeks to answer several important questions about peacetime access. Where is basing risky and where is it reliable? That is, where are U.S. forces at risk of being expelled or having their basing rights limited? Conversely, which nations are likely to provide reliable peacetime access for the foreseeable future? Finally, how have the threats to peacetime access changed over time? To answer these questions, we developed a framework to assess peacetime access risk and compiled data on challenges to U.S. basing rights since 1950.

Assessing Peacetime Access Risk

Chapter Two detailed the internal challenges to the U.S. military presence overseas.[2] Nevertheless, significant domestic opposition does not always result in a loss of peacetime access, which is puzzling. During

---

[2] This section is drawn from Pettyjohn and Vick, 2013, Chapter Four.

the 1980s, for instance, sizable antibase movements emerged in several European countries, but most of these protests did not result in the closure of U.S. bases. Between 1981 and 1983, there were large and widespread protests against the plan to station U.S. Pershing II intermediate-range nuclear missiles in West Germany, but the Bundestag still authorized the deployment.[3] In contrast, Spanish popular opposition compelled the United States to relinquish two particularly controversial air bases in 1988.[4] Similarly, since 1996, the United States has been closing bases on the Japanese island of Okinawa in an effort to improve relations with the local population. There are also instances in which antibase sentiments have led to the complete expulsion of U.S. forces, such as in the Philippines, Panama, and Kyrgyzstan. What explains these varied outcomes? Why are U.S. bases highly contested in some nations, while they are generally accepted, if not welcomed, in others? We argue that peacetime access risk is a product of two factors: a host nation's regime type and the nature of its access relationship. We combined these two variables to create a composite risk metric that helps distinguish between hosts likely to be dependable and those that are likely to be problematic.

Regime Type

Several studies have argued that a host nation's domestic political institutions influence the likelihood that U.S. basing rights will be challenged, but Alexander Cooley has provided the most detailed explanation for why this is the case.[5] Cooley argues that regime type (authoritarian, democratizing, or consolidated democracy) affects whether a state will abide by its international commitments, especially basing agreements.[6] According to Cooley, consolidated democracies

---

[3]   Baker, 2004, pp. 86–89.

[4]   Sandars, 2000, p. 256–257.

[5]   Cooley, 2008; Calder, 2007.

[6]   Cooley's argument is more nuanced than presented here and includes two variables: regime type (which he describes as the contractual credibility of a country's institutions) and a regime's dependence on the United States, although the former offers the most explanatory power. Combining these two factors, he explains when basing contracts will be accepted,

are the most dependable host nations; democratizing states are the least dependable host nations; and authoritarian states fall somewhere in between. We amend this argument. When considering the robustness of long-term basing rights, we argue that, while consolidated democracies are indeed more dependable than other nations, authoritarian states are the least reliable host nations, while democratizing nations are the ones that fall in between. Table 3.1 outlines how regime type affects access risk.

During the Cold War, anticommunist dictators were thought to be steadfast allies and good hosts because they were not beholden to public opinion.[7] Yet because decisionmaking in authoritarian states

Table 3.1
Regime Type and Peacetime Access Risk

Regime Type	Impact on Basing Agreements	Access Risk
Consolidated democracy	• Legitimate agreements • Established party system moderates officials' positions on bases • Technocratic administration of agreement routinizes U.S. presence	Low
Democratizing	• Previous agreement lacks legitimacy • Weak institutions lead candidates to appeal to nationalism, politicizing U.S. bases • Opportunity to forge a more equitable and legitimate agreement	Medium
Authoritarian	• Agreements lack popular legitimacy • Unconstrained decisionmaking enables leaders to make sudden changes to U.S. access • Contingent on the leader who made agreement • Unlikely to persist beyond the regime	High

indifferent, politicized, and contested. According to Cooley, democratizing states "have been the most politically volatile of base hosts" because they have often politicized and contested U.S. basing rights (Cooley, 2008, p. 250). In democratizing states, new political actors often take a populist antibase stance to gain political support, and newly empowered branches of government (e.g., legislatures or courts) may assert their power over basing related issues. In contrast, authoritarian states politicize U.S. base rights when they want to renegotiate the contract, extract additional concessions in terms of quid pro quo, or evict U.S. forces. For more see Cooley, 2008 pp. 18–23, 249–253.

[7]   Cooley, 2008, pp. 14–15; Calder, 2007, pp. 115–119.

tends to be centralized and relatively unconstrained, dictators can break agreements or revise basing decisions with little warning. In 1962, for instance, Saudi Arabia abruptly decided to terminate the U.S. lease to Dhahran Airfield.[8] As a result, the United States lost all the investments it had made in the facility to support USAF bomber operations. Authoritarian states, therefore, are less likely to honor their basing agreements than other types of regimes. In addition to the uncertainty created by a personalized and informal decisionmaking process, bases in authoritarian states are at risk because they are not likely to persist beyond the regime that makes the agreement. When a dictator falls, the new government almost invariably challenges the U.S. military presence to distinguish itself from its unpopular predecessor and burnish its nationalist credentials.[9] For example, Libyan revolutionary leader Muammar Qaddafi wasted little time before expelling the United States from Wheelus Air Base after deposing King Idris in 1969.[10] Due to its cooperation with the late regime, the United States was widely discredited because many believed that it turned a blind eye toward past repression to maintain its basing rights.[11] In short, a U.S. military presence in autocratic nations inevitably associates the United States with detested rulers and often leads to blowback if they fall.

While all regime transitions are likely to generate challenges to an existing U.S. military presence, nations that are transitioning to democracy can be especially problematic because the introduction of political competition in the absence of strong institutions incentivizes elites to politicize the basing issue. Yet, in contrast with other transitioning states, this tends to be a relatively short-term phenomenon; as democratic institutions mature, a more-dependable (although probably more constrained) form of access may take hold. Although democratization is generally viewed as being a core U.S. interest, it usually hurts U.S. basing rights—at least in the near term—because leaders com-

---

[8]   Bronson, 2008, p. 79.

[9]   Calder, 2007, pp. 112–114.

[10] Pargeter, 2012, pp. 44–46, 71.

[11] Gerson, 1991, p. 17.

peting for votes for the first time often appeal to nationalism to gain public support.[12] In this context, existing basing agreements lack legitimacy because they were made through an undemocratic process. Thus, promising to revise or annul U.S. basing rights is an attractive position that resonates with the public and can help propel aspiring politicians into office. Yet, once elected, candidates who demanded radical changes to a U.S. military presence often moderate their stance because they are reluctant to forfeit the financial benefits or security that accompanies U.S. bases. In sum, democratization encourages elites within a host nation to politicize U.S. bases, which in turn frequently results in lost or significantly reduced U.S. access.

For example, when Greece reverted back to democracy in 1974, after seven years of military rule, U.S. basing rights became a hotly contested national issue that dominated bilateral relations for nearly a decade. Suspicions that the United States had orchestrated or at a minimum backed the military regime led to widespread anti-Americanism, which candidates for office exploited to enhance their standing. As a result of these dynamics, basing agreements were frequently revised to constrain U.S. rights, while at the same time requiring greater compensation.[13]

Nevertheless, democratization also offers the chance to renegotiate basing agreements with a legitimate government, thereby creating a more-stable foundation for peacetime access. Moreover, if a state succeeds in becoming a consolidated democracy, U.S. basing rights tend to fade as a national political issue. Consolidated democracies have several features—legitimacy, stable institutions, and a well-developed party

---

[12] Cooley, 2008, pp. 16–18. According to Cooley, 2008, p. 16, democratizing nations are those that are "undergoing a democratic transition from authoritarian rule." Yet, a democratic transition is only "the interval between one political regime and another" (Guillermo O'Donnell and Philippe Schmitter, *Transitions from Authoritarian Rule: Tentative Conclusions About Uncertain Democracies*, Baltimore, Md.: Johns Hopkins University Press, 1986, p. 6). Because Cooley's case studies suggest that democratization can last for decades, well after a new regime has taken power, it seems that his real argument is that nonconsolidated democracies—not just states in the midst of a transition—are unreliable hosts. To avoid confusion, we maintain Cooley's usage of the word *democratizing* but actually mean nonconsolidated democracies.

[13] Sandars, 2000, pp. 263–266.

system—that together help depoliticize the issue of U.S. bases.[14] First, basing agreements reached by democratic governments are viewed as legitimate because they have been negotiated by freely elected leaders and/or ratified by a legislature or through a public referendum, which helps to defuse nationalist criticism. Second, consolidated democracies are characterized by strong institutions, which have clearly defined roles and responsibilities. As a result of this stable institutional framework, technocrats manage basing issues, which routinizes and depoliticizes the matter. Additionally, the presence of multiple bureaucracies increases the number of actors involved in basing decisions, making it more difficult to modify policies. Third, consolidated democracies have well-developed party systems that encourage elected officials to temper their positions. In democratizing states, which lack strong parties, candidates often employ radical nationalist and populist campaign pledges to win votes, while in consolidated democracies, robust party systems moderate the views of candidates and elected officials.

To understand the effects of democratic consolidation, it is useful to return to the example of Greece in the 1980s. As Greek democracy matured, U.S. basing rights became depoliticized and generally accepted. For instance, Constantine Mitsotakis ran for parliament in 1989 on a platform of upholding the basing agreement with the United States and won handily. Ultimately, the United States decided to close most of its bases in Greece in the 1990s, but its remaining base, Souda Bay, has generated little controversy.[15]

In sum, consolidated democracies that are characterized by procedural legitimacy, institutional stability, and well-regulated political competition are the most reliable partners and host nations because

---

[14] According to Linz and Stepan, a regime is a consolidated democracy when the "institutions, rules, and patterned incentives and disincentives has become, in a phrase 'the only game in town.'" Juan J. Linz and Alfred Stepan, "Toward Consolidated Democracies," *Journal of Democracy*, Vol. 7, No. 2, 1996. Cooley, 2008, pp. 15–18. For more on contractual credibility, see Charles Lipson, *Reliable Partners: How Democracies Have Made a Separate Peace*, Princeton, N.J.: Princeton University Press, 2003; and Lisa L. Martin, *Democratic Commitments: Legislatures and International Cooperation*, Princeton, N.J.: Princeton University Press, 2000.

[15] Sandars, 2000, p. 268.

they cannot arbitrarily modify or abandon their agreements. This does not mean a complete absence of opposition to a U.S. military presence but rather that basing rights are not a highly charged national political issue. Local pragmatic opposition to U.S. bases might persist but typically remains limited and is unlikely to shape national policy. High-profile incidents related to U.S. bases—such as an accident or a crime committed by U.S. military personnel—can temporarily gain significant attention, but their impact tends to be fleeting. Aside from these infrequent high-profile events, U.S. bases tend to recede from the national political discourse because of the particular institutional features of consolidated democracies.

Access Relationships

While regime type influences the reliability of peacetime access, arguments that focus solely on domestic politics are incomplete because they ignore ideational and strategic variables in addition to bargaining incentives that can either contain or exacerbate domestic political opposition.[16] A second variable—the type of access relationship—captures these different factors and significantly affects the level of peacetime access risk. Although the decision to provide the United States with access is often multifaceted, the primary factor often falls into one of three categories: a desire for material benefits (transactional), a shared perception of threat (mutual defense), or a deep security consensus (enduring partnership). Table 3.2 shows the different type of access relationships and the attendant level of access risk.

Transactional Relationships

In the transactional model, a country makes bases on its territory available to the United States to secure material benefits.[17] In this situation,

---

[16] Yeo, 2011, p. 187.

[17] Pettyjohn, 2012, pp. 103–104. A number of studies of U.S. overseas bases have asserted that the transactional model is predominant, but these studies typically focus on negotiations after the base has already been established. They therefore neglect a critically important part of the life cycle of an overseas base: why and under what terms it was initially created. By doing so, these studies underestimate the importance of security interests in driving the original basing agreement. See Cooley, 2008, pp. 46–47; Cooley and Spruyt, 2009, pp. 103–

Table 3.2
Type of Access Relationship and Peacetime Access Risk

Type of Access Relationship	Host-Nation Motive for Providing Access	Effect on Access	Access Risk
Transactional	Material benefits	Volatile	High
Mutual defense	Perception of shared threat	Stable when facing common threat	Medium
Enduring partnership	Elite security consensus	Depoliticized	Low

compensation may take many forms, including straightforward rent payments, economic assistance, or arms sales. Compensation-driven access creates an unstable situation because the host nation has every reason to emphasize the problems associated with an American military presence in an effort to extract larger payments. In particular, the host government stresses and perhaps even exaggerates its domestic constraints—namely, public opposition to a U.S. military presence—to gain leverage in negotiations with the United States and ultimately to secure more compensation.[18]

In a transactional relationship, a host nation will attempt to take advantage of any missteps by U.S. forces—either accidents or crimes committed by U.S. personnel—to obtain a better deal. Because the negotiations are iterative, transactional agreements will be characterized by short-term contracts, which enables the host government to renegotiate frequently. In addition, a host government might try to intentionally enflame nationalist sentiment and encourage popular demonstrations to strengthen its bargaining leverage, especially in the lead-up to or during basing negotiations. Although the central government might engineer or encourage nationalist outrage, domestic oppo-

---

111; Blaker, 1989, pp. 105–114; Calder, 2007, pp. 127–140, 136–148; and Duncan L. Clarke and Daniel O'Connor, "U.S. Base Rights Payments After the Cold War," *Orbis*, Vol. 37, No. 3, Summer 1993. In contrast, Harkavy, 1989, pp. 320–358, argues that mutual security interests were dominant for the first several decades of the Cold War but that, more recently, access relationships are becoming more transactional.

[18] Robert D. Putnam, "Diplomacy and Domestic Politics: The Logic of Two-Level Games," *International Organization*, Vol. 42, No. 3, Summer 1988, p. 450.

sition to transactional basing agreements is also likely to emerge organically because it is clear that the bases serve the interests of the United States more than they do those of the host nation. Moreover, corrupt elites often misappropriate the rents from basing agreements, fueling the public's anger toward the U.S. military presence. However, if a host government attempts to generate opposition to U.S. bases, it risks becoming entrapped by its own rhetoric and may be forced to follow through on its bluffs to limit or terminate U.S. access. Consequently, transactional basing agreements typically result in a vicious bargaining cycle, escalating payments, and restrictions on (or the loss of) access.[19]

Mutual-Defense Relationships

In the second model, nations offer to host American forces when there is a common threat.[20] This is a fairly stable foundation for a basing agreement, so long as the U.S. military presence remains focused on countering this mutual security challenge. The perception of a shared and growing threat is the most frequent reason that other nations consent to the establishment of a peacetime U.S. military presence. In this type of mutual-defense relationship, however, the United States is likely to encounter difficulties if it tries to use bases or forces for unrelated operations.[21] Moreover, if a host nation's threat perception declines or diverges from that of the United States, basing rights can become increasingly tenuous, and access is more likely to be rescinded.[22]

Today, there is no longer any single, overriding, and unambiguous global threat akin to the one the Soviet Union posed during the Cold War. While the United States confronts a variety of security challenges in different regions, most other nations today face geographi-

---

[19] This is similar to what Calder calls *bazaar-type* basing. Calder, 2007, pp. 140–151.

[20] Pettyjohn, 2012, pp. 102–103.

[21] During the Cold War, when the United States wanted to use its European bases or the forces stationed at these facilities for other operations, it often encountered resistance. See Grimmett, 1986; Walter J. Boyne, "El Dorado Canyon," *Air Force Magazine*, Vol. 82, No. 3, March 1999; and Siegel, 1995.

[22] Pettyjohn, 2012, pp. 104–105; Stephen Walt, *The Origins of Alliances*, Ithaca, N.Y.: Cornell University Press, 1987; Calder, 2007, pp. 69–72.

cally discrete challenges.[23] Moreover, because the United States often seeks access arrangements that enable it to use bases for a range of different operations, it is more difficult to create a direct and enduring tie between U.S. bases and the security of a host nation, which complicates obtaining and preserving access.[24] Many nations are also hesitant to allow U.S. forces to be stationed on their soil to counter unspecified future threats because the host nation will be implicated in any operations that these forces conduct.[25] As a result, the United States is likely to find that the mutual defense model yields access that is more restricted and less enduring than access during the Cold War.[26]

Enduring Partnerships

Finally, there is the enduring partnership model. All the countries that fall into this category had initially granted the United States basing rights for a reason (either shared threat or compensation) that has since disappeared.[27] Yet, these nations have continued to host U.S. forces because of an elite security consensus that the U.S. military plays a stabilizing role in the world and that the host nation has broad shared

---

[23] The war on terrorism that was launched after 9/11 provided an initial basis for mutual defense, but the threat has tended to be more localized than during the Cold War. Moreover, the United States has, at times, found itself deeply involved in local political disputes because a host government manipulated the parameters of the war on terrorism to bolster its position internally. For example, Uzbek President Islam Karimov used the war on terrorism as a guise for cracking down on all types of dissent (Cooley, 2008, pp. 224–226).

[24] Andrew Krepinevich and Robert O. Work, *A New Global Defense Posture for the Transoceanic Era*, Washington, D.C.: Center for Strategic and Budgetary Assessments, 2007, p. 190.

[25] Lincoln P. Bloomfield, Jr., "Politics and Diplomacy of the Global Defense Posture Review," in Carnes Lord, ed., *Reposturing the Force: U.S. Overseas Presence in the Twenty-First Century*, Newport, R.I.: Naval War College Press, 2006, pp. 61–62.

[26] Another potential difference between the mutual defense model today and the Cold War is the duration of the threat. If shared threats do not persist for decades, such a relationship may not produce an identity change and therefore may not create enduring partnerships.

[27] This is similar to the notion of alliance persistence: "An alliance is said to 'persist' when it is renewed or continued even after the initial conditions that gave rise to it have disappeared or been so transformed as to eliminate the original need" (Stephen A. Walt, "Why Alliances Endure or Collapse," *Survival*, Vol. 39, No. 1, 1997, p. 134).

interests that are advanced by hosting U.S. forces.[28] Shared threat can contribute to the development of a strong security consensus, but other factors, such as common values, identity, and history, also play an important role, resulting in ties that are more durable than just mutual defense.[29] For instance, NATO is today founded on a "collective identity of liberal democracies," which generally supports a continued U.S. military presence in Europe.[30]

When there is a strong security consensus, host-nation elites are able to contain antibase movements that might emerge, preventing them from gaining enough traction to alter national policy. In an effort to defuse antibase movements, elites can use a variety of strategies, including campaigns to shape public opinion or co-option. As long as elite solidarity persists, enduring partners are likely to successfully minimize the impact of antibase movements, resulting in only small changes in basing policy (compared with severe limitations or the loss of access).[31] That is not to say that the enduring partner may never deny the United States permission to use a base for a particular operation or that the relationship is entirely trouble free, but, in general, this is the most secure type of peacetime access.

All the U.S. enduring partners provided basing access during the Cold War and continued to do so after the dissolution of the Soviet

---

[28] *Elites* are defined as foreign and defense policy opinion leaders. This is a broad group of people, including government officials, politicians, members of the diplomatic corps or defense establishment, academics, and policy analysts (Yeo, 2011, pp. 14–15).

[29] This is not to suggest that collective beliefs cannot change, but they tend to be fairly durable. For more on how norms and identities can change, see Paul Kowert and Jeffery Legro, "Norms, Identity, and Their Limits: A Theoretical Reprise," in Peter J. Katzenstein, ed., *The Culture of National Security: Norms and Identity in World Politics*, New York: Columbia University Press, 1996, pp. 470–474, 488–490.

[30] Thomas Risse-Kappen, "Collective Identity in a Democratic Community: The Case of NATO," in Katzenstein, 1996, p. 395. Going even further, Monteleone claims that Europeans do not perceive U.S. bases to be a threat or a violation of their sovereignty because of the existence of a Euro-Atlantic pluralistic security community (Carla Monteleone, "The Evolution of the Euro-Atlantic Pluralistic Security Community: Impact and Perspectives of the Presence of American Bases in Italy," *Journal of Transatlantic Studies*, Vol. 5, No. 1, 2007, p. 69).

[31] Yeo, 2011, pp. 25–27.

Union in 1991. Because the Soviet Union was the shared threat that yielded many of the U.S. overseas bases, it is not surprising that the end of the Cold War often precipitated the shift into the enduring partnership model, which demonstrates that basing relationships are not static. Instead, over time, a host nation's rationale can change, shifting from one type of access relationship to another. (See Table 3.3 for examples.)

Measuring Peacetime Access Risk

We have found that the regime type and access relationship variables interact with each other, and that particular combinations are especially stable or volatile (see Table 3.4 for examples). For instance, to date, all U.S. enduring partners have been consolidated democracies, producing an especially durable foundation for peacetime access. Well-entrenched democratic institutions make it difficult for governments to modify or abandon existing basing agreements, while the shared identity fostered by a common form of government embeds U.S. access in a broader set of security cooperation activities, helping to depoliticize the issue of U.S. bases.

The second most durable type of access has been based on shared threat with consolidated democracies. Only one country in this cat-

Table 3.3
Examples of Different Access Relationships

	Transactional Model	Mutual Defense Model	Enduring Partnership
United Kingdom		1946–1990	1991–2014
Australia		1955–1990	1991–2014
UAE		1990–2014	
Djibouti	2002–2014		
Kyrgyzstan	2001–2014		
Japan[a]		1951–1990	1991–2014
Philippines	1956–1992	2001–2014	

[a] This coding is for the main Japanese islands. We would code Okinawa as a special triangular transactional relationship. See Pettyjohn and Vick, 2013, p. 51, fn. 126.

Table 3.4
Regime Type and Access Relationship Combined

	Enduring Partnership	Mutual Defense	Transactional
Consolidated democracy	• UK, 1991–2014 • Germany, 1991–2014 • Spain, 1988–2014 • Portugal, 1996–2014	• Romania, 2001–2014 • South Korea, 2004–2014 • UK, 1946–1990 • France, 1952–1967[a]	• Portugal, 1988–1995 • Greece, 1990–1998 • Panama, 1999[a]
Democratizing	• None	• Japan, 1951–1969 • South Korea, 1988–2004 • Philippines, 2000–2014 • Thailand, 1973–1975[a]	• Philippines, 1986–1992[a] • Ecuador, 1999–2009[a] • Greece, 1976–1989 • Turkey, 1980–2014 • Portugal, 1975–1987 • Panama, 1990–1998 • Kyrgyzstan, 2010–2014[a]
Authoritarian	• None	• UAE, 1990–2014 • Singapore, 1990–2014 • Saudi Arabia, 1990–2003[b] • Bahrain, 1971–2014 • Iran, 1950–1979[a] • Thailand, 1961–1973	• Libya, 1954–1970a • Saudi Arabia, 1945–1961[a] • Uzbekistan, 2001–2005[a] • Pakistan, 1959–1969[a] • Djibouti, 2002–2014 • Kyrgyzstan, 2001–2010 • Ethiopia, 1953–1977[a] • Panama, 1977–1989

[a] These nations entirely revoked U.S. access.
[b] The United States decided to leave Saudi Arabia because of growing restrictions on its access.

egory has evicted U.S. forces (France in 1967). However, this result was certainly skewed by the dynamics of the Cold War—the existence of a single, unifying global threat that persisted for decades. Future threats, which are likely to be shorter and contained to one region, may not yield the same result.

In contrast, the most unstable combination involves authoritarian states that enter into transactional basing agreements with the United States. In this situation, dictators who are unfettered by institutional constraints can arbitrarily threaten to evict U.S. forces unless the United States meets their terms. Consequently, the United States is forced to accept contracts that restrict its access, are of short duration, and obligate it to make increasing payments. As a result, these relationships are unpredictable, and U.S. access is always in question. Moreover, autocrats who are interested only in compensation have entirely revoked U.S. access more than any other type of regime and access relationship.[32]

Similarly, democratizing nations that are in transactional relationships with the United States usually restrict or at times even rescind U.S. access. In this situation, host-nation elites foment nationalist opposition by denouncing past U.S. support for dictators and demanding that U.S. bases be removed or that access be renegotiated on more-favorable terms. This anti-American furor is partly a ploy elites use to win popular support, but at the same time, the host government leverages this sentiment to obtain larger payments. While democratization combined with compensation-based relationships nearly always results in instability and limitations on U.S. access, it also offers an opportunity to revise the existing basing agreement so that it is more equitable and provides more-stable access.

Alternatively, when a democratizing nation is in a shared threat relationship, it is still likely to restrict access, but at the same time more likely to want some type of U.S. military presence to remain. In contrast, when a democratizing state is in a transactional relationship, the incentive for greater compensation fuels rather than contains the nationalism that emerges as a part of the transition from authoritarian to democratic regimes.

---

[32] Examples of authoritarian states that have completely rescinded U.S. access include Ethiopia (1977), Morocco (1962), Libya (1970), Saudi Arabia (1962), Uzbekistan (2005), and Pakistan (1969).

Some of the combinations of regime type and access relationship have never or rarely existed. For instance, only two consolidated democracies had transactional relationships with the United States: Portugal (1988–1995) and Greece (1990–1998).[33] In these instances, stable democratic institutions restrained Portuguese and Greek leaders, leading them to abide by the existing basing agreements. Yet, one would also expect transactional dynamics to push the host nation to request that the agreement be renegotiated in an effort to secure larger payments.

Similarly, the United States has never had enduring partners that were authoritarian regimes or undergoing a transition to democracy. One would expect, however, that a security consensus in an authoritarian regime would provide stability but that the consensus would be unlikely to persist if there were a regime change. Moreover, if the state were to democratize, one can imagine that there is a higher probability that it will experience a shift in elite beliefs that could erode the previous security consensus.

Given the complexities of combining these two variables, we used a minimum rule (taking the lowest score) to create a composite access risk metric for a number of current host nations (see Figure 3.1). To identify a country's regime type, we used Freedom House's Freedom Rating, which categorizes countries as free, partly free, or not free.[34] *Free* corresponds with consolidated democracies, which we assign the a low risk rating (green). *Partly free* represents nonconsolidated democracies or democratizing states, which we assign a moderate risk score (yellow). *Not free* indicates that the government is authoritarian and has a high risk rating (red).

For access relationship, we explored the historical record to determine the primary reason each nation hosts U.S. forces. This qualitative assessment was necessary because no easily observable and quantifiable metric can accurately identify whether an American military presence

---

[33] Okinawa's hidden transactional model is a special case; see Pettyjohn and Vick, 2013, p. 51, fn. 126.

[34] Arch Puddington, *Freedom in the World 2013: Democratic Breakthroughs in the Balance*, Washington, D.C.: Freedom House, 2013, p. 32.

Figure 3.1
Composite Peacetime Access Risk with Select Host Nations

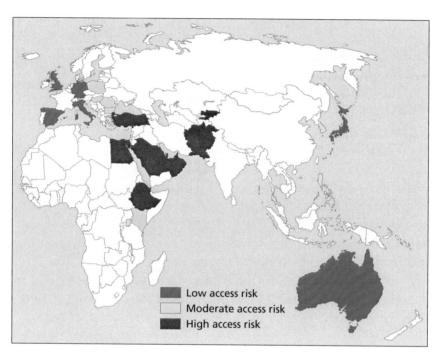

SOURCE: Pettyjohn and Vick, 2013.
RAND *RR1339-3.1*

is based primarily on a shared identity, shared threat, or a transactional dynamic. This is due in part to the fact that the U.S. government does not admit that it pays for basing rights, preferring to adhere to the pretense that all of its bases overseas provide defense against common threats.[35] Although the United States frequently provides significant economic and security assistance to enduring partners or countries facing a shared threat, this is not necessarily the *primary* reason a nation provides the United States with access. Rather, the presence of

---

[35] Clarke and O'Connor, 1993.

economic assistance and arms sales may be due to the broader security relationship or the existence of a common threat.[36]

Because enduring partners are reliable host nations, they were given the lowest risk score (green). The mutual defense model offers a stable foundation for countering the shared threat and therefore receives a moderate risk score (yellow). Finally, transactional relationships are very unstable, so they are given a high risk score (red). The scores for regime type and access relationship were then combined by assigning each country the lower of its two scores. For instance, if a nation was partly free and transactional, it received a yellow regime type score and a red access relationship score, which would make its composite risk score red.

Figure 3.1 displays the scores of a select subset of countries on this composite risk metric. Not surprisingly, the U.S. Western European partners—which are consolidated democracies and enduring partners—are the most reliable host nations, along with a few close Asian allies. Nevertheless, in the regions that have been identified as the highest priority—the Middle East and Southeast Asia—the United States faces greater uncertainty. In the Middle East, most of the U.S. closest allies are hereditary monarchies. Given the unexpected and dramatic fashion in which many Middle Eastern dictators fell as a part of the Arab spring, it is clear that popular pressure poses a significant challenge to Middle Eastern autocrats. In Southeast Asia, the United States is on better ground because access is based on shared threat and some of its closest partners, such as Thailand and the Philippines, are democracies—although imperfect ones.

Peacetime Access Challenges Across Time

In addition to the risk assessment, we also wanted to gain a better understanding of how often and when host nations have challenged

---

[36] Harkavy, 1989, concludes that other nations provide the United States with bases in return for arms sales. This, however, is likely a spurious relationship. See also Pettyjohn, 2012, p. 66.

U.S. basing rights. Several excellent studies on the subject of peacetime access risk use case studies to explore when and why opposition to U.S. bases emerges, but to date, no one has systematically compiled data on threats to U.S. peacetime access over time. Therefore, to complement the longitudinal data we have gathered on contingency access, we also created a data set on peacetime access challenges from 1950 to 2014.

Unlike contingency access, no obvious metric for peacetime access challenges also lends itself to data collection across many decades. Conceivably, any number of variables could serve as proxies for contested access, including the frequency, number, or size of antibase protests; statements of high-ranking government officials denouncing or calling for the removal of U.S. bases; or actions legislators or courts take to restrict or revoke U.S. basing rights. Yet, all these criteria attest only to the fact that there was opposition to a U.S. military presence; they do not indicate whether this opposition negatively affected U.S. basing rights. Consequently, we chose not to use any of the above measures but instead to focus on the status and content of U.S. basing agreements. In particular, we gathered information on when basing agreements were prematurely terminated or allowed to lapse, when limitations were placed on U.S. peacetime access, and when the United States was forced to provide greater compensation to retain access. The complete list is available in Appendix A. It is important to note that these data include only changes to the U.S. peacetime presence that were at least in part involuntary. When the United States chose to reduce its presence or close a base on its own accord, it was not responding to host-nation pressure, and the event is therefore not included in the data.

We identified three primary challenges to peacetime access: evictions, restrictions, and increased quid pro quo. Evictions include instances in which access was revoked, while restrictions curtailed U.S. basing rights in one of the following ways:

- *consultation*: an explicit requirement that the United States, at a minimum, confer with the host nation or seek its explicit approval before making changes to its military presence or using the bases for particular operations

- *duration:* a provision that reduces the length of the U.S. lease relative to prior agreements.
- *sovereignty:* a change that asserts the host nation's jurisdiction over facilities the United States or its military personnel use
- *limits on the type of forces:* prohibitions on certain types of forces or activities
- *contraction:* decreases in the size of the U.S. military presence, either in terms of the number of facilities that U.S. forces have access to or the number of forces or platforms permitted at any one time.

Increased quid pro quo captures when the United States had to provide larger aid packages or pay higher rents to retain access. Figure 3.2 shows the number of times that U.S. peacetime access has been revoked, restricted, or become more expensive between 1950 and 2014. Not surprisingly, there have been more restrictions (57) than evictions (17), while compensation packages were increased 38 times. Evictions and restrictions are mutually exclusive, but at times, host nations placed limits on U.S. rights *and* raised the price of access. The

Figure 3.2
Peacetime Access Challenges, 1945–2014

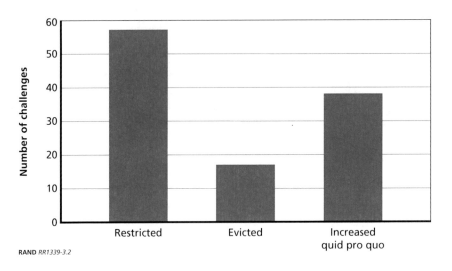

RAND *RR1339-3.2*

United States made larger payments in return for more-limited rights 18 times.

Figure 3.3 shows the total number of peacetime access challenges (i.e., restrictions, evictions, and increased compensation) that occurred each year and reveals that there have been three particularly difficult periods.[37] During the first of these episodes (1954–1969), there were 36 challenges to U.S. access. By the late 1950s, many nations began to question the very generous terms of the initial post–World War II access agreements signed with the United States. These one-sided agreements had largely been a product of the overwhelming economic, military, and political dominance of the United States in the early postwar era. As the rest of the world recovered, host nations sought inevitably to

Figure 3.3
Number of Peacetime Access Challenges, by Year, 1954–2014

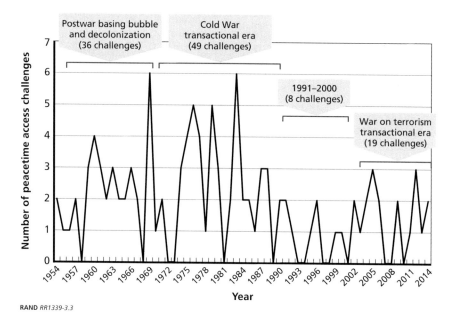

---

[37] An agreement that included any provision restricting U.S. basing rights was counted once, even if that agreement imposed multiple types of limitations on the United States. One thing worth noting is that the periods identified in Figure 3.3 were of different lengths, which is likely to have affected the number of challenges in each one.

redress this imbalance by renegotiating basing accords.[38] Also during the 1950s and 1960s, the process of decolonization proved to be troublesome, with newly independent states insisting on revising imperial basing agreements on terms less favorable to the United States.

Between 1970 and 1990, the majority of U.S. basing problems were products of transactional basing agreements with authoritarian or democratizing states. During this period, 34 of the 49 challenges occurred in states that fit both these characteristics. Five nations (Philippines, Greece, Turkey, Spain, and Portugal) were especially problematic, accounting for 67 percent (33) of the challenges to access.

In the 1990s, challenges to U.S. basing rights dramatically declined; only eight challenges occurred. This drop-off was a product of two factors. First, given the more-benign security environment, the United States stopped paying exorbitant amounts for base access, thereby ending the nearly continuous transactional basing negotiations that had been so prevalent during the latter part of the Cold War.[39] Second, many of the previously troublesome host nations had successfully democratized. Consequently, if U.S. bases remained in these states, they became less controversial. Two major incidents during this period were exceptions to this general trend. The first major challenge emerged in Japan, after the rape of a young Okinawan schoolgirl by U.S. servicemen led to the Special Action Committee on Okinawa agreement to reduce the number of U.S. bases on the Japanese island. The second challenge was the result of a terrorist attack on a U.S. facility in Saudi Arabia. As a result of this incident, U.S. forces were consolidated and relocated to a remote air base in the desert to reduce the visibility and vulnerability of U.S. bases.

The 9/11 terrorist attacks on the United States marked the beginning of the most recent period of basing troubles. In response, the United States embarked on a global war against terrorism, which required acquiring access in new places. But many of these new partners have proven to be difficult hosts. Between 2002 and 2014, there

---

[38] For more on why countries were able to successfully challenge U.S. basing rights, see Cooley and Spruyt, 2009, pp. 107–109.

[39] Clarke and O'Connor, 1993.

were 19 challenges to U.S. basing rights. As in previous eras, many (12) of these incidents were caused by authoritarian or democratizing states that had transactional relationships with the United States. In particular, the United States has faced repeated issues with Central Asian host nations and the small African state of Djibouti.

While challenges as a whole have been quite common, evictions have been less frequent. Figure 3.4 shows the 17 countries that have thrown out U.S. forces since 1945. During the Cold War, host nations expelled U.S. forces nine times, all between 1962 and 1979. Since the 1990s, seven host nations have revoked U.S. basing rights, with five of these incidents occurring since 2003.

Figure 3.5 presents detailed information on the types of restrictions host nations have imposed on the United States. This vertical axis of this graph counts the number of restrictions, while the color of the bar indicates the number and specific types of constraints. One agreement may have imposed multiple different constraints on the United States. By the late 1950s, it became common for host nations to curb U.S. basing rights, although the specific types of restrictions varied considerably. Over time, however, contraction and limits on type have become the most frequent types of restrictions. This is probably due to the fact that, for existing basing agreements, earlier revisions had already dealt with the balance of sovereign rights and such issues as

Figure 3.4
Countries That Have Evicted the United States

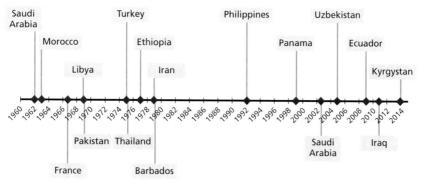

RAND RR1339-3.4

Figure 3.5
Number and Type of Restrictions, by Year

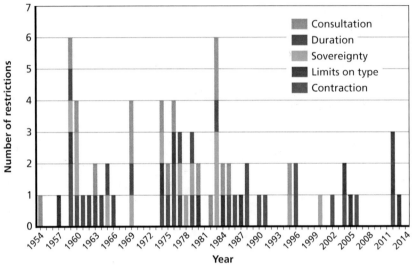

RAND RR1339-3.5

consultation, and new base contracts were likely to be more constrained from the beginning than those that had been made during the early years of the Cold War.

Figure 3.6 shows the number of times each year the United States was forced to pay higher rents to maintain its bases. By the mid-1950s, host nations' growing appetites for compensation were already becoming a problem. Moreover, paying one nation more tended to have a ripple effect as other nations demanded similar deals, which helps explain why the challenges tended to cluster together temporally. As Frank Nash, a DoD official in the Eisenhower administration, observed, "the price paid for facilities in one country becomes known to other nations similarly situated, and an increase in the quid pro quo granted to one is likely to create new demands in other countries."[40] Maintaining peacetime access became increasingly costly during the Cold War as the United States was forced to provide greater aid packages or compensation 26 times. This practice has been far less frequent

---

[40] Nash, 1957, p. 50.

Figure 3.6
Increased Quid Pro Quo, by Year

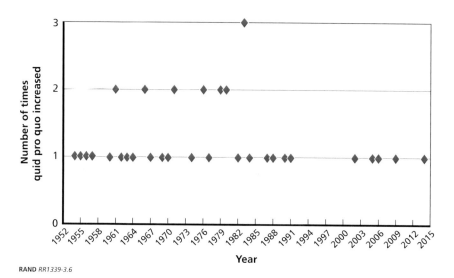

in the post–Cold War era; however, it reemerged as a common practice in the post-9/11 era.

Conclusion

Since the United States established an extensive overseas military presence after World War II, its global network of bases has faced persistent challenges. Host nations have restricted U.S. basing rights, evicted U.S. military personnel, and demanded greater amounts of compensation in return for permitting U.S. forces to remain in peacetime. In this chapter, we developed a methodology to identify dependable host nations and those countries that are likely to restrict or rescind U.S. basing rights. Using this approach, we then identified the levels of risk associated with current host nations and recommended that, wherever possible, the United States prioritize hosts that are stable democracies and those having a shared threat or enduring partnership.

We also compiled information on peacetime challenges to U.S. access and found that U.S. peacetime basing rights had been under the most duress during the last several decades of the Cold War. Since that peak, peacetime access challenges have abated. In large part, this is due to the fact that the United States has fewer bases in high-risk countries (transactional relationships in authoritarian or democratizing regimes) than it did during the Cold War. It is worth noting, however, that the United States has secured access in many countries since 2001 that do pose a significant access risk. If this trend continues, peacetime access challenges are likely to spike once again. Moreover, there has been a marked increase in the number of evictions in the past decade.

One thing that our data do not capture is broad changes in the international environment, in particular the fact that most new access agreements are starting from a much more constrained baseline than those that had been reached in the early years of the Cold War.[41] The era of U.S. forces having carte blanche to do what they please is long gone. Instead, host nations generally do limit U.S. freedom of action and demand ultimate jurisdiction over the facilities and U.S. person-nel. While this is appropriate, it is not clear that U.S. officials and military personnel have fully accepted this fact. Many Americans still expect access to foreign territory to be forthcoming and are irritated and surprised when other countries limit or deny basing privileges. These outdated attitudes must be shed. U.S. officials need to embrace the fact that all host nations, even close allies and enduring partners, are going to demand that U.S. respect their sovereignty. By being con-siderate guests, the United States may help defuse some of internal challenges that pose a risk to its peacetime access. In addition to steady-state basing rights, the United States also needs access to foreign bases, territory, and airspace during contingencies. The next chapter consid-ers the issue of contingency access and identifies the factors associated with access permissions and denials.

---

[41] It is also worth pointing out that the number of U.S. bases overseas has also declined dra-matically. Since the United States maintains far fewer bases and forces overseas than it did during the Cold War, its network of bases is more brittle, and access problems could have a larger impact than in past decades.

CHAPTER FOUR

Contingency Access

On April 14, 1986, nearly 60 USAF aircraft took off from four bases in the UK, beginning an approximately 2,800-nautical mile–long combat mission to Libya.[1] Because of the lengthy journey around the Iberian Peninsula through the Straight of Gibraltar to the Mediterranean, the 24 F-111s of the 48th Tactical Fighter Wing based at RAF Lakenheath and the 5 EF-111s of the 42nd Electronic Combat Squadron stationed at RAF Upper Heyford had to be supported by 29 Strategic Air Command tankers operating from RAF Mildenhall and RAF Fairford (see Figure 4.1).[2] As it had been originally conceived, the mission to punish Libyan leader Muammar Qaddafi for his support for terrorism was considerably less arduous. The USAF had intended to fly through French airspace en route to targets near Tripoli, which would have significantly shortened the aircraft's transit times from their UK bases to Libya. Yet, when the French and Spanish governments refused to permit USAF aircraft to overfly their nations, Operation El Dorado Canyon turned into the longest fighter combat mission in history, lasting 13 hours and requiring as many as 12 aerial refuelings for each aircraft.[3]

---

[1] "Briefing by Shultz and Weinberger on Strikes Against Libya," *New York Times*, April 15, 1986.

[2] About 90 minutes into the mission—after the first aerial refueling—six of the F-111s and one of the EF-111s returned to their bases in the UK (Boyne, 1999, p. 60).

[3] Boyne, 1999, pp. 59–60; Judy G. Endicott, "Raid on Libya: Operation ELDORADO CANYON," in Timothy Warnock, ed., *Short of War: Major USAF Contingency Operations, 1947–1997*, Washington, D.C.: Air Force History and Museums Program, 2000, p. 150;

Figure 4.1
Operation El Dorado Canyon: The 1986 Strikes Against Libya

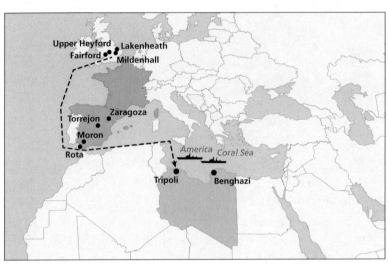

Despite the complications of such a grueling mission, U.S. officials decided that USAF aircraft were needed for the operation to increase the probability of a successful retaliatory attack against all five targets in both Tripoli and Benghazi at acceptable risk to U.S. forces. Two carrier battle groups were nearby, in the Tyrrhenian Sea, but the 6th Fleet forces in the vicinity were, by themselves, incapable of carrying out a simultaneous attack on all the desired targets, which was deemed to be necessary to maximize surprise and to complete the mission before Libyan air defenses had the chance to respond.[4] During this joint oper-

---

Joseph T. Stanik, *El Dorado Canyon: Reagan's Undeclared War with Qaddafi*, Annapolis, Md.: Naval Institute Press, 2003, pp. 150–152. The United States reportedly asked Spain for overflight and, failing that, permission for U.S. tankers based in Spain to refuel the combat aircraft en route to Libya, but the Spanish government rejected both propositions (George J. Church, David Beckwith, Barrett Seaman, and Christopher Ogden, "Hitting the Source: U.S. Bombers Strike at Libya's Author of Terrorism, Dividing Europe and Threatening a Rash of Retaliations," *Time*, Vol. 127, No. 17, April 28, 1986).

[4] To reduce the risk to U.S. forces, which had to penetrate heavily defended Libyan airspace, the President determined that the attacks against all five Libyan targets had to be carried out simultaneously and that each aircraft would be permitted to make only one pass at

ation, USAF F-111s struck at western targets near Tripoli, including the Azziziyah barracks, the Sidi Bilal training complex, and the Tripoli airport. At the same time, carrier aircraft from the USS *America* and USS *Coral Sea* battle groups flew combat air patrols, suppression of the enemy air defense missions, and attacked targets at Beninia Air Base and Jamahiriyya Barracks, which were near Benghazi.

This example raises a number of important questions: Which countries can the United States rely on for access to bases and airspace during a contingency? Are the same nations that offer reliable peacetime access also likely to provide basing rights and overflight for operations? In particular, will U.S. permanent foreign bases be available when the United States wants to use them? In 1986, for example, the United States did not have a military presence in France, but it maintained several air bases in Spain that it could not use for the strike against Libya.[5] If permanent bases may not be accessible for contingencies, this calls into doubt some rationales for retaining many of these facilities.

Additionally, have there been factors that were regularly associated with contingency access permissions and denials across time? In the Libya case, as in many others, U.S. officials seemed to be surprised when another nation refused to allow U.S. forces to use its territory or airspace, which forced last-minute changes to military plans.[6] If contingency access outcomes could be predicted, DoD could anticipate when states may be uncooperative and develop operational plans to avoid these issues instead of being forced to hastily adapt when a country refuses to allow U.S. forces to operate from or above its territory.

---

its target. This increased the force structure required to carry out the operation (Boyne, 1999, pp. 59–60; Stanik, 2003, pp. 152–154).

[5]   Church et al., 1986. On the return trip to the UK, one F-111 was forced to make an emergency divert to Rota Air Base, which was allowed (Boyne, 1999, p. 62).

[6]   Other instances of U.S. officials being taken by surprise by access problems include Austria, Switzerland, Israel, Saudi Arabia, and Greece denying overflight and basing rights for the 1958 U.S. intervention in Lebanon; Albania declining to host U.S. Army Task Force Hawk during Operation Allied Force; all neighboring states withholding basing rights for a 1996 U.S. strike against Iraq; and Turkey spurning the U.S. request to stage the IV Infantry Division for Operation Iraqi Freedom.

Finally, many people have drawn attention to the problems the United States has encountered securing access for particular operations and have suggested that it is increasingly likely that U.S. forces might find themselves "locked out" from bases that they need and therefore unable to carry out a military operation.[7] Despite this, there has been no systematic effort to explore the frequency and determinants of contingency access outcomes over time. Existing studies have focused exclusively on documenting access denials, and there have been few efforts to identify the factors that may have influenced these decisions. No one has attempted to understand how much of a problem securing contingency access permissions has been for the United States or to establish whether access denials are actually becoming more common.

We aim to fill these gaps in the existing literature by taking a more-comprehensive and methodologically sound approach that examines the full spectrum of contingency access outcomes. Given the limitations of any one methodology, we used two complementary approaches to compensate for the shortcomings of each one alone. First, we constructed a large data set of formal access requests between 1945 and 2013 and statistically tested for the relationship between access outcomes and a number of variables. This allowed us to systematically examine the relationship between numerous factors and access outcomes instead of pointing to isolated examples as evidence that proves or disconfirms a hypothesis. Second, we also examined ten cases in greater depth to get at issues that do not lend themselves to large-scale data analysis, such as *why* states provided or denied access; such factors as shared interests, perception of threat, or how much effort the U.S. government devoted to securing access permissions; and issues of self-censorship—that is, when U.S. officials choose not to ask a country for access because they expect a negative response. This chapter presents the results of the statistical analysis, while Chapter Five discusses the qualitative analysis.

---

[7]   Siegel, 1995, p. 27; Cote, 2001.

Contingency Access Statistical Analysis

Creating the Data Set

This section briefly describes the approach and methods that we used to identify and code the access requests that are included in the data set. For a more-thorough description of our quantitative methods, see Appendix B. Because there were no existing contingency access data sets and because few sources focused exclusively on access to foreign territory, we compiled information from many different sources. The data set includes only documented nonroutine requests to access another country's territory or airspace for a particular operation. For many operations, the United States asked multiple countries for access, which are all included. A nation may even be listed twice for a particular operation if it modified its access permission during the operation. For example, in Operation Blue Bat—the U.S. intervention in Lebanon in 1958—Greece is listed three times because it first granted U.S. forces overflight and transit rights, then entirely revoked those permissions, and finally allowed U.S. aircraft supporting the Middle Eastern operation to use its bases within certain well-defined bounds. In short, Greece made three different access decisions during the operation that are all captured in the data set.

The data set, therefore, excludes steady-state requests for access to support forward-based forces and regular peacetime exercises that were not in response to a particular stimulus. Consequently, the data do not include normal bilateral and multilateral exercises, such as REFORGER during the Cold War or Foal Eagle today. The data also do not include forced entry operations because, in these instances, the host nation did not consent to the U.S. military presence. The 2003 invasion of Iraq is not listed as an access request because Iraq did not have a say in whether U.S. forces operated in its territory. In contrast, Kuwait, Turkey, Saudi Arabia, the United Arab Emirates (UAE), Qatar, and other nations that hosted or were asked to host U.S. invasion forces are entered in the data set.

Because we built this data set from the ground up, we began by relying heavily on a number of USAF historical documents. We found that focusing on USAF was a good starting point because it is involved in the vast majority of U.S. military operations that require access to foreign territory. For instance, mobility aircraft are needed to transport and support Army units and to supply ground forces, including Marines, who are ashore for operations that last for more than a few weeks. Moreover, USAF tankers are often required to support sea-based air operations. To code the cases, we examined additional sources that provided more details about the operations. As the data set grew, we cross-checked it with existing lists of U.S. military operations for completeness, but we included only operations for which there was a record of the United States asking for or receiving access to foreign bases or airspace. For more recent operations whose USAF and U.S. government histories remain classified, we drew on secondary sources and periodicals.

The contingency access data set, like all data sets, is not without its limitations. First, this data set includes only *formal* U.S. requests for contingency access. In reality, the U.S. decisionmaking process involves at least two steps: a period of deliberation that may involve informal or secret discussions with the host nation to gauge the likelihood that an American access request will be received positively and then a formal request for access, which may be either approved or denied. Because we focused only on the second step (the formal access request), there may be selection effects—omitted variables that influence whether a host nation grants or denies a formal U.S. request for contingency access.[8] In particular, U.S. officials' prior beliefs about the probability that a request will be granted may affect the likelihood of formally requesting access. For instance, the United States may unofficially probe a host government to get a sense of whether it is favorably inclined toward allowing U.S. forces on its soil or in its airspace for a particular operation. If the host nation seems disinclined, American officials may decide to forgo a formal request for access because they anticipate a negative response. As discussed in Chapter Six, the case studies

---

[8] For more on selection effects, see James D. Fearon, "Selection Effects and Deterrence," *International Interactions*, Vol. 28, No. 5, 2002, pp. 5–29; James D. Morrow, "Capabilities, Uncertainty, and Resolve: A Limited Information Model of Crisis Bargaining," *American Journal of Political Science*, Vol. 33, No. 4, November 1989, pp. 941–972.

reveal that this process of self-denial has happened, although relatively infrequently. Moreover, other work on contingency and peacetime access negotiations confirms that base negotiations are often carried out secretly.[9] Nevertheless, our research included the exploration of many declassified documents, and while we found that self-denial does occur, especially when U.S. officials fear that a formal request for contingency access may jeopardize U.S. peacetime basing rights, it was not pervasive. Still, it is likely that the cases included in the data set do suffer from selection effects that will influence the analysis somewhat. Specifically, if the data set does not capture cases of the United States choosing not to ask for access because of a belief that access would be denied, our estimates of how often U.S. access requests are granted will be somewhat inflated. Putting that aside, our analysis of the data set is still useful because the analysis provides insight into the factors associated with access being granted (and the type of access granted) when the United States did make a formal access request. Future work looking more extensively into the magnitude and implications of these selection effects may be valuable.

Second, because the contingency access data set is based entirely on unclassified sources, it doubtlessly excludes many clandestine or special operation forces operations. Some more-recent operations— particularly politically sensitive access requests—may not entirely be accurately reflected in the data. Third, the data on overflight requests and en route stops are often incomplete. Most of the sources that we examined discuss where an operation began and ended but do not always mention the intervening stops or the flight paths of the U.S. aircraft. Our suspicion is that overflight and en route access requests are usually mentioned when there is a problem and frequently excluded when no obstacles were encountered. But since we included only documented and formal requests for access in the data set, we ran statistical tests with and without the overflight entries to ensure that these omissions were not biasing or driving our results. And we found that

---

[9] Jonathan N. Brown, "The Sound of Silence: Power, Secrecy, and International Audiences in U.S. Military Basing Negotiations," *Conflict Management and Peace Science*, Vol. 31, No. 4, 2014b, pp. 406–431; Brown, 2014a.

the results did not significantly change. Despite these limitations, we are quite confident that the data set includes all major U.S. operations and that it is a representative sample of the types of operations that the United States military has conducted over this time.

Explanatory and Dependent Variables

There has been very little work done to identify the factors associated with contingency access permission and denials. Moreover, some of the variables that are believed to influence contingency access outcomes, such as close military ties, shared interests and objectives, hopes for closer ties with the United States, domestic public opinion, and fear of reprisals, do not lend themselves to quantitative analysis.[10] It is difficult, if not impossible, to collect information on these dimensions for all the countries queried and over the nearly 70 years covered by the data set. For instance, public opinion data are not readily available in many authoritarian nations, certainly not for the full range of dates included. Moreover, other factors, such as the amount of effort U.S. officials devoted to securing access, cannot easily be captured quantitatively.

Consequently, based on a review of the literature and historical research, we identified 12 explanatory variables that could plausibly have a significant impact on access permissions and for which data could be acquired for the entire period covered by the data set:

- the operation name and operation location
- the operation type (e.g., combat, humanitarian assistance [HA], etc.)
- the nation asked for access and the region of that nation
- whether the operation occurred during or after the Cold War
- whether the operation occurred before or after 9/11
- whether the nation asked for access is geographically contiguous with the area of the operation
- whether access was granted or denied

---

[10] One of the only studies that explicitly identifies factors that may make a state more inclined or disinclined to provide access is Shlapak et al., 2002, p. 37. However, the authors did not systematically test the effects of these variables but, instead, offer anecdotal evidence of the effects.

- the type of access granted (combat or nonlethal troops, transit, overflight)
- whether the nation asked for access had permanent U.S. bases
- whether the operation received authorization from an international organization
- the nature of the access relationship between the nation asked for access and the United States (transactional, mutual defense, enduring partnership)
- the regime type of the nation asked for access.[11]

For a more detailed discussion of the variables, see Appendix C.

Results of the Statistical Analysis

The results of the data analysis are striking: The United States has been incredibly successful in securing contingency access during this period.[12] Since 1945, 90 percent of U.S. formal requests have been granted, with only 5 percent restricted and 5 percent denied (see Figure 4.2). This finding calls into question the claims of the alarmists who contend that political access problems have been a serious impediment to U.S. military operations overseas.[13] Instead, we have found that the United States has only infrequently encountered contingency access denials. Moreover, while access problems have hindered U.S. operations, often making a mission more complicated or risky, they have not prevented its successful execution.

That is not to suggest that obtaining contingency access was easy, or that the United States is going to be able to replicate these results in the future. Skilled U.S. civilian and military officials devoted considerable effort and time to produce these stunning results. Moreover, throughout the entire period examined, the United States was

---

[11] Regime type was based on a nation's Polity IV score. Polity IV is a data set that assesses the how democratic a nation's political institutions are. For more details, see Monty G. Marshall, *Polity IV Project: Political Regime Characteristics and Transitions, 1800–2013*, Center for Systemic Peace and Societal Systems Research, July 16, 2016.

[12] The full regression results are documented in Appendix B.

[13] Siegel, 1995, p. 27; Cote, 2001, p. 82.

Figure 4.2
Contingency Access Requests in the Dataset Approved, Restricted, and Denied

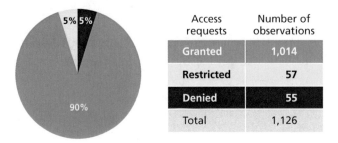

Access requests	Number of observations
Granted	1,014
Restricted	57
Denied	55
Total	1,126

RAND *RR1339-4.2*

the dominant state in both the economic and military realms. If U.S. ascendency does not last, it seems plausible that the United States could encounter greater difficulty acquiring contingency access in the future.

The statistical analysis also reveals that denials and restrictions have not become more prevalent since the end of the Cold War. In fact, somewhat surprisingly we found that the United States was less likely to receive contingency access during the Cold War than in the post–Cold War era. There is not, therefore, an increasing chance that U.S. forces may be unable to carry out an operation because they have been denied access to bases, as some have asserted. In all likelihood, this misperception is due to a focus on a few recent, high-profile instances of access denial, such as Turkey's unwillingness to allow U.S. ground forces to launch an invasion of Iraq from its territory in 2003.

Access outcomes also have no relationship to whether they occurred before or after the September 11, 2001, Al-Qaeda attacks on the United States. Instead, as Figure 4.3 demonstrates, at least 75 percent of U.S. requests for access have been approved in all but a few years.[14] Moreover, unsuccessful requests are fairly evenly distributed across the entire period. It is also worth noting that, contrary to popu-

---

[14] The years that fall below the 75 percent threshold are 1958 (Blue Bat), 1973 (Nickel Grass), 1986 (El Dorado Canyon), 1987 (Earnest Will), 1996 (Desert Strike), 1999 (Allied Force), and 2003 (Iraqi Freedom).

Figure 4.3
Percentage of Successful Contingency Access Requests, 1947–2013

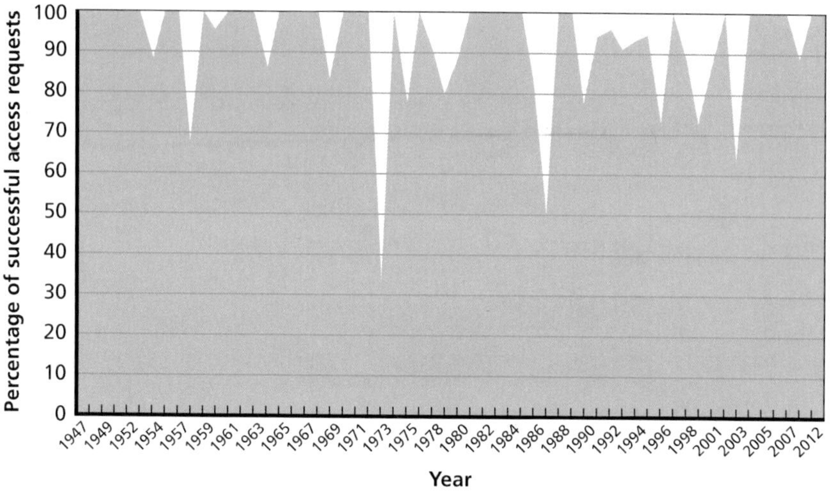

NOTE: Includes only requests for which access was fully granted. Restricted access
and denied access were considered unsuccessful.
RAND RR1339-4.3

lar wisdom, contingency access problems first emerged relatively early
during the Cold War, in the mid-1950s.

Type of Operation

At the aggregate level, access denials have been relatively infrequent;
however, the United States has had more difficulty obtaining access
for some types of operations than others. Figure 4.4 shows the percentage and number of access requests that were approved, denied,
and restricted for each different type of military operation included
in the data set. Not surprisingly, access is nearly automatic for generally noncontroversial operations, such as HA and disaster relief (DR).
At the other end of the spectrum, major combat operations (MCOs)
and limited punitive strikes have posed greater access challenges.[15]
According to the statistical analysis, strike operations are more likely to

---

[15] The predicted probabilities suggest that unrestricted access is less likely for both limited
strike operations and MCOs, but keep in mind that the sample size for both of these categories (especially limited strikes) was very small.

Figure 4.4
Percentage and Number of Access Permissions, Denials, and Restrictions, by Operation Type

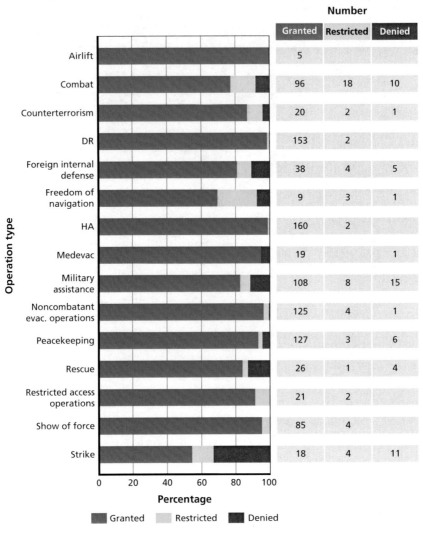

RAND RR1339-4.4

receive restricted access than other types of operations,[16] with 33 percent (11) of U.S. requests having been refused, while only 54 percent
(18) were approved and 12 percent (4) restricted.[17] In contrast, only
8 percent (10) of access requests for MCOs have been denied outright,
but more—15 percent (18)—were restricted-access permissions, and
77 percent (96) were approved. These findings suggest that the United
States should anticipate and plan for how to deal with access problems,
particularly with limited punitive strike operations, while it should
expect to face some restrictions on access for MCOs.

The fact that limited strikes have posed a greater access challenge
than MCOs have indicates that access denials are driven by something
more than the fact that U.S. forces are engaged in combat operations.
Our hypothesis, which was confirmed by the case study analysis, is
that other nations are particularly reluctant to allow limited punitive
strike operations to be carried out from their territory because such
operations seem especially likely to invite retaliation. Unlike MCOs,
which aim to seriously degrade the capabilities of an adversary, limited punitive strikes often do not significantly weaken a target; instead,
they are intended to be a public but also carefully calibrated rebuke.
Host nations fear that such strikes will only provoke a target that will
remain capable and has every reason to lash out at nearby states that
supported the attack.[18]

Region

The United States has also had more problems securing access in some
regions than others. In particular, securing access for unrestricted operations taking place in Southwest Asia is less likely (30 percent as likely
as other regions) than other regions. See Figure 4.5 for the distribution
of access decisions by region.

---

[16] This result was statistically significant at the $p < 0.01$ level, although the substantive size of
the effect is small due to the small number of limited strike operations and the small number
of cases with restricted access.

[17] For the full results of the statistical analysis, see Appendix B.

[18] Additional evidence for this finding is the fact that proximate states are less likely to offer
the United States unrestricted access than those that are not located adjacent to the country
where the operation is taking place. See Appendix B for the full regression results.

Figure 4.5
Access Outcomes, by Region of the Operation

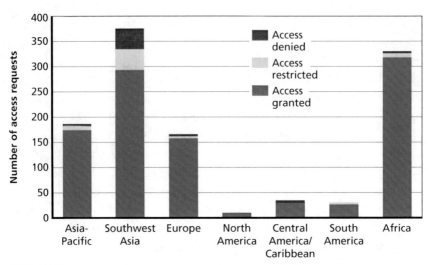

RAND RR1339-4.5

Additionally, as shown in Figure 4.6, nations in Southwest Asia are less likely to provide unfettered access (30 percent as likely) than countries in other regions. This outcome should not be surprising, given that a U.S. military presence in Middle Eastern nations is often quite controversial. Moreover, the United States has repeatedly sought access for operations against Iraq that were unpopular in the region. Somewhat surprisingly, we also found that European nations are also less likely to grant unrestricted access (approximately one-half as likely) as nations in other regions. This finding, however, seems to be driven by the sheer number of times European states have been asked for access, which far outstrips all other regions. European nations may have granted the largest number of requests but have also made more refusals than other, less-often-queried, regions.

Permanent Bases

Conventional wisdom holds that the likelihood that the United States will gain access during a contingency depends in part on whether it has large permanent bases in a country. According to this view, maintaining a permanent presence in a nation during peacetime increases the

Figure 4.6
Access Outcomes, by Region of the Nation Queried

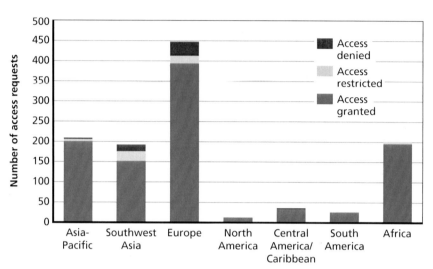

RAND *RR1339-4.6*

probability of being allowed to use its bases during a crisis. Conversely, if the United States does not have a permanent military presence in a country, it is supposedly less likely to be granted temporary permission to operate from a nation's military facilities. In short, contingency access is largely a function of having an enduring peacetime presence.

Statistical analysis demonstrates that countries hosting a large U.S. military presence are no more likely to grant U.S. access requests than other nations (see Figure 4.7). In fact, countries that did not have a large peacetime U.S. military presence have granted U.S. access requests somewhat more often (527 times) than those with permanent U.S. bases (487 times). Similarly, there is no discernable difference between countries with and without permanent bases and the number of restrictions and denials. In short, the presence of permanent bases alone does not improve the probability of securing contingency access.

That should not be taken to mean that permanent bases have not been essential enablers of U.S. operations overseas. In at least 59 percent of the 402 operations in the data set, U.S. forces used permanent bases to carry out its operations. This should not come as a surprise.

Figure 4.7
Permanent Bases and Access Outcomes

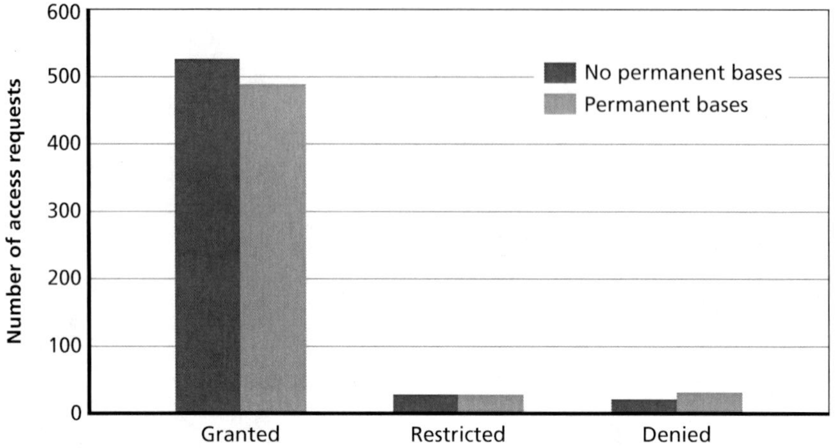

RAND RR1339-4.7

The United States is more likely to ask countries in which it has permanent bases for access than those in which it does not because it is more familiar with those facilities and has all the infrastructure, equipment, and manpower in place that it needs to operate from that location.

Additionally, the statistical analysis revealed that, if they have agreed to grant U.S. forces access to their territory, countries in which the United States has permanent bases provide more freedom of action to the United States.[19] In particular, countries with permanent bases are nearly twice as likely to allow U.S. combat forces to operate from their territories than those without (see Figure 4.8).

Enduring Partners Are the Most Likely to Provide Contingency Access

Having a permanent military presence does not, by itself, improve the probability of securing contingency access permissions. Nevertheless, some types of peacetime access are associated with access approvals.

---

[19] This finding about the type of access granted should be caveated by the fact that, in general, more-permissive types of access, in particular those permitting nonlethal forces, are more common than less-permissive types of access.

Figure 4.8
Type of Access Granted and Presence of Permanent Bases

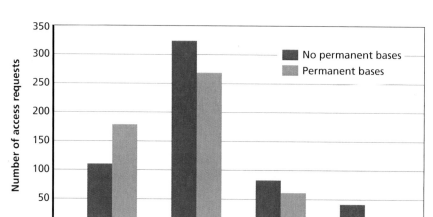

RAND *RR1339-4.8*

In Chapter Three, we established that one of the key factors associated with reliable peacetime access is the type of access relationship. Our statistical analysis reveals that the underlying access relationship is also a predictor of contingency access permissions and denials and that enduring partners are the most likely to grant the U.S. access to their facilities (see Figure 4.9). An astounding 97 percent of the time, enduring partners have permitted U.S. forces to have unrestricted access to their bases and airspace. In contrast, transactional partners are the least reliable and have granted the United States access only 81 percent of the time.[20] Notably, transactional partners are less likely to provide the United States with access than nations in which it has no peacetime presence, which have approved 91 percent of U.S. access requests. In short, a large peacetime military presence correlates only with a high probability of receiving access during a contingency in enduring partner nations.

This finding is incredibly important. The same nations that offer the most dependable peacetime access, enduring partners, are also the

---

[20] There is no statistically significant relationship between transactional and mutual defense partners and contingency access outcomes; see Appendix B.

Figure 4.9
Type of Access Relationship and Contingency Access Permissions

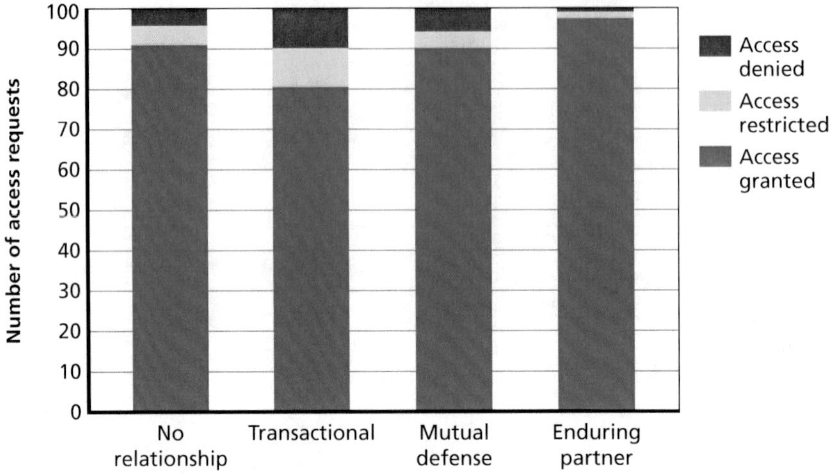

RAND *RR1339-4.9*

most likely to allow forces to operate from their territory during a crisis. Equally important, transactional partners are the least reliable during both peacetime and contingencies. This suggests that the United States should not delude itself into thinking that paying for peacetime basing rights is worth it because these bases will be available when it needs them. Instead, host nations that are primarily interested in material benefits should not be counted on to come through in a pinch, certainly not unless more money is offered. But the example of Turkey in 2003 suggests that even offering very large payments is not enough to guarantee positive outcomes.[21] It is worth noting, however, that

---

[21] The Bush administration reportedly agreed to provide Turkey with a $6 billion aid package in return for allowing the United States to use Turkey's territory and bases for Operation Iraqi Freedom. This figure included $2 billion in military assistance and $4 billion in economic assistance, which was to be used to secure $24 billion in loan guarantees. As a part of the agreement, the U.S. Treasury's Exchange Stability Fund also would have immediately granted Turkey a bridge loan of $8.5 billion that would have later been repaid with the funds from the $24 billion in private loans (Carol Migdalovitz, "Iraq: Turkey, the Deployment of U.S. Forces, and Related Issues," Washington, D.C.: Congressional Research Service, May 2, 2003).

despite the relative unreliability of transactional partners, they have still granted access 80 percent of the time.

Concluding Thoughts

The critics are wrong. Contingency access has not been as debilitating a problem as they suggest. In fact, quite the opposite is true; 90 percent of the United States formal access requests have been approved. Neither have denials become more common in recent years. Denials and restrictions were more common during the Cold War than they have been in recent years. Moreover, difficulty securing access for a particular operation has certainly hindered and at times complicated U.S. missions but has rarely prevented an operation from being carried out.

The statistical analysis established that most of the variables we examined are not correlated with contingency access outcomes. Notably, this includes countries in which the United States has permanent bases. These nations are no more likely to grant the United States access than are nations lacking a peacetime U.S. military presence. Nevertheless, if nations do decide to permit U.S. forces to operate from their bases, countries with U.S. garrisons are more likely to provide more-permissive types of access (i.e., allow combat forces) than are other nations.

Two variables—the type of operation and the type of access relationship—had the most significant influence on contingency access outcomes (see Appendix B for the full results). A nation is most likely to refuse a U.S. request for access for a limited punitive strike operation, while there is a greater chance that it will place limits on access for MCOs. Access permissions and denials are associated with the type of peacetime access relationship. Enduring partners are the most likely to approve access requests, while transactional partners are the least likely. To complement this quantitative analysis, Chapter Five details the results from ten case studies and explores why nations decided to approve or refuse specific U.S. requests.

Other Factors That Influence Access Success or Failure

Several factors that seem to contribute to contingency access success or failure are not easily incorporated in a statistical analysis but can be explored qualitatively. Therefore, to add depth to the quantitative analysis, we surveyed a number of cases to identify the factors that influenced states' contingency access decisions. Although the cases confirm that the decision to grant or deny U.S. forces access for a particular operation is quite context dependent, they also uncovered some general trends that were not apparent in the large-scale data analysis. In particular, four factors—self-interest, perceived legitimacy, the fear of retaliation, and domestic politics—appeared to be associated with access permissions and denials across the cases.

For the qualitative analysis, we began by constructing a list of the most important U.S. military operations since 1945 and then chose cases from this list that varied along key dimensions, such as year; region; type of operation; and, most important, the severity of the access problems encountered (see Table 5.1). We deliberately selected operations that would be considered both access successes, such as Desert Storm and Odyssey Dawn, and access failures, such as El Dorado Canyon and Nickel Grass. We wanted to examine cases with various degrees of access problems so that we could begin to identify the reasons states were so cooperative in some instances and unwilling to host U.S. forces in others.

The case studies confirm that the reasons that other countries provided or denied U.S. forces contingency access were varied and at times

Table 5.1
Case Studies

Operation	Location	Date	Type of Operation	Severity of Access Problem
Blue Bat	Lebanon	1958	Foreign internal defense	Medium
Dragon Rouge	Congo	1964	Rescue	Medium
Vietnam War	Vietnam	1964–1975	Combat	Low
Nickel Grass	Israel	1973	Military Assistance	High
Mayaguez	Cambodia, Gulf of Thailand	1975	Rescue	Medium
El Dorado Canyon	Libya	1986	Strike	High
Desert Shield to Iraqi Freedom	Iraq	1990–2003	Combat, no-fly zone, strikes	Low to High
Allied Force	Kosovo	1999	Combat	Medium
Enduring Freedom	Afghanistan	2001–2014	Combat	Low
Odyssey Dawn	Libya	2011	No-fly zone	Low

idiosyncratic. Nevertheless, some patterns emerged, although this list is by no means exhaustive; neither is the relationship between access outcomes and the factors identified below absolute. In general, another nation either has its own reasons for supporting U.S. military operations or, failing that, wants to be able to justify its actions to internal and external audiences. Given these considerations, states are more likely to support an operation that can be convincingly depicted as legitimate. Additionally, we also found that the fear of retaliation and domestic political considerations often thwart U.S. efforts to secure contingency access.[1] These two factors do not always result in access denials or restrictions but do frequently come up as reasons for access problems and have played prominent roles in the cases most often identified as access failures.

---

[1]   Shlapak et al., 2002, pp. 39–41, also highlights these factors.

Self-Interest: Is an Operation Likely to Help or Harm a Nation's Well-Being?

A common reason other nations have provided U.S. forces with contingency access is that it is in their interests to do so. This rather banal explanation shows up with some frequency in the case studies. During Operation Blue Bat, for instance, the governments in Turkey and Lebanon felt threatened by radical Arab nationalism and thus strongly supported the U.S. intervention against these forces in the Levant. Not surprisingly, other countries whose citizens were being held hostage in the Congo in 1964—Belgium and the UK—also had a vested interest in the rescue operation and therefore granted access to their bases.[2] In fact, because the vast majority of the hostages were Belgian, Belgian paratroops led the operation, which suited both the U.S. and British governments as they sought to avoid an international backlash.[3]

Frequently, U.S. and partner-nation interests align because they share a common enemy. During the Vietnam War, Thailand became a hub for U.S. forces in Southeast Asia because Thai officials viewed communism as a serious threat.[4] Mutual antipathy toward communism, therefore, formed the foundation of the U.S.-Thai relationship from the mid-1960s to the mid-1970s and was the reason that Bangkok allowed U.S. aircraft to engage in essentially unrestricted combat in Vietnam, Laos, and Cambodia.[5] Similarly, after 9/11, many nations welcomed U.S. forces on their soil to combat terrorist groups that the countries had been battling for many years. For instance, both the Philippines and Uzbekistan embraced security cooperation with the

[2] The hostages included 60 Americans, 300 British, and more than 1,000 Belgians. Daniel L. Haulman, "Rebellion in the Congo: Operation DRAGON ROGUE," in Warnock, 2000, p. 55.

[3] Odom, 1988, pp. 46–37.

[4] In 1963, Ambassador Graham Martin identified Thailand as "the hub of U.S. Security efforts in Southeast Asia" (Robert James Flynn, *Preserving the Hub: United States–Thai Relations During the Vietnam War, 1961–1976*, dissertation, Lexington, Ky.: University of Kentucky, 2001, p. 1; see also Randolph, 1986, p. 64).

[5] Flynn, 2001, pp. 4–7.

United States to counter indigenous radical Islamic organizations, which included stationing U.S. forces in their countries.[6]

In contrast, between the first and second Gulf Wars, Turkey was notorious for restricting or denying U.S. access for operations against Iraq out of concern that they might strengthen the Kurds, which were viewed as a threat to Turkey's territorial integrity.[7] This concern also influenced Turkey's decision to prohibit the U.S. Army's 4th Infantry Division from using its territory to open a northern front during the 2003 invasion of Iraq.[8] Yet, Turkey had a change of heart when the U.S. and Iraqi governments failed to reach a new SOFA that would allow U.S. troops to remain in Iraq past 2011. Absent U.S. forces, the Turkish government feared that the Kurdistan Workers' Party—a militant Kurdish separatist organization located in northern Iraq—would be strengthened and more capable of launching attacks against Turkey. Consequently, the Turks reportedly implored the United States to station MQ-1 predator drones at Incirlik Air Base to help Turkey monitor and counter the Kurdistan Workers' Party.[9] In short, Turkey has welcomed U.S. forces when they have helped contain the Kurdish threat but has been a reluctant or unwilling host when U.S. actions strengthened Kurdish groups.

---

[6] Renato Cruz de Castro, "Philippine Defense Policy in the 21st Century: Autonomous Defense or Back to the Alliance," *Pacific Affairs,* Vol. 78, No. 3, Fall 2005, pp. 416–419; Renato Cruz de Castro, "The US-Philippine Alliance: An Evolving Hedge Against an Emerging China Challenge," *Contemporary Southeast Asia,* Vol. 31, No. 3, 2009, pp. 406–407; Cooley, 2012, p. 31.

[7] James E. Kapsis, "From Desert Storm to *Metal Storm*: How Iraq Has Spoiled US-Turkish Relations," *Current History,* Vol. 104, No. 685, November 2005, pp. 382–387; Micah Zenko, *Between Threats and War: U.S. Discrete Military Operations in the Post–Cold War World,* Palo Alto, Calif: Stanford University Press, 2010, pp. 37–38; F. Stephen Larrabee, *Troubled Partnership: U.S.-Turkish Relations in an Era of Global Geopolitical Change,* Santa Monica, Calif.: RAND Corporation, MG-899-AF, 2010, pp. 14–16, 82–84.

[8] Ian O. Lesser, "Turkey, the United States and the Delusion of Geopolitics," *Survival,* Vol. 48, No. 3, Autumn 2006, pp. 84, 88; and Kapsis, 2005, pp. 381–385.

[9] Craig Whitlock, "U.S. Considering Ankara's Request to Base Predators in Turkey to Fight a Kurdish Group in Northern Iraq," *Washington Post,* September 10, 2011.

Legitimacy

Nevertheless, there are many examples of states offering access to the United States when it was not directly in their interest. In these cases, access was most forthcoming when a nation could easily defend its decision to support a U.S. military operation or when it could insulate itself against potential negative repercussions. These conditions are likely to obtain if an operation is seen as legitimate, especially among nations one considers to be peers. It may be easier to acquire access for operations seen as legitimate because foreign leaders truly believe that it is the right thing to do. But it is equally plausible that legitimacy facilitates access by making it easier for a government to justify its support for a U.S. operation to domestic and international audiences or because, to legitimize a mission, the United States voluntarily subjects itself to certain constraints in how it conducts the operation. Legitimacy may thus be important because it provides cover for a decision or credibly conveys information about how the operation will be carried out, not because those making the decision believe it is the morally correct course of action.

It is often assumed that legality and legitimacy are nearly synonymous or at least that they typically go hand in hand. This, however, is not necessarily true because the use of force is only legal if it falls under the self-defense clause of the UN charter or if it is explicitly authorized by the UN under Chapter VII.[10] In contrast, legitimacy is subjective and rests on the beliefs of the actors.[11] The statistical analysis included one variable that was intended to measure legitimacy or legality— formal authorization by an international organization. Given how infrequently, international organizations have expressly sanctioned military operations, it was not entirely surprising to find that this vari-

---

[10] Sarah E. Kreps, "Multilateral Military Interventions: Theory and Practice," *Political Science Quarterly*, Vol. 123, No. 4, Winter 2008, pp. 584–585; Bruno Simma, "NATO, the UN and the Use of Force: Legal Aspects," *European Journal of International Law,* Vol. 10, No. 1, 1999, pp. 4–5. In some cases, however, gaining authorization from an international organization is constitutionally mandated. We thank Alex Cooley for pointing this out.

[11] Erik Voeten, "The Political Origins of the UN Security Council's Ability Legitimize the Use of Force," *International Organization*, Vol. 59, No. 3, Summer 2005, p. 534.

able was not a statistically significant determinate of access decisions. Nevertheless, that does not mean that legitimacy should be dismissed as being unimportant. It does mean that international authorization, in and of itself, does not facilitate access permission. But because legitimacy is a nebulous concept that rests on perceptions, it is a concept that is better explored qualitatively. Our qualitative analysis found that there are a number of different factors that can influence perceptions of legitimacy, including whether a mission is in response to unambiguous aggression, an operation has explicit or implied UN Security Council (UNSC) authorization, or it is endorsed by a regional international organization. Legitimacy may also be tied to the terms of the U.S. basing agreement with the host nation. For instance, some countries— such as Italy and Turkey—at times have emphasized that their bases can be used only for NATO operations.[12] Ensuring that an operation has international legitimacy may be particularly important in nations where it is constitutionally mandated that the legislator approve access requests, as is the case in Turkey, for example.[13]

Responses to Clear Aggression

One of the most widely accepted reasons that a nation may resort to force is individual or collective self-defense, which is enshrined in Chapter VII of the UN charter.[14] One would think that, if the United States claimed to be exercising its right to self-defense, its actions would be seen as not only legal but also legitimate and that it would have little difficulty obtaining the access that it needed to execute a mission. But because many states have invoked their right to self-defense under dubious circumstances, this assertion is not always believed. The right to self-defense has most often been accepted when the United States

---

[12] Grimmett, 1986, pp. 23, 51–52.

[13] Cooley, 2008, p. 118.

[14] The UN charter prohibits members "from the threat or use of force against the territorial integrity or political independence of any states, or in any other manner inconsistent with the Purposes of the United Nations" except under Article 51, which allows for the "inherent right of individual or collective self-defense if an armed attack occurs against a Member of the United Nations." See United Nations, Charter of the United Nations, June 26, 1945, Chapter 1, Article 2(4), and Chapter 7, Article 51.

has been responding to clear belligerence or what appears to be the imminent threat of aggression. Several of the cases that can be characterized as access successes (Desert Shield/Desert Storm, Vigilant Warrior, and Enduring Freedom) were also instances of overt international aggression. Some of these cases correlate with authorization from an international organization, but responses to aggression are implicitly understood to be legitimate and do not necessarily require additional authorization. Of course, blatant aggression does not always trigger an international military response but, clearly, creates a relatively favorable context for securing international support for military action.

During the first Gulf War, for example, there were "uniquely favorable conditions" for forging a broad coalition against Saddam Hussein.[15] UN Secretary General Boutros Boutros-Ghali noted that "The Iraqi invasion and occupation of Kuwait was the first instance since the founding of the Organisation [UN] in which one Member State sought to completely overpower and annex another."[16] Wars of conquest are prohibited by international law, and in this instance, there was no disguising the fact that Saddam Hussein had forcibly annexed Kuwait. This helped build support for military action, particularly after diplomatic solutions were pursued and failed.[17] For the defense of Saudi Arabia (Operation Desert Shield), 21 nations provided basing, transit, or overflight rights, with only two outright denials. For the offensive against Iraq (Operation Desert Storm), 17 countries provided basing, transit, or overflight rights, and several nations that initially had restricted U.S. access removed the limitations.

At times, even preparations for what appears to be an impending military offensive have been sufficient to elicit strong support for a U.S. military operation. In 1994, for example, when the United States

---

[15] Thomas A. Keaney and Eliot A. Cohen, *Revolution in Warfare? Air Power in the Persian Gulf*, Annapolis, Md.: Naval Institute Press, 1995, p. 163

[16] Quoted in Christine Gray, "From Unity to Polarization: International Law and the Use of Force Against Iraq," *European Journal of International Law*, Vol. 13, No. 1, 2002, p. 2.

[17] For more on how the United States built international and domestic support for Operation Desert Storm, see Evan Braden Montgomery, "Counterfeit Diplomacy and Mobilization in Democracies," *Security Studies*, Vol. 22, No. 1, 2013, pp. 58–64.

already had its hands full with crises in Bosnia, Haiti, and North Korea, it appeared as if Hussein was going to try to take advantage of these diversions to invade Kuwait again. On October 7, Iraq began to build up its forces near its southern border by mobilizing two elite Republican Guard divisions; within days, there were nearly 71,000 Iraqi forces near Kuwait.[18] Although the United States had aircraft in Saudi Arabia to enforce the no-fly zone over southern Iraq, there were not enough ground or air forces in the theater to hold off an armored Iraqi incursion of that size.[19] U.S. President William Clinton wasted little time before ordering a number of "precautionary steps" that involved rapidly deploying reinforcements to the Persian Gulf.[20] Given the urgency of the situation and the fear of repeating the mistakes of 1990, the United States had little trouble finding places to bed down its forces in theater.[21] All six members of the Gulf Cooperation Council (GCC) quickly granted the United States basing rights.[22] Operation Vigilant Warrior deterred an Iraqi offensive against Kuwait, but it also taught Hussein to adopt more subtle tactics in the future that made it more difficult to forge a unified international response.

---

[18] W. Eric Herr, *Operation Vigilant Warrior: Conventional Deterrence Theory, Doctrine, and Practice,* Maxwell Air Force Base, Ala.: School of Advanced Airpower Studies, June 1996, p. 26.

[19] By one count, the United States had 12,165 U.S. troops in the vicinity of the Persian Gulf before the October 1994 crisis (Paul K. White, *Crises After the Storm: An Appraisal of U.S. Air Operations in Iraq Since the Persian Gulf War,* Washington, D.C.: Washington Institute for Near East Policy, 1999, p. 30).

[20] William J. Clinton, "The President's News Conference," The American Presidency Project website, October 7, 1994. For details on the U.S. forces dispatched, see Herr, 1996, pp. 26–28; White, 1999, p. 31.

[21] By October 12, the United States had 36,000 troops on the ground in the Persian Gulf, including 28,000 combat soldiers (White, 1999, pp. 31–32). Pollack claimed that, by the end of the operation, the United States had approximately 60,000 troops in the area, including an 18,000-strong Marine Expeditionary Force; 16,000 troops from the 24th Mechanized Infantry Division; and 350 additional aircraft (Kenneth Pollack, *The Threatening Storm: What Every American Needs to Know Before an Invasion in Iraq,* New York: Random House, 2002, p. 70).

[22] Herr, 1996, p. 34.

While both of the prior cases involved conventional interstate aggression, U.S. forces have received access for counterattacks against terrorist organizations and the states that have sponsored them. The best example of this is Operation Enduring Freedom, the U.S. Afghan campaign against Al-Qaeda and the Taliban, which was launched in response to the 9/11 terrorist attacks. The international community not only recognized the U.S. right to retaliate against Al-Qaeda under Article 51 of the UN charter but also supported the more-ambiguous goal of eradicating international terrorism.[23] As part of the outpouring of international support for the United States, 89 nations offered over-flight clearances, while 58 nations offered basing rights.[24] Moreover, for the first time in its history, NATO invoked the alliance's mutual defense clause and stated that its members were "ready to provide the assistance that may be required as a consequence of these acts of barbarism."[25]

Notably, support for Operation Enduring Freedom came not only from close U.S. allies, such as those in Europe, but also from nations that the United States has a more complicated and, at times, strained relationship, such as Russia and China.[26] Russian backing was particularly important in terms of facilitating access to bases in the former Soviet republics.[27] Although the Russian defense minister ini-

---

[23] Andrew J. Pierre, *Coalitions: Building and Maintenance: Gulf War, Kosovo, Afghanistan, War on Terrorism*, Washington, D.C.: Institute for the Study of Diplomacy Edmund A. Walsh School of Foreign Service, Georgetown University, 2002, p. 77. By passing Resolution 1373, the UNSC endorsed the right of the United States to defend itself against terrorism and, therefore, de facto authorization for the United States to intervene in Afghanistan (Voeten, 2005, p. 530).

[24] Pierre, 2002, p. 39. For a list of publicly announced pledges of support as of October 17, 2001, see David J. Gerleman, Jennifer E. Stevens, and Steven A. Hildreth, *Operation Enduring Freedom: Foreign Pledges of Military & Intelligence Support*, Washington, D.C.: Congressional Research Service, October 17, 2001.

[25] Quoted in Benjamin S. Lambeth, *Air Power Against Terror: America's Conduct of Operation Enduring Freedom*, Santa Monica, Calif.: RAND Corporation, MG-166-1-CENTAF, 2006, p. 26.

[26] Pierre, 2002, p. 47.

[27] Cooley, 2012, pp. 53–54; Lambeth, 2006, pp. 26–30.

tially vetoed the idea of U.S. or NATO bases in Central Asia, Putin overruled this decision, telling U.S. President George W. Bush that he had "no objection to a U.S. role in Central Asia," provided that it was temporary and limited to counterterrorism operations.[28]

Even when the U.S. right to act in self-defense is not as widely accepted, evidence tying the intended target to terrorist attacks has helped to secure access with critical states. In 1986, proof that Qaddafi was linked to the bombing of a discotheque in Berlin that killed two American servicemen swayed British Prime Minister Margaret Thatcher. She alone among European leaders provided support for the Reagan administration's strikes against Libya—the state that had aided the terrorist group that had planted the bomb—on the condition that the retaliation was proportional and that the United States targeted only sites directly connected to terrorism.[29] In defense of her decision, Thatcher explained to the British Parliament that "[i]t was inconceivable to me that we should refuse U.S. aircraft and U.S. pilots to be able to defend their own people." Because she believed that the "United States was entitled to use its inherent right of self-defense," she permitted USAF F-111s to fly from bases in Britain for the operation.[30]

Explicit or Implied UNSC Authorization

The preeminent mechanism for legitimizing military operations is the UNSC. Given the size and heterogeneity of the UN's membership, it is clear why it stands above other international organizations.[31] While

---

[28] Quoted in Bob Woodward, *Bush at War*, New York: Simon and Schuster, 2003, p. 118.

[29] David C. Martin and John Walcott, *Best Laid Plans: The Inside Story of America's War Against Terrorism*, New York: Harper and Row Publishers, 1988, pp. 286–290.

[30] Quoted in E. J. Dionne, Jr. "Attack on Libya; Reproaches from Far and Wide; West Europe Generally Critical of U.S.," *New York Times*, April 16, 1986. It seems likely that Thatcher was also influenced by a sense of indebtedness to the Reagan administration for the "splendid support" which was "far beyond the call of duty" that it provided during the Falklands war (quoted in "The Iron Lady Stands Alone," *Time*, April 28, 1986, Vol. 127, No. 17, p. 24).

[31] Thompson argued that an international organization's legitimacy is tied to its neutrality and its independence, which in part is a function of the size and diversity of its members. Neutral organizations cannot be controlled by one state and therefore because the decision

nations have long looked to the UN to judge the appropriateness of international behavior, since the end of the Cold War, the institution has taken on an even more central role because of its increased willingness to endorse the use of force. Given the stature of the UN, many nations, including the United States, have expended considerable time and effort trying to convince the UNSC to sanction their military operations. Although it is indisputable that a UNSC mandate confers legitimacy, there is disagreement over why this is the case. Some believe that the UNSC's standing is based on the fact that the organization stands for a set of moral and legal standards.[32] Consequently, a UNSC resolution authorizing a military operation suggests that a nation is not pursuing its own narrow self-interest but rather is acting in the name of a broader set of generally accepted principles.[33] Others maintain that the real power of the UNSC stems from its ability to credibly convey information to various audiences about a state's intentions and the likely consequences of a military operation.[34]

Regardless of the specific mechanism at work, an explicit mandate from the UNSC has clearly helped the United States secure access for several operations. In 1992, for instance, the UNSC passed Resolution 781, which prohibited military flights over Bosnia and Herzegovina and endorsed the establishment of a no-fly zone in an effort to stabilize the situation and enable the delivery of HA. After repeated violations of the no-fly zone, the UNSC invoked Chapter VII in Resolution 816, which authorized member states or regional organizations to take "all

---

to work through an international organization imposes costs on a state, it also conveys credible information to the international community (Alexander Thompson, "Coercion Through IOs: The Security Council and the Logic of Information Transmission," *International Organization*, Vol. 60, No. 1, January 2006, pp. 7–10, 27).

[32] Inis L. Claude, Jr., "Collective Legitimization as a Political Function of the United Nations," *International Organization*, Vol. 20, No. 3, Summer 1966, pp. 367–379; Ian Hurd, "Legitimacy, Power, and the Symbolic Life of the UN Security Council," *Global Governance*, Vol. 8, No. 1, January 2002, pp. 35–51.

[33] Finnemore made this argument more generally about multilateralism (Martha Finnemore, *The Purpose of Intervention: Changing Beliefs About the Use of Force*, Ithaca, N.Y.: Cornell University Press, 2003, p. 82).

[34] Voeten, 2005, pp. 541–544; Thompson, 2006, pp. 9–12.

necessary measures . . . to ensure compliance with the ban on flights."[35] Given its proximity to the former Yugoslavia, Italian air bases offered an ideal location for enforcing the UN-sanctioned no-fly zone. The Italian government, however, feared that its public was opposed to military intervention in Bosnia and, until early 1994, advocated a political solution to the conflict. Despite these concerns, Italy allowed U.S. and NATO forces to operate from its territory in large part because of the UNSC mandates.[36]

UNSC Resolution 1973 played a similar role in fostering support for the 2011 U.S.-led intervention in Libya and securing access to critical southern European air bases.[37] Italy was particularly reluctant to support military operations against the government of Muammar Qaddafi because of Italy's historic and economic ties with Libya. Moreover, in 2008, Italy and Libya had reaffirmed these connections with a treaty of friendship, partnership, and cooperation, which included a nonaggression clause that prohibited the use of Italian bases for offensive operations against Libya. Consequently, before the UNSC vote, Italy had only permitted the United States to use a strategically located air base on the island of Sicily for humanitarian operations and to evacuate U.S. civilians from Libya. Italian Foreign Minister Franco Frattini explained that, since there was "no consensus among members of the Security Council," it would be premature to provide access for other operations. Yet he conceded that, "if and when the Security Council members took the decision, then we would consider it."[38] Ultimately, after Resolution 1973 was passed, Italy allowed U.S. and other allied forces to use several bases to carry out operations against Qaddafi.

---

[35] Bradley S. Davis, "The Planning Background," in Robert C. Owen, ed., *Deliberate Force: A Case Study in Effective Air Campaigning*, Maxwell AFB, Ala.: Air University Press, 2000, pp. 40–41.

[36] Paolo Bellucci and Pierangelo Isernia, "Massacring in Front of a Blind Audience? Italian Public Opinion and Bosnia," in Richard Sobel and Eric Shiraev, eds., *International Public Opinion and the Bosnia Crisis*, Lanham, Md.: Lexington Books, 2003, pp. 187–188.

[37] This resolution authorized the use of "all necessary measures" to protect civilians and to enforce a no-fly zone. UNSC, Resolution 1973, 2011.

[38] Quoted in Silvia Aloisi, "Italy Says Would Consider Libya No-Fly Zone Request," Reuters, February 28, 2011.

The UNSC mandate also influenced the willingness of the Spanish and Greek governments to make their military bases available to coalition forces. Spain's Prime Minister Jose Luis Rodriguez Zapatero, who had withdrawn Spanish forces from Iraq in 2003, called Resolution 1973 "decisive and historic."[39] Given the UN endorsement, Zapatero's government elected to support the Libyan intervention by allowing "foreign forces acting under the umbrella of the resolutions (UNSC resolutions 1970 and 1973)" to use Spanish bases.[40] Moreover, while the Greek government preferred a nonviolent solution to the Libyan crisis, after the UNSC issued Resolution 1973, Greek Foreign Minister Dimitris Droutsas announced that Greece was "ready to contribute, in cooperation with our partners and allies, to the effort of ensuring that international law is respected."[41] Greek forces did not participate in the Libyan operations, but the government did permit U.S. and other partner nations to use several of its air bases.

Nevertheless, the case studies also confirm the statistical analysis's finding that formal authorization from the United Nations is neither necessary nor sufficient for securing contingency access. The United States has obtained enough access to execute numerous operations that lacked a UNSC mandate (e.g., Allied Force, Enduring Freedom, and Iraqi Freedom) but has encountered some access difficulties when carrying out explicitly UN-sanctioned operations (e.g., with Turkey during the lead up to the first Gulf War). This finding suggests that the perception of legitimacy matters more than strict legality in the form of a UNSC mandate.

At times, an implied UNSC authorization has been enough to legitimize an operation. When it has proven impossible for the United States to secure an explicit UNSC mandate to use of force (i.e., "all necessary means"), U.S. officials have justified their actions by point-

---

[39] Quoted in Adam Gabbatt, Mark Tran, Haroon Siddique, and Richard Adams, "Libya Military Action—Friday 18 March," news blog, *Guardian*, March 18, 2011.

[40] Miguel Gonzalez, "Spain Sets Own Rules of Engagement for Libya Mission," *El Pais* (English), March 24, 2011.

[41] "Greece to Let Bases Be Used for NATO Operations in Libya," *Kathimerini* (English), March 18, 2011.

ing to resolutions that espouse the same objectives, even if they do not endorse military operations. When it established the no-fly zones over Iraq, for instance, the United States claimed that its actions were in support of Resolution 688, which "condemn[ed] the repression of the Iraqi civilian population" and encouraged states to take action to help the beleaguered Iraqis but did not provide a mandate for the use of force. Instead, the United States took the controversial step of claiming that Resolution 678, which was passed prior to Operation Desert Storm, provided the legal basis to establish the Iraqi no-fly zones because it had authorized the use of "all necessary means" to expel Iraqi forces from Kuwait and restore peace and stability.[42]

Despite the questionable legality of the no-fly zones, few in the international community objected to the U.S. actions, and Turkey and Saudi Arabia readily agreed to host the U.S. aircraft responsible for patrolling Iraqi airspace. Moreover, the United States did not have many problems finding neighboring nations willing to support limited strikes or shows of force against Iraq through 1995.[43] Over time, however, international support for the Iraqi sanctions regime eroded; as a result, fewer states were willing to back coercive U.S. military operations against Hussein.[44] As former National Security Council staffer Kenneth Pollack has noted, "by any measure, the Saudis have become less supportive of limited U.S. military operations against Iraq" and increasingly refused to allow combat operations to be carried out from their bases.[45] A growing number of critics in the Arab world accused the United States of having a double standard because it refused to punish Israel for violating UNSC resolutions but repeatedly used force to punish Iraq. They also questioned the U.S. commitment to interna-

---

[42] Jeremiah Gertler, Christopher M. Blanchard, Catherine Dale, and Jennifer K. Elsea, *No Fly Zones: Strategic, Operational, and Legal Considerations for Congress*, Washington, D.C.: Congressional Research Service, May 3, 2013, pp. 5–6; Gray, 2002, p. 9.

[43] Turkey was the only host nation that refused to support U.S. offensive operations against Iraq.

[44] Alfred B. Prados, *Iraq Challenges and US Responses: March 1991 Through October 2002*, Washington, D.C.: Congressional Research Service, November 20, 2002, p. 25.

[45] Pollack, 2002, p. 188. For views on all of the states see, pp. 186–200.

tional law, especially after the Clinton administration announced that its goal in Iraq was regime change.[46] In sum, the legal basis for U.S. actions had not changed, just the world and especially the Arab states' perception that U.S. sanctions and strikes were no longer legitimate because they were harming Iraqi civilians more than the regime.[47]

Operation Allied Force—the air war over Kosovo—was also based on an implied UNSC mandate. In October 1998, NATO Secretary General Javier Solana threatened to use force against Yugoslavia to compel compliance with UNSC Resolutions 1160, 1199, and 1998. However, this was a specious argument because the only reason that the UNSC had passed these resolutions was because they did not include an express provision for the use of force.[48] At the same time, Solana justified NATO's actions on the notion of humanitarian intervention, which he directly tied to the UN charter to further enhance its legitimacy.[49] Toward this end, the North Atlantic Council—NATO's governing body—also met with UN Secretary General Kofi Annan in January 1999 in a "highly symbolic and important meeting," in which Annan tacitly endorsed NATO's coercive strategy.[50] When asked by the press about the necessary conditions for military intervention in Kosovo, Annan reportedly replied that "normally a UN Security Council Resolution is required."[51] Solana then used the meeting with Annan and the Secretary-General's statements to convey the impression NATO had the UN's support to use force if Yugoslav President Slobodan Milosevic did not concede.[52] Because many U.S. European

---

[46] Marc Lynch, *Voices of the New Arab Public: Iraq, Al-Jazeera, and Middle East Politics Today*, New York: Columbia University Press, 2006, pp. 130–131.

[47] Gray, 2002, p. 10; Lynch, 2006, pp. 97–138.

[48] Gray, 2002, p. 13.

[49] Simma, 1999, p. 7. For full text, see also Gray, 2002, p. 13.

[50] Simma, 1999, p. 8; Ivo H. Daalder and Michael E. O'Hanlon, *Winning Ugly: NATO's War to Save Kosovo*, Washington, D.C.: Brookings Institution Press, 2000, p. 75.

[51] Quoted in Simma, 1999, p. 8.

[52] Solana said to the press: "You have seen from the visit of the United Nations Secretary-General to NATO earlier today that the United Nations shares our determination and objectives." Quoted in Simma, 1999, pp. 8–9.

allies were quite apprehensive about undertaking this mission without a UNSC mandate, these steps helped allay their concerns.[53] Despite the fact that the UNSC had not specifically authorized NATO's offensive actions in Kosovo, the United States had few problems securing access for its air operations.[54]

Authorization by a Regional International Organization

Although the UNSC may offer the preferred imprimatur, it may, at times, be impossible to get the permanent members to set aside their differences and agree to authorize the use of force. This was clearly the case during the Cold War, when UNSC mandates were extremely rare because of enduring U.S.-Soviet competition. When the UNSC cannot come to agreement, the backing of a regional organization can sometimes help the United States obtain access. Working through a regional international organization offers similar benefits to those of working through the UNSC, although the legitimacy and signaling effects are likely to be somewhat diminished because the organization may be seen as less neutral. Nevertheless, endorsement from a regional international organization can bolster an operation's legitimacy and can also convey information about how the United States intends to carry out the operation—that it will abide by certain limits and that its actions will be subject to greater scrutiny than if they were undertaken outside the organization.[55] Additionally, a mandate from a highly institutionalized regional international organization, such as NATO, may also incentivize its members to cooperate by providing the United

[53] Patricia A. Weitsman, *Waging War: Alliances, Coalition, and Institutions of Interstate Violence*, Stanford, Calif.: Stanford University Press, 2014, pp. 93–94; John E. Peters, Stuart Johnson, Nora Bensahel, Timothy Liston, and Traci Williams, *European Contributions to Operation Allied Force*, Santa Monica, Calif.: RAND Corporation, MR-1391-AF, 2001, pp. 60–61.

[54] There were, however, more-serious reservations about deploying ground forces.

[55] Thompson, 2006, p. 10.

States with access, even if they would otherwise prefer not to support the operation.[56]

These mechanisms were all apparent during Operation Allied Force. Because China and Russia would have likely vetoed any resolution expressly sanctioning the use of force in Kosovo, the United States turned to NATO to legitimize the air war over Kosovo. As previously discussed, NATO cultivated the impression that it had an implicit UNSC mandate, but the North Atlantic alliance offered its own complimentary source of legitimacy. In light of the UN's failure to act in a timely and effective fashion in Bosnia, some commenters even suggested that, at the time, NATO had greater legitimacy than the UN.[57]

Additionally, most states readily agreed to grant U.S. forces basing rights for the Kosovo operation because they recognized that its actions would be seriously constrained by the alliance's consensus-based decisionmaking process.[58] Before launching an attack on a particular site, the North Atlantic Council and all 19 of NATO's members had to sign off on each target.[59] Not surprisingly, "combat operations by committee" introduced "inefficiencies," which frustrated U.S. military officials, who believed that an intensified bombing campaign was needed to force Milosevic to capitulate.[60] Nevertheless, this thorough and lengthy targeting process was part of the reason many states were willing to provide basing rights and helped the alliance maintain cohesion throughout an air war that lasted much longer than expected. The controls imposed by working through NATO reassured allies about U.S.

---

[56] Sarah Kreps, "Elite Consensus as a Determinant of Alliance Cohesion: Why Public Opinion Hardly Matters for NATO-led Operations in Afghanistan," *Foreign Policy Analysis*, Vol. 6, No. 3, July 2010, p. 192.

[57] Daniel W. Drezner, "Regime Proliferation and World Order: Is There Viscosity in Global Governance?" paper presented at McGill University, Montreal, November 2007, p. 21

[58] This also was true of U.S. operations (Deny Flight and Deliberate Force) in Bosnia. In fact, the Bosnia operations were even more constrained than Allied Force because there was a dual-key arrangement, in which each target had to be approved by both the UN and NATO.

[59] After several weeks, the North Atlantic Council removed itself from the targeting authorization process. For more, see Peters et al., 2001, pp. 25–29.

[60] Benjamin S. Lambeth, *NATO's Air War for Kosovo: A Strategic and Operational Assessment*, Santa Monica, Calif.: RAND Corporation, 2001, p. 185.

intentions and allowed members of the alliance to exert control over the process, thereby increasing their willingness to allow U.S. forces to operate from their territories.

The fact that Allied Force was a NATO operation proved to be particularly important in securing and maintaining basing rights in two critical members—Greece and Italy—that faced significant domestic opposition to the war. Despite countervailing domestic pressures, neither the Greek nor the Italian government wavered in its provision of steadfast access for the air war. This was due in part to the fact that "member states valued the alliance itself, perhaps even more than the conflict at hand."[61] Longstanding formal alliances that are highly institutionalized can help induce cooperation. States that have benefited in the past from alliance membership and have made open-ended pledges to collaborate are likely to go along with alliance decisions because they want to ensure future returns and avoid gaining a reputation for being unreliable.[62]

In Greece, for example, the public fiercely opposed Allied Force due to Greeks' religious and historic ties to Serbia. Consequently, there were extensive anti-U.S. and anti-NATO protests during the operation, and at one point, as many as 96 percent of the Greeks polled were against NATO's air campaign.[63] Additionally, Greek judges challenged the operation's legality, claiming that the air war was in breach of the UN charter and, therefore, that the Greek government was violating its own constitution by providing bases for an offensive war. It is unclear whether the judges had jurisdiction over this issue, but the incident reveals the serious domestic problems that the Greek government faced in supporting Allied Force.[64] While Greece maintained that it preferred a peaceful solution to the Kosovo crisis, and thus did not directly participate in the air war, it also did not veto the operation and satisfied its alliance commitments by providing access to its ports, fuel lines, and

---

[61] Weitsman, 2014, p. 92.

[62] Kreps, 2010, p. 202.

[63] Carol Migdalovitz, "Greece," in Karen Donfried, ed., *Kosovo: International Reactions to NATO Air Strikes*, Washington, D.C.: Congressional Research Service, April 21, 1999.

[64] Peters et al., 2001, p. 61, fn. 13.

an air base on Crete.[65] Ultimately, the Greek government decided that it would weather the domestic turmoil because it was more important to be a good ally and a part of the broader Western community than to appease public opinion.[66]

Similarly, Italy's left-leaning government faced significant public opposition to Allied Force in addition to internal differences over the appropriate policy toward Kosovo. The weakness of Prime Minister Massimo D'Alema's position was revealed on March 26 when the Chamber of Deputies passed a motion by 388 to 188 urging NATO to halt its attacks and for Italian forces to assume a "defensive posture" so that negotiations could restart.[67] While parts of D'Alema's coalition strongly backed NATO's actions and even indicated support for the deployment of ground forces, communist members dissented and threatened to withdraw from the government if this occurred. Despite this, Italy remained committed to the NATO operation, which was crucial because most of the combat operations were flown from its bases.

During the 2011 air campaign over Libya, several regional international organizations played a central role in helping the United States first acquire and then preserve access to Mediterranean air bases for the duration of the operation. In this instance, transitioning operational control from the United States to NATO did not significantly affect the mission's legitimacy.[68] Instead, Operations Odyssey Dawn and Unified Protector were legitimized by the support of several Arab and Islamic regional organizations that took the unprecedented step of calling for the UN to intervene in Libya on humanitarian grounds.[69]

---

[65] Migdalovitz, 1999; GAO, 2001, p. 6

[66] Daalder and O'Hanlon, 2000, p. 129.

[67] Paul Gallis, "Italy," in Donfried, 1999, p. 5.

[68] Odyssey Dawn was the U.S.-led mission, which lasted from March 19 to March 29, 2011, while Unified Protector began on March 30, when NATO assumed command of the operation. Jeremiah Gertler, *Operation Odyssey Dawn (Libya): Background and Issues for Congress*, Washington, D.C.: Congressional Research Service, March 30, 2011, p. 1.

[69] The Arab states' support for a UN intervention was in part due to the fact that Qaddafi had alienated most of his peers, particularly the Saudis. Clearly, their endorsement did not

On March 7, the ministerial council of the GCC issued a statement condemning the "crimes committed against civilians" by Qaddafi's regime and "demand[ing] that the Security Council take the steps necessary to protect civilians, including a no-fly zone in Libya."[70] The next day, the Organization of the Islamic Conference's Secretary General, Ekmeleddin Ihsanoglu, also "ask[ed] for a no-fly zone in Libya" and "call[ed] on the Security Council to do its duty in this regard."[71] Then, on March 12, the Arab League exhorted the UNSC "to take all the necessary measures to impose immediately a no-fly zone on Libyan military aviation and to establish safe areas."[72] Because these organizations and their member states have historically opposed Western interference in their internal affairs, their about-face had a significant effect on international opinion and helped legitimize the military intervention against Qaddafi. In short, by urging the international community to act, these regional international organizations facilitated the passage of a UNSC resolution authorizing military action.[73] In contrast to the past, Western nations found themselves in an unusual position in which the use of force seemed to offer an opportunity to burnish their image in the Arab and Islamic world, which in turn made them more willing to support the operation.[74]

Although NATO's involvement did not significantly enhance the legitimacy of Operation Unified Protector, which had already been secured, it helped to assure access in several member states that were

---

reflect a deep belief in protecting basic human rights; around the same time that the crisis broke out in Libya, Saudi Arabia and the UAE sent forces under the aegis of GCC to put down popular demonstrations in Bahrain (Christopher S. Chivvis, *Toppling Qaddafi: Libya and the Limits of Liberal Intervention*, New York: Cambridge University Press, 2014, p. 54).

[70] Quoted in Kareem Shaheen, "GCC Wants No-Fly Zone Over Libya," *National UAE,* March 8, 2011.

[71] Quoted in "OIC Chief Backs No-Fly Zone Over Libya," Emirates 24/7 News website, March 8, 2011.

[72] Arab League, "The Outcome of the Council of the League of Arab States Meeting at the Ministerial Level in Its Extraordinary Session on the Implications of the Current Events in Libya and the Arab Position," Cairo, March 12, 2011.

[73] Weitsman, 2014, p. 183.

[74] Chivvis, 2014, p. 54.

reluctant to support the campaign against Qaddafi. In particular, placing the operation under NATO command encouraged Germany, Italy, and Turkey to cooperate by providing various levels of access for forces carrying out the air campaign. Domestic politics and the desire to avoid a protracted conflict led the German government to abstain during the vote over UNSC Resolution 1973. While Germany refused to allow its military personnel—even those assigned to NATO's Airborne Warning and Control System—to contribute to the mission, it did permit U.S. (480th fighter squadron based at Spangdahlem) and NATO forces (E-3A component based at Geilenkirchen) to deploy from its bases and participate in the operations. Additionally, the U.S.-led phase of the air campaign was controlled by the air operations center at Ramstein Air Base.[75] After realizing that the abstention had damaged its relationship with other members, Germany took several indirect steps to support the Libya operations and rehabilitate its image, including sending its own Airborne Warning and Control System to Afghanistan to free other NATO intelligence, surveillance, and reconnaissance assets and resupplying deployed Belgian and Dutch fighter units in the Mediterranean.[76] According to German Defense Minister Thomas de Maiziere, his nation's willingness to expand its surveillance flights over Afghanistan was a "political sign of our solidarity with the alliance."[77]

Initially, Turkey and Italy opposed taking military action against Qaddafi because of domestic public opinion and economic ties to Libya but eventually pushed for NATO to take command to give them some control over the operation.[78] For the NATO operation, Turkey allowed allied forces to use the air operations center located in Izmir. Qatari

---

[75] Stefanie Torres, "General Ham Visits Air Operations Center Responsible for Operation Odyssey Dawn Air Campaign," U.S. Air Forces in Europe, Air Forces Africa website, March 23, 2011.

[76] Christian F. Anrig, "The Belgian, Danish, Norwegian, and Dutch Experiences," in Karl P. Mueller, ed., *Precision and Purpose: Airpower in the Libyan Civil War*, Santa Monica, Calif.: RAND Corporation, RR-676-AF, 2015, p. 293.

[77] "Germany's Libya Contribution: Merkel Cabinet Approves AWACs for Afghanistan," *Spiegel Online International*, March 23, 2011.

[78] Chivvis, 2014, pp. 73–74

aircraft deploying to the Mediterranean were also permitted to transit through Incirlik Air Base.[79] Not surprisingly given its more proximate location, Italian facilities were in higher demand than those in Turkey, and NATO forces ultimately flew operations from seven Italian air bases.[80]

It is worth pointing out that not all types of multilateral support will have an equal effect on legitimacy and access. Depending on the particular situation, certain nations or regional organizations are likely to have more weight than others. In general, there are countries and organizations that are expected to endorse or contribute to U.S. operations, and then there are those that typically oppose U.S. military activities. The reasons that a nation or international organization usually supports or opposes the United States are varied and may include that they are longstanding allies, that they share a culture, that there are domestic political sensitivities, or that they typically follow a neutral or nonaligned foreign policy. If a country or international organization that falls into the former camp fails to come out in favor of a particular U.S. operation, it is likely to raise questions about the legitimacy of the operation. Take Germany's lack of support for UNSC Resolution 1973, for example: "[T]he abstention was taken in Washington as tantamount to a vote against" because "Germany was expected to vote with its allies, as it traditionally had."[81] If the closest U.S. partners have reservations, it may give other states pause and reason to think that a mission is suspect. In contrast, when a country or international organization that falls into the latter category extends its support, it should have an outsized influence on the perceived legitimacy of the operation, as the GCC, Organization of the Islamic Conference, and Arab League endorsements did for the establishment of a no-fly zone over Libya.[82]

---

[79] Bruce R. Nardulli, "The Arab States' Experiences," in Mueller, 2015, p. 350.

[80] Gertler, 2011, p. 19.

[81] Chivvis, 2014, p. 61.

[82] The international responses to the U.S. decision to intervene in Grenada in 1983 is also illustrative. The inability of United States to convince the UN or Organization of American States to sanction intervention forced the Reagan administration to draw attention to

Fear of Retaliation

Concern about reprisals played a critical role in some of the most prominent cases of access failure, although the type of retaliation has varied. For instance, during Operation Nickel Grass, Western European leaders acted to avoid an Arab oil embargo. Because Western Europe imported approximately 80 percent of its oil from the Middle East, supporting the U.S. resupply of Israel appeared likely to have serious economic repercussions. Consequently, all the U.S. European allies—except for Portugal—refused to allow their bases to be used to support the airlift to Israel.

Then–Department of State (DoS) spokesman Robert J. McCloskey observed that "a number of our allies [went] to some lengths to separate themselves publicly from us" in response to the threat of Arab economic coercion.[83] Even before being asked for access, many of the European states preemptively declared their neutrality, making it clear that they would not allow U.S. aircraft to use their territories or airspace to resupply Israel.[84] Initially, West Germany reportedly had been willing to look the other way when the United States moved some arms based in its territory to Israel, but when the press got wind of the fact that U.S. weapons were being loaded onto Israeli ships at Bremerhaven, the German government publicly demanded that the United States immediately stop shipments "from and over" Western German

---

a request to restore democracy in Grenada from a little-known international organization, the Organization of Eastern Caribbean States. The organization's appeal was not based on a formal vote, and the organization itself had little consequence, so this request was seen as a transparent attempt by the Reagan administration to manufacture legitimacy for the operation, which ultimately failed. Close U.S. allies—including the UK, France, and Italy—in addition to most other Latin American countries voiced strong objections to the intervention. Ultimately, the United States had to veto a UNSC Resolution "deploring" the invasion of the Caribbean nation (Edward C. Luck, "The United States, International Organizations, and the Quest for Legitimacy," in Stewart Patrick and Shepard Forman, eds., Multilateralism and U.S. Foreign Policy, Boulder, Colo.: Lynne Rienner Publishers, 2002, pp. 62–63).

[83] David Binder, "Bonn Is Singled Out," *New York Times*, October 27, 1973

[84] Dan Morgan, "Western Europe Keeping Out of Middle East Crisis Moves," *Washington Post*, October 26, 1973.

territory.[85] In contrast, Portugal was less susceptible to the effects of an Arab oil embargo than many other European states because it could import nearly 150,000 barrels of oil daily from its West African colony, Angola.[86] Nevertheless, the Portuguese government consented to allow the United States to use Lajes Air Base in the Azores (but not air bases on the Portuguese mainland) only under heavy U.S. pressure.[87]

While economic coercion was quite effective at limiting U.S. basing options during the 1973 Arab-Israeli War, it was the fear of terrorist reprisals that created access problems for United States in 1986. Many Western European governments opposed the U.S. strike against Qaddafi because they thought that it would not only be ineffective at stopping terrorism but was likely to lead to more attacks against their countries. For instance, Italian Prime Minister Bettino Craxi warned that an attack on Qaddafi would precipitate "a further explosion of fanaticism and extremism."[88] The French government later explained that it refused the U.S. request for overflight because it feared escalating "the chain of violence" by aiding the U.S. operation.[89] In addition to terrorist attacks within its country, France was also worried about retribution against its citizens who were being held hostage in Lebanon.

In this case, the difference of opinion between the United States and its allies was rooted in geography, which influenced the likelihood of terrorist attacks on one's soil. The European states feared that Washington's actions would provoke Qaddafi; while the United States could retreat to safety across the Atlantic Ocean, it would leave the more proximate Western Europeans to bear the brunt of Libyan revenge.[90] Moreover, since many Western European countries hosted

---

[85] Alvin Shuster, "Alert Puzzles Europeans," *New York Times*, October 27, 1973.

[86] Kenneth L. Patchin, *Flight to Israel: A Historical Documentary of Strategic Airlift to Israel, 14 October–14 November 1973*, Scott Air Force Base, Ill.: Military Airlift Command, April 30, 1974, declassified November 18, 1993, pp. 36–37.

[87] Interview with William B. Quandt, May 29, 2013.

[88] Dionne, 1986.

[89] Church et al., 1986.

[90] Brian Lee Davis, *Qaddafi, Terrorism, and the Origins of the U.S. Attack on Libya*, New York: Praeger, 1990, p. 157.

U.S. forces, the governments worried that they would inevitably be drawn into the crossfire. This turned out to be true; Qaddafi's first attempt at vengeance targeted Italy, a nation that was not even asked to support Operation El Dorado Canyon but that did host a number of U.S. bases. Seizing on the closest and, therefore, the easiest target, Libya fired two Scud missiles at a U.S. Coast Guard station on the Italian island of Lampedusa, which fortunately missed their mark. In the wake of the U.S. strike, there were also a string of Libyan-sponsored terrorist attacks, including the attempted assassinations of American diplomats in Sudan and South Yemen, the killing of three U.S. and British hostages in Lebanon, and thwarted plots against an airport in the UK and a U.S. officers' club in Turkey.[91]

At other times, states have denied the United States basing rights or restricted its freedom of action because they feared that supporting a U.S. operation would make them targets for conventional retaliation. Not surprisingly, this concern is often an issue when the United States wants to use a nation as a staging ground for offensive attacks. While proximate states are ideal for air and ground strikes, this same characteristic also makes them vulnerable to counterattacks. For instance, during Desert Storm, the majority of Turks feared "that Iraq would strike against Turkey in revenge for American strikes" and thus opposed supporting U.S. operations against Iraq.[92] These concerns restrained President Turgut Özal from offering U.S. combat forces access until after the war had begun.[93] Throughout the sanctions era, Iraqi retribution continued to weigh on Turkish officials' minds and contributed to their reluctance to allow offensive missions against Iraq to be flown from their territory. Despite this fact, Hussein continued to threaten to punish Turkey for hosting Operation Northern Watch aircraft. To ease Turkish fears and ensure continued access to Incirlik Air Base for the no-fly zone, the United States deployed the 69th Air Defense Artil-

---

[91] Martin and Walcott, 1988, pp. 313–314; "The Iron Lady Stands Alone," 1986.

[92] Lawrence Freedman and Efraim Karsh, *The Gulf Conflict 1990–1991: Diplomacy and War in the New World Order*, Princeton, N.J.: Princeton University Press, 1993, p. 354.

[93] Freedman and Karsh, 1993, p. 354.

lery Brigade from Germany to bolster Turkey's defense in early 1999.[94] In the late 1990s, reprisals also became a growing concern for the Gulf states, especially Saudi Arabia and the UAE, which, as a result, were increasingly reluctant to support combat operations against Iraq. They saw great risk and little benefit to abetting limited offensive operations that were only likely to provoke Saddam, while leaving him in power and able to retaliate against them.[95]

Similarly, during the air campaign over Kosovo, many of the countries sharing a border with Yugoslavia were hesitant to provide NATO forces with basing and overflight rights. This was particularly true of the states that were not members of the North Atlantic Alliance—Bulgaria, Croatia, and Macedonia—which demanded that NATO guarantee their security and territorial integrity before supporting the operation. But even this was not sufficient to secure unfettered access because Bulgaria and Macedonia would not permit offensive operations from their territories.[96] When Macedonia made this announcement, it upended U.S. plans to deploy Task Force Hawk, an Army detachment consisting of artillery and attack helicopters, and forced U.S. officials to scramble to find an alternative host.[97] Even newly minted NATO member Hungary refused to host a second U.S. artillery unit out of concern for the well-being of the ethnic Hungarian minority in Vojvodina, a northern province of Serbia.[98]

Domestic Politics

At times, domestic politics have prevented governments that were disposed toward providing access to U.S. forces from doing so. When a country's population is opposed to a mission for any reason, it can

[94] Anthony H. Cordesman, *The Air Defense War Since Desert Fox: A Short History*, Washington, D.C.: Center for Strategic and International Studies, July 1, 1999, p. 15.

[95] Prados, 2002, p. 25.

[96] Donfried, 1999, pp. 4–11.

[97] Nardulli et al., 2002, pp. 63–64.

[98] Nardulli et al., 2002, p. 63, fn. 15; Donfried, 1999, pp. 4–5.

place tremendous pressure on a government to refuse a U.S. request for access. And if a government chooses to ignore its public's preferences, it may be accused of subordinating its own nation's interests and well-being to another country, which, in turn, can hurt not only its popularity but also its legitimacy. On first blush, it would seem that democratic governments, which are directly accountable to their citizens, would be more attuned to the domestic political consequences of access decisions. This is certainly true in nations that require legislature approval to host foreign forces on their soil. The 1987 Philippine constitution, for instance, prohibits the establishment of foreign military bases and the deployment of foreign troops unless a decision is ratified by its senate and passes a popular referendum.[99] Similarly, Turkey's 1982 constitution stipulates that only the Grand National Assembly can agree to the stationing of foreign troops in Turkey, which frustrated U.S. efforts to secure access in the lead-up to Operation Iraqi Freedom.[100]

Yet, somewhat surprisingly, nondemocratic governments have also been constrained by public attitudes. In fact, some authoritarian governments seem almost more conscious of and beholden to domestic opinion than democratic leaders when it comes to making access decisions. For example, Arab political sensitivities have frequently impeded U.S. efforts to obtain contingency basing rights in the Middle East and North Africa. As far back as the 1958 U.S. intervention in Lebanon, Saudi Arabia refused to allow U.S. aircraft to overfly its territory because the story had been picked up in the press.[101] Similarly, Libyan King Idris was only willing to allow U.S. forces to operate from Wheelus Air Base if it was done covertly.[102]

In the 1980s, Middle Eastern leaders continued to view an overt U.S. military presence as politically unacceptable, which complicated U.S. efforts to assist Kuwait during the Iran-Iraq War. Although the Gulf nations welcomed the protection U.S. naval convoys afforded

---

[99] Sandars, 2000, p. 124.

[100] Sandars, 2000, p. 278; Larrabee, 2010, pp. 12–13.

[101] "Document 205: Memorandum of a Conference with the President, White House, Washington, July 20, 1958, 3:45 pm." *FRUS 1958–1960*, Vol. XI, 1992, p. 348.

[102] Lemmer, 1963, p. 32.

Kuwaiti tankers, these nations preferred that the U.S. military presence remain as inconspicuous as possible. This led to an unconventional arrangement in which Kuwait, Bahrain, and Saudi Arabia agreed to pay for and support moored barges that were used as staging facilities for U.S. surveillance and countermine aircraft and special forces.[103] By using ships in international waters instead of land bases, the GCC nations could distance themselves from the U.S. operation and truthfully claim that U.S. forces were not stationed on their soil.

The presence of foreign, particularly non-Muslim, troops in many Middle Eastern countries has long been controversial, but it became an even larger problem when these forces were implementing deeply unpopular policies, such as enforcing sanctions or carrying out punitive strikes against Saddam Hussein's regime for not complying with UN weapon inspections. Fueled by the rise of new media, such as Al-Jazeera, "Iraq became a focal point" of Arab discourse in the 1990s.[104] Throughout this period, the Arab street passionately debated the international community's policies toward Iraq and increasingly reached the conclusion that the sanctions regime was unfair and inhumane. By the late 1990s, U.S. actions, and in particular its bombing of Iraq, galvanized Arab critics, who not only condemned the United States but also their governments for enabling the attacks. As a result, the Arab states became increasingly reluctant to cooperate publicly with the United States, especially for offensive operations. Moreover, most governments, including close partners, became increasingly critical of U.S. actions in public and routinely expressed their sympathy for the plight of the Iraqi people.[105] After the 1998 bombing of Iraq, for example, there were widespread protests in the Middle East, leading Egyptian President Hosni Mubarak, a longstanding U.S. ally, to demand that President Clinton "end military operations on Iraq as quickly as possible," because the attacks were exacerbating Iraqi suf-

---

[103] Anthony H. Cordesman and Abraham R. Wagner, *The Lessons of Modern War*, Vol. II: *The Iran-Iraq War*, Boulder, Colo.: Westview Press, 1990, p. 300.

[104] Lynch, 2006, p. 12.

[105] For more on the evolution of Arab public opinion during the 1990s, see Lynch, 2006.

fering.[106] Because of the pervasive anti-American sentiment, if Arab governments were willing to support U.S. operations against Iraq, they generally would only do so privately. This widening gap between Arab governments and their publics led the Clinton administration to avoid additional high-profile bombing campaigns in favor of low-intensity offensive actions that generally remained out of the headlines and did not require U.S. partners to make controversial access decisions.[107]

Domestic political challenges also played a role in Turkey's and Spain's decisions to restrict U.S. access during Operation Desert Shield. As the United States rapidly deployed hundreds of thousands of troops to defend Saudi Arabia in 1990, Turkey's President Özal was unwilling to take the incredibly unpopular step of receiving additional U.S. forces, particularly when it was unclear whether the United States would decide to use force to restore Kuwait's independence. Given that Özal also faced strong opposition within his government, he did not want to have to pay the price domestically if the U.S. operation amounted to little more than a massive show of force. Yet, once the U.S. ambassador to Turkey, Morton Abramowitz, personally appealed to the Turkish president the night that the air campaign began, Özal leveraged his party's commanding position in the national assembly to push through a resolution permitting U.S. combat operations from Turkish bases.[108]

Spanish Prime Minister Felipe Gonzalez also faced domestic pressures that made it difficult for him to unreservedly support the movement of U.S. forces to the Persian Gulf. At the time, the issue of permanent U.S. bases in Spain was extremely contentious and the United States was in the midst of closing several major bases at the request of the Spanish government. Consequently, Gonzalez's government placed

---

[106] Quoted in Eugene Robinson, "U.S. Halts Attacks on Iraq After Four Days," *Washington Post,* December 20, 1998.

[107] Lynch, 2006, p. 128; Michael Knights, *Cradle of Conflict: Iraq and the Birth of the Modern U.S. Military,* Annapolis, Md.: Naval Institute Press, 2005, pp. 217–238, 255–260.

[108] Morton Abramowitz, "The Complexities of American Policymaking on Turkey," in Morton Abramowitz, ed., *Turkey's Transformation and American Policy,* New York: Century Foundation, 2000, pp. 153–155.

limits on the types and numbers of U.S. aircraft that were allowed at Spanish bases at any one time. Of particular concern was Torrejón Air Base, located near Madrid, which was one of the facilities that the United States was in the process of vacating. Given the sensitivities surrounding the highly visible installation, Gonzalez's government restricted the number of A-10 aircraft that could be present. Additionally, the Spanish prime minister was initially unwilling to allow the United States to bed down B-52 bombers on Spanish territory, for fear of generating controversy. Like Turkey, however, once the war began, Spain removed all its restrictions on U.S. access.

In several of the cases (Blue Bat, El Dorado Canyon, Desert Shield, Desert Fox, Allied Force), both the fear of retaliation and domestic political opposition were present, making it even more difficult for a state to provide U.S. forces with unrestricted access. Table 5.2 shows the access problems the United States encountered in the case studies and the primary reason(s) that states did not respond positively to a U.S. access request.

Conclusion

Looking in greater detail at ten case studies highlighted several recurring factors that were associated with access success and failure and that could not be captured in the large-scale data analysis because they are embedded in the case's specific context. In general, host nations are more likely to provide the United States with contingency access if it is in their own interests to do so or if they view the operation as legitimate and therefore defendable to critical domestic and international audiences. Conversely, host nations are less likely to offer to provide such access if they face significant opposition at home or if fear that supporting a U.S. operation is likely to make them targets for retaliation. Chapter Six draws on both the quantitative and qualitative peacetime and contingency access analyses to highlight some additional findings that are of interest.

Table 5.2
Reasons for Access Restrictions and Denials

Operation	Domestic Politics	Retaliation	Other
Blue Bat	Israel Saudi Arabia Libya	Israel Greece	Austria Switzerland
Dragon Rogue			Spain
Vietnam War	Philippines		
Nickel Grass		10 European allies	
Mayaguez	Thailand		
El Dorado Canyon	Spain	Spain France	
Desert Shield	Jordan Turkey Saudi Arabia Spain Egypt	Jordan Turkey	
Desert Storm	Jordan	Jordan	
Desert Strike	GCC States Turkey Jordan		
Desert Fox	Saudi Arabia UAE Turkey	Saudi Arabia UAE Turkey	
Allied Force	Bulgaria Macedonia	Bulgaria Macedonia Hungary	Austria France
Enduring Freedom (initial phase, 2001–2002)	Uzbekistan[a] Saudi Arabia Tajikistan	Turkmenistan	
Iraqi Freedom	Saudi Arabia UAE Turkey		Austria Switzerland
Odyssey Dawn and Unified Protector		Malta	

NOTES: Blue indicates access was limited; red indicates access was denied. If a country's access decision changed during the course of the operation, the most restrictive decision is reflected in the color.

[a] Later, in 2005, Uzbekistan revoked the United States' access to Karshi-Khanabad air base due to U.S. criticism of Uzbek security forces actions against protestors in Andijan.

CHAPTER SIX

Integrated Insights

Bringing together the different analyses yielded some important observations about the relationship between peacetime and contingency access and the behavior of certain types of states. Although decisions about peacetime and contingency access are often made separately, the two types of access are interrelated, and actions in one area can affect the other, although often in ways that are not expected. Additionally, we found that there are two generic types of states that can present access challenges—vacillators and repeat offenders. Each of these issues will be discussed further below.

Interaction Between Peacetime and Contingency Access

The relationship between steady-state basing rights and permission to use a base for a particular operation is often assumed to be positive and to move in one direction, which is represented the first row in Figure 6.1. According to this logic, peacetime access increases the probability of securing access permissions during a contingency. We found that this was far from the only or even the most likely case. The relationship between peacetime and contingency access is complicated and multidirectional. One type of access can clearly influence the other type, but often in unexpectedly negative ways. For instance, the statistical analysis demonstrated that large permanent garrisons by themselves do not improve the likelihood of securing contingency access, thereby debunking the relationship often presumed to be true. Only

Figure 6.1
The Interaction Between Peacetime and Contingency Access

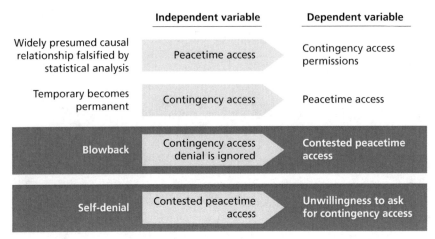

RAND *RR1339-6.1*

enduring partner nations are more likely to provide U.S. forces with access during a contingency.

Yet, as shown in Figure 6.1, one type of access can lead to another. Access that was initially temporary and limited to a particular mission can lead to steady-state basing rights, especially if the operation lasts for a long time. This occurred in several Persian Gulf nations that originally provided the United States with access for Operation Desert Storm but then allowed U.S. forces to stay to enforce UN sanctions and the no-fly zone against Saddam Hussein.

The reverse is also true, meaning that access problems in one domain can spill over into the other area, which are depicted in the two shaded rows in Figure 6.1. For instance, if the United States carries out a mission against the host nation's wishes, it may lead to limitations on or the revocation of U.S. peacetime basing rights (blowback). Alternatively, when there are serious internal challenges to U.S. bases, the United States has been reluctant to further strain the relationship and to risk its peacetime access by asking to use these bases for a particular operation, especially one that is likely to be controversial. In these situations, the United States engages in self-denial. In short, peacetime and contingency access are related but in more varied and complicated ways than is typically assumed. We next discuss the two issues that have received less recognition—blowback and self-denial.

Unheeded Access Denials and Blowback

Some might think that the issue of access—particularly overflight—is overstated because the U.S. military can often do what it wishes with impunity. Other countries either do not have the technological capabilities to detect U.S. military movements or the capability to respond to U.S. violations of their airspace or territory. Generally, this has not proven to be the case. In fact, it has been quite difficult for the United States to ignore diplomatic clearances, and when U.S. officials have disregarded a host nation's instructions, there has usually been blowback. These repercussions have been particularly severe in nations where the United States has a permanent peacetime presence.

In Operation Blue Bat, for instance, U.S. officials had intended to proceed regardless of whether they received overflight and basing authorizations.[1] According to Chairman of the Joint Chief of Staff General Nathan F. Twining, while U.S. forces "would need base rights and overflight rights in several countries" to execute Operation Blue Bat, he "was in agreement with the State Department position that this was no time to ask any country for them. Once the operation began,

---

[1] While the United States deliberately disregarded host nations' access decisions in 1958, it has accidentally done so at other times. For instance, during a 1964 hostage rescue operation in the Democratic Republic of the Congo (DRC), Operation Dragon Rogue, the United States inadvertently overstepped its bounds by landing uncleared aircraft at Moron Air Base in Spain. Although the Spanish government had agreed to allow USAF C-130s carrying a battalion of Belgian paratroopers to pass through its airspace and refuel at Spanish bases, U.S. officials had failed to ask for permission to stage an additional squadron of C-130s from Pope Air Force Base in Spain. Deputy Secretary of Defense Cyrus Vance wanted the extra C-130 squadron from the 464th Tactical Airlift Wing to be on alert in the event that rapid reinforcements were needed. In this instance, a honest oversight angered the Spanish government, which responded by prohibiting returning U.S. aircraft from using its bases or airspace, forcing them to navigate around the Iberian Peninsula. At best, this was a modest punishment because Madrid permitted U.S. aircraft to refuel in the Canary Islands. (Thomas P. Odom, *Dragon Operations: Hostage Rescues in the Congo, 1964–1965*, Fort Leavenworth, Kan.: Combat Studies Institute, U.S. Army Command and General Staff College, Leavenworth Papers 14, 1988, p. 75; Thurston Maccauley, *History of the 322nd Air Division (MATS): 1 July–December 1964*, Military Air Transport Service, undated.)

the United States "would ignore the requirements."[2] Yet, in practice, this turned out to be difficult.

Initially, the United States paid little attention to Austria's protests against the violation of its airspace by USAF aircraft. Nevertheless, when the Austrian government threatened to shoot down U.S. planes that failed to comply with its injunction, U.S. officials were forced to abandon their plans to fly over central Europe and to embark on a more circuitous trip that involved stops in France, Italy, and Greece or Libya.[3] Later in the operation, when U.S. aircraft were resupplying British troops in Jordan, Israel closed its airspace to U.S. and UK aircraft and declared that the Israeli Defense Forces would fire on any transgressors, inducing U.S. compliance.[4] In these instances, it was not only Austrian and Israeli threats to protect their airspace that influenced U.S. decisionmaking but also the fear of bad publicity that the Soviet Union could exploit. U.S. officials were concerned that flagrantly ignoring access decisions would damage the U.S. reputation and have reverberations in the global struggle against communism. In short, even in countries where the United States did not have permanent bases, it found it difficult to ignore access denials.

The United States also discovered that deploying forces presumptively was a brazen and ultimately counterproductive approach that alienated even states that strongly supported the U.S. intervention in Lebanon and resulted in restrictions on its peacetime basing rights. Turkey, for instance, was informed (not asked) only after the operation had began that the United States was using Incirlik Air Base to stage Army and USAF forces.[5] Because the Turkish government did not want to impede the U.S. operation, it did not respond to the high-handed treatment by restricting or denying U.S. basing rights during Operation Blue Bat. But this incident left a lasting impression on the affronted Turkish officials, who were increasingly protective of their nation's sovereignty. Subse-

---

[2] "Memorandum for the Record of the State-Joint Chiefs of Staff Meeting, Pentagon, Washington, May 16, 1958, 11:30 a.m.," *FRUS 1958–1960*, Vol. XI, 1992, p. 60.

[3] Dragnich, 1970, pp. 66–68.

[4] Dragnich, 1970, p. 68.

[5] Nur Bilge Criss, "U.S. Forces in Turkey," in Duke and Krieger, 1993, p. 346.

quently, the Turkish government insisted that the United States officially ask for permission to use Turkish bases and was less inclined to make the bases available for non-NATO operations.[6]

One time when the United States blatantly disregarded a host nation's wishes was during the rescue of a hijacked U.S. merchant vessel, the SS *Mayaguez,* in the Gulf of Thailand in 1975 seven years after North Korea had seized the USS *Pueblo,* a USN intelligence ship.[7] President Gerald Ford was determined to prevent another protracted hostage crisis.[8] Moreover, U.S. officials felt the need to demonstrate U.S. resolve and military prowess because the North Vietnamese had just captured Saigon a few weeks earlier.[9] These considerations led President Ford to order U.S. forces to find and liberate the crew of the *Mayaguez,* hopefully before its members were taken ashore in Cambodia, which would have made any rescue operation much more difficult. By this time, there were no U.S. ground forces in Thailand, but the USAF still had aircraft at four Thai bases, which were deployed immediately to search for the missing ship and once, it was located, monitor its activities.[10] In an effort to contain the *Mayaguez* and its crew

[6]   Criss, 1993, pp. 349–350.

[7]   For more on this incident, see Ralph Wetterhan, *The Last Battle: The Mayaguez Incident and the End of the Vietnam War,* New York: Plume Group, 2002; Clayton K. S. Chun, *The Last Boarding Party: the USMC and the SS Mayaguez 1975,* Oxford, UK: Osprey Publishing, 2011; George M. Watson, Jr., "The Mayaguez Rescue," *Air Force Magazine,* July 2009; Daniel L. Haulman, "Crisis in Southeast Asia: Mayaguez Rescue," in Warnock, 2000.

[8]   Wetterhan, 2002, pp. 37–39.

[9]   Henry Kissinger was the most vocal proponent of this view (see "Minutes of National Security Council Meeting, Washington, May 13–14, 1975, 10:40 pm–12:25 am," *FRUS 1969–1976,* Vol. X: *Vietnam, January 1973–July 1975,* ebook, Washington, D.C.: U.S. Government Printing Office, 2010, document 295).

[10]   At the time of the *Mayaguez* incident, U.S. forces in Thailand included the 307th Strategic Wing at U-Tapao Air Base; the 41st Aerospace Rescue and Recovery , 388th Tactical Fighter, and 347th Tactical Fighter wings based at Korat Air Base; the 432nd Tactical Fighter Wing at Udorn Air Base; and the 56th Special Operations and 41st Aerospace Rescue and Recovery wings at Nakhon Pahnom Air Base (Chun, 2011, p. 20). For more on the USAF's role in the storming of Koh Tang, see Thomas D. Des Brisay, *Monograph 5: Fourteen Hours at Koh Tang,"* in A. J. C. Lavalle, ed., *USAF Southeast Asia Monograph Series Vol. III, Monographs 4 and 5,* Washington, D.C.: Office of Air Force History, U.S. Air Force, 1985.

near Koh Tang island, USAF aircraft attacked and sunk three Cambodian patrol boats trying to depart the island. These activities were undertaken without asking for the Thai government's permission.[11] In fact, the American chargé d'affaires, unaware of the ongoing U.S. military operations, assured Thai Prime Minister Kukrit Pramoj that the United States would consult with him before using Thai territory for any *Mayaguez*-related operations.[12]

For its part, Thailand did not want to cross the newly installed Khmer Rouge government in Cambodia and was afraid of inadvertently being drawn into a larger conflict with its communist neighbors by the *Mayaguez* incident.[13] Despite the Thai government's protests, the U.S. National Security Council authorized a rescue operation using Thai air bases, which included seizing the *Mayaguez*, a Marine assault on the island of Koh Tang, and strikes against the Cambodian mainland, but this effort was delayed until a Marine battalion landing team and several USN ships arrived in theater. After being informed about the deployment of U.S. Marines to U-Tapao Air Base, Thai Prime Minister Kukrit expressly prohibited the United States from using Thai air bases to support the rescue operation and demanded that the United States withdraw the Marines "immediately."[14] While the civilian Thai leaders warned that U.S.-Thai "good relations and cooperation

---

[11] Randolph, 1986, pp. 180–181.

[12] "Telegram from the Embassy in Thailand to the Department of State, Bangkok, May 13, 1975, 1116Z," *FRUS 1969–1976*, Vol. X, 2010, document 292. The U.S. ambassador to Thailand assumed it was an accident that he was not informed about the use of Thai-based U.S. aircraft, but this was not actually the case. From the beginning, members of the cabinet recognized that the Thai government was not likely to support any U.S. efforts to rescue the *Mayaguez* and, therefore, deliberately chose not to inform the ambassador about the planned military activities. ("Telegram from the Embassy in Thailand to the Department of State, Bangkok, May 13, 1975, 1315Z," *FRUS 1969–1976 ebook*, Vol. X, 2010, document 289; and "Minutes of National Security Council Meeting, Washington, May 12, 1975, 12:05–12:50 p.m.," *FRUS 1969–1976*, Vol. X, 2013, document 285; especially "Telegram from the Department of State to the Embassy in Thailand, Washington, May 13, 1975, 1754Z," *FRUS 1969–1976*, Vol. X, 2010, document 292).

[13] Randolph, 1986, p. 182; Flynn, 2001, pp. 297–298.

[14] "Telegram from the Embassy in Thailand to the Department of State, Bangkok, May 14, 1975, 1406Z," *FRUS 1969–1976*, Vol. X, 2010, document 296.

. . . would be exposed to serious and damaging consequences," unless the Marines were removed, Thai military leaders quietly indicated that they "extremely pleased" with the forceful U.S. response, although in public they supported their prime minister.[15]

Ultimately, the United States chose to ignore the Thai politicians and to instead proceed with the rescue operation based on an implicit green light from the Thai generals.[16] The United States succeeded in retaking the *Mayaguez* and securing the release of its crew, although at considerable cost in terms of the American lives lost. Moreover, the decision to use Thai bases without official clearance significantly damaged the U.S.-Thai relationship by undermining public support for a post–Vietnam War U.S. military presence. Although the Thai government worked to contain the anti-U.S. protests that broke out in the wake of this incident, it ultimately created a inhospitable political climate that undercut efforts to extend U.S. basing rights. After the incident, the U.S. and Thai governments sought to draw down the U.S. force in Thailand significantly, but, ultimately, both sought to preserve a residual U.S. presence.[17] In the midst of renegotiating U.S. basing rights, Kukrit called for new elections, which further politicized the issue.[18] In a desperate attempt to win reelection, Kukrit played to nationalist sentiment by demanding that the United States agree to seven principles—the most contentious of which was that U.S. forces be subject to Thai jurisdiction—or withdraw all its troops within four months. Given Thai domestic sensitivities about the extraterritorial privileges extended to U.S. troops, Kukrit refused to compromise, which led to an impasse and the withdrawal of the last U.S. troops in Thailand in summer 1976.[19]

---

[15] "Minutes of National Security Council Meeting, Washington, May 14, 1975, 3:52–5:42 p.m.," *FRUS 1969–1976*, Vol. X, 2010, document 298. See also Randolph, 1986, p. 184.

[16] Randolph, 1986, p. 184.

[17] Thai officials still saw the presence of U.S. forces as an important hedge against their communist neighbors (Flynn, 2001, pp. 301–302).

[18] These events support Cooley's argument that U.S. basing rights are often threatened in democratizing states.

[19] Randolph, 1986, pp. 186–193; Flynn, 2001, pp. 308–310.

At times, U.S. leaders have chosen to execute a military operation using a foreign base or airspace without that nation's permission; however, this has generally created blowback that hurt U.S. basing rights over the long run. Even close U.S. allies resent being treated like subordinates and have taken action to punish the United States when it has failed to consult with them about the use of their bases. Blowback is particularly likely if an access violation is publicized. While foreign leaders might be willing to overlook high-handed U.S. behavior, the public is much less willing to do so. The United States, therefore, must be cognizant of and take steps to respect the sovereignty of host nations.

Self-Denial

Another issue that was highlighted in the case studies was the matter of self-denial, that is, situations in which the United States decided not to ask a country for contingency access because it anticipated a negative response or serious complications. This is a classic situation of the dog that did not bark, which makes it difficult to assess how frequently this phenomenon occurs. However, it stands to reason that, throughout the Cold War, for example, the United States did not ask the Soviet Union or China for overflight rights or basing access, even if it would have dramatically reduced the complexity of an operation, because U.S. officials expected that its communist foes would not cooperate. The same is likely true today of Iran or North Korea. Additionally, there may be times when U.S. officials informally discuss the prospect of securing contingency access for an operation with foreign officials; if a nation indicates that it will not respond positively to such a request, the United States refrains from formally asking. There is thus likely a selection bias that is not captured in the data set. Although we cannot determine the frequency of this self-denial, the case studies do provide cursory support for this idea. Moreover, self-denial seems most likely to happen when U.S. officials are worried about jeopardizing their peacetime basing rights.

During Operation Dragon Rogue, the DoS prevented USAFE from asking to use a Libyan air base for the hostage rescue operation in the DRC. Military planners had identified Wheelus Air Base—one of the few U.S. bases on the African continent—as their preferred location for staging the C-130s transporting Belgian paratroopers to the DRC. Access to Wheelus would have simplified the logistical requirements for the operation because it was a USAFE air base with all the needed supplies and equipment in place and offered shorter flying times, provided that overflight clearances could be obtained from several African nations.

In addition to Wheelus, U.S. planners also considered Roberts Field in Liberia and Ascension Island, which was owned by the British, but were disinclined to use these coastal or offshore airfields because the distance using them would add to the operation and the lack of infrastructure and critical supplies, such as fuel, at these locations.[20] Staging forces at Ascension also necessitated obtaining access to an additional refueling base on the African continent, but DoS insisted on the British island for several reasons. First, and most important, the department was concerned that using the base for this controversial operation would jeopardize ongoing U.S. negotiations to extend its peacetime rights to the Libyan air base. The Libyan government had already been under intense pressure from Egyptian President Nasser to evict U.S. forces. At an Organization of African Unity meeting in February 1964, Nasser had demanded that all member states expel foreign military forces and had explicitly called on Libyan King Idris to abrogate U.S. basing rights.[21] DoS officials feared that, if U.S. forces used Wheelus Air Base in this charged environment, U.S. personnel would be subject to attack; the U.S. operation would be condemned in the Organization of African Unity and the United Nations; and the price that the United States would have to pay to retain access to Wheelus would go up significantly.[22] Second, DoS officials argued that Ascension was the better choice because the operation was less likely to

---

[20] Odom, 1988, pp. 35–37, 47.

[21] Thomas Sturm, *USAF Overseas Forces and Bases: 1947–1967*, Washington, D.C.: Office of Air Force History, 1969, p. 88.

[22] The DoS concern about public demonstrations and attacks was likely correct. In Kenya, mobs bombed diplomatic cars parked around the U.S., UK, and Belgian embassies, and there were attacks on embassies in Czechoslovakia, Egypt, and the USSR (Fred E. Wagoner, *Dragon Rouge: The Rescue of Hostages in the Congo,* Washington, D.C.: National Defense University, 1980, pp. 160, 191).

be prematurely exposed to the public.[23] In the end, USAFE was forced to accede to the DoS's wishes and never asked to use Wheelus for the insertion or retrograde of forces from the DRC.[24]

Similarly, during the Vietnam War, the United States wanted to base B-52s near South Vietnam to increase their responsiveness but was unwilling to pursue permanent basing at some of the most logical locations (Okinawa or the Philippines) because of the likely political fallout. As the air war over Vietnam escalated, the United States found that operating B-52s from Andersen Air Force Base on Guam was insufficient to meet the growing demand for the Arc Light close air support and interdiction missions. According to the commander of U.S. Forces in Vietnam, General William Westmoreland, "Guam is barely adequate as a base from which to support the war in Vietnam" because "strike reaction time . . . is much too long, and many valuable targets are lost due to this delay."[25]

When a typhoon forced the bombers to relocate from Guam to Kadena Air Base on Okinawa in July 1965, the United States seized the opportunity to conduct bombing operations from the closer air base. Operating from Kadena instead of Andersen shaved two and half hours off the bombers' reaction time; however, it also caused a furor in Japan.[26] The U.S. embassy in Japan recommended that, unless absolutely essential, the USAF should refrain from carrying out additional bombing raids from Okinawa to avoid further inflaming Japanese public opinion.[27] While Undersecretary of State George Ball noted that, because the United States directly administered Okinawa, its

---

[23] Odom, 1988, p. 37.

[24] Wagoner, 1980, p. 136.

[25] Quoted in Graham A. Cosmas, *The Joint Chiefs of Staff and the War in Vietnam, 1960–1968*, Part 2, Washington, D.C.: Office of Joint History, Office of the Chairman of the Joint Chiefs of Staff, 2012, p. 467.

[26] Thomas R. H. Havens, *Fire Across the Sea: The Vietnam War and Japan, 1965–1975*, Princeton, N.J.: Princeton University Press, pp. 76–77; Headquarters U.S. Military Assistance Command Vietnam, *B-52 Study*, 1 December 1966, p. 1.

[27] "Telegram from the Embassy in Japan to the Department of State Tokyo, July 30, 1965, 1001Z," *FRUS 1964–1968*, Vol. XXIX, Part 2: *Japan*, Washington, D.C.: U.S. Government Printing Office, 2006, pp. 110–111.

rights were "theoretically unlimited." Further, because there was not even "a formal obligation . . . to consult or notify the Japanese," he felt, "in the wake of this week's strike and its publicity . . . that some form of discussion was required as a matter of courtesy." Moreover, Ball concluded that "recurrent use of the Okinawa bases . . . will seriously heighten pressures in Japan on the issue of Okinawa generally, and indeed will significantly affect the whole atmosphere of our relations with Japan in every sphere." Consequently, he advised that the United States "take a very hard look indeed before we get into a situation where the use of Okinawa would in fact be frequent."[28] Due to these considerations, additional B-52 operations from Okinawa were avoided, and the bombers were returned to Guam as soon as the situation allowed.[29]

Although the USAF's experience of operating the bombers on Okinawa did not go well, the requirement for an additional, closer B-52 base grew. By December 1965, the Joint Staff recommended that DoD find a forward base for at least 30 B-52s to improve reaction time, reduce the cost of operations, reduce tanker requirements, decrease congestion at Andersen, and serve as an additional divert location.[30] In a formal study of the possible B-52 operating locations, the USAF considered air bases in Taiwan, Okinawa, and the Philippines. As shown in Figure 6.2, all these options would significantly reduce the distance flown for each bombing sortie and would therefore have helped to achieve the Joint Staff's objectives. Because Kadena or U-Tapao air base would have required fewer improvements to the exist-

---

[28] "Letter from the Under Secretary of State (Ball) to Secretary of Defense McNamara, Washington, July 31, 1965," *FRUS 1964–1968*, Vol. XXIX, Part 2, 2006, pp. 111–113.

[29] In response to several simultaneous crises in 1968 (the hijacking of the USS *Pueblo* and the Tet offensive), the United States once again temporarily deployed B-52s to Okinawa. In this instance, the Japanese government made it clear that it had no intention of asking for the removal of the Air Force bombers. Nevertheless, U.S. officials felt the need to assure the Japanese that the bombers would remain on the island only for the duration of the crisis, which lasted for approximately one year ("Document 117: Editorial Note," *FRUS 1964–1968*, Vol. XXIX, Part 2, 2006, pp. 266–267).

[30] At the beginning of 1966, the USAF had only 30 B-52s at Andersen for operations in South Vietnam but was upgrading the base so that, by the end of the year, it could support 70 bombers (Cosmas, 2012, p. 466).

ing infrastructure, military planners considered these the most expedient options and recommended that DoD reconsider the costs and risks associated with using Okinawa as a B-52 base.

Around the same time, President Lyndon B. Johnson was "struck by the obvious geographic and logistic advantages" of moving B-52 operations from Guam to the Philippines.[31] Consequently, the National Security Council asked DoS to assess the political situation in the Philippines and whether it would be feasible to station B-52s in the Southeast Asian nation. Assistant Secretary of State for Near Eastern Affairs William Bundy believed that Philippine President Ferdinand Marcos would be amenable to the idea, but that because this decision would

Figure 6.2
Distance from Bases Considered for B-52 Operations During the Vietnam War

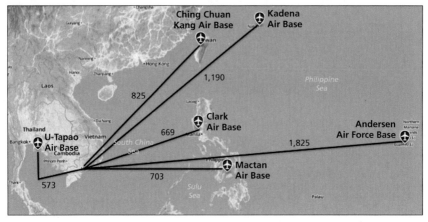

SOURCE: Edward Vallentiny, *USAF Posture in Thailand January–December 1967: Project CHECO Southeast Asia Report*, Hickam AFB, Hawaii: Pacific Air Forces, March 25, 1969, p. 35.
NOTE: Distances in nautical miles.
RAND RR1339-6.2

---

[31] "Memorandum from the Assistant Secretary of State for Far Eastern Affairs (Bundy) to William J. Jorden of the National Security Council Staff Washington, August 22, 1966," in *FRUS 1964–1968*, Vol. XXVI: *Indonesia; Malaysia-Singapore, Phillippines*, Washington, D.C.: U.S. Government Printing Office, 2000, pp. 741, fn. 2.

"involve[e] great political costs at home," Marcos would demand "a substantial quid pro quo" from the United States. Additionally, Bundy concluded that Marcos would likely "need to obtain a formal resolution of approval by the Philippine Congress," which would involve a "long and bloody fight."[32] For these reasons and because of the costs associated with making the improvements needed at the Philippine air bases to support B-52 operations, this option was not formally pursued.[33]

Ultimately, the United States also decided against basing the bombers on Okinawa to avoid upsetting U.S.-Japan relations, even though the Joint Staff affirmed that Kadena was one of the best options. Instead, in January 1967, the United States asked Thailand to base B-52s at U-Tapao; after three months of negotiations, the Thai government agreed, on the condition that the real purpose of the new construction was concealed.[34] By mid-1967, Arc Light operations began at U-Tapao, eliminating the need for aerial refueling and cutting approximately ten hours off the mission time from Guam.[35]

The case studies suggest that there are indeed selection effects that are not captured in the quantitative analysis. In the examples discussed above, U.S. officials avoided requesting access in certain countries— even when the host government would likely have given its permission—because the officials feared that doing so would anger the local population and ultimately jeopardize U.S. peacetime basing rights. In short, it appears that the United States has refrained from asking countries where it has permanent bases for contingency access when its peacetime access has been challenged by internal access threats. Therefore, instead of peacetime access assuring contingency access, we found

---

[32] "Memorandum from the Assistant Secretary of State for Far Eastern Affairs (Bundy) to William J. Jorden of the National Security Council Staff Washington, August 22, 1966," in *FRUS 1964–1968,* Vol. XXVI, 2000, pp. 741–743.

[33] Taiwan was similarly dismissed because of cost and political complications (Cosmas, 2012, p. 467).

[34] Vallentiny, 1969, p. 35.

[35] William P. Head, *War From Above the Clouds: B-52 Operations During the Second Indochina War and the Effects of the Air War on Theory and Doctrine,* Maxwell Air Force Base, Ala.: Air University Press, 2002, p. 29.

that endangered peacetime access can prevent U.S. officials from even asking for permission to use bases during a contingency.

Vacillators and Repeat Offenders

The integrated analysis also revealed two additional observations that have direct implications for U.S. policymakers. First, contingency access permissions may be revised during the course of an operation. This suggests that some nations are prone to changing their minds and that U.S. officials need to recognize that contingency access negotiations are an ongoing process that must be managed. Even after a nation grants access, the United States may need to work to maintain that access. Alternatively, even if a nation denies or restricts U.S. access for an operation, continued deliberations could turn a no or qualified yes into unrestricted access. Second, access challenges have historically been more common in some nations than in others. Because these repeat offenders have often restricted or denied U.S. basing rights in peacetime and contingencies, U.S. officials may want to seek alternative locations when possible or be prepared for difficult negotiations if access in these states is truly needed.

Contingency Access Permissions Are Dynamic

It is often assumed that contingency access is binary and fixed, meaning that a nation either allows or prohibits U.S. forces from using its territory for the duration of an operation. In some instances, this is clearly true. In El Dorado Canyon, for instance, Spain and France firmly held to the position that no U.S. aircraft would be granted overflight or basing rights during the strike against Libya. But in other cases, access permissions may change by the day or even the hour. This is particularly likely for longer operations that last for weeks, months, or even years.

Take Operation Blue Bat—the 1958 U.S. intervention in Lebanon—for example. On July 14, 1958, a radical Arab nationalist coup overthrew the pro-Western Hashemite monarchy in Iraq, which in turn precipitated the deployment of U.S. troops to Lebanon to shore up the government of another shaky ally. Middle Eastern leaders aligned with the West feared that their regimes were at risk of suffering a similar fate and encouraged the United States to take action to stem the tide of Arab nationalism by deploying troops to bolster the most vulnerable governments. In particular, Lebanese President Camille Chamoun invoked the Eisenhower Doctrine—the pledge U.S. President Dwight D. Eisenhower had made that the U.S. military would come to the aid of any Middle Eastern country whose independence was threatened by communism—and, on July 14, requested that the United States dispatch forces to support his government.[36] Concerned about the regional and international consequences of U.S. inaction, President Eisenhower quickly agreed to this request. During the course of this operation, which lasted for over three and a half months, three countries (Greece, Austria, and Israel) changed their access permissions ten times.

On July 15, the United States began Operation Blue Bat, which involved three Marine battalions landing near Beirut, airlifting two airborne battle groups from France and Germany to Lebanon, steaming most of the 6th Fleet to the Eastern Mediterranean, and deploying a USAF composite strike air force to Turkey.[37] Given the limited range of many U.S. aircraft at the time, moving forces to the Middle East from Europe and the United States required significant access to foreign territory. As depicted in Figure 6.3, access permissions were forthcoming from West Germany, France, Italy, Portugal, and Turkey, while Libya only allowed U.S. forces to land at Wheelus Air Base on the conditions that this presence was kept secret and that the forces did

---

[36] For more on the Eisenhower Doctrine, see Salim Yaqub, *Containing Arab Nationalism: The Eisenhower Doctrine and the Middle East,* Chapel Hill, N.C.: University of North Carolina Press, 2004, pp. 57–117.

[37] For more on this operation, see Dragnich, 1970; Robert D. Little and Wilhelmine Burch, *Air Operations in the Lebanon Crisis of 1958,* USAF Historical Division Liaison Office, October 1962, declassified February 23, 1982; Jack Shulimson, *Marines in Lebanon 1958,* Washington, D.C.: Historical Branch, G-3 Division, Headquarters, U.S. Marine Corps, 1966; Roger J. Spiller, *"Not War but Like War": The American Intervention in Lebanon,* Fort Leavenworth, Kan.: Combat Studies Institute, U.S. Army Command and General Staff College, Leavenworth Papers 3, 1981.

not stay overnight.[38] Throughout the operation, the Swiss government refused to grant U.S. military aircraft en route to Lebanon overflight clearances.[39] On July 17—just two days into the operation—U.S. officials had to revise their plans after Austria and Greece denied U.S. aircraft transit and overflight rights. Austria had announced a policy of "perpetual neutrality" in 1955 and felt that it was violating this pledge if it authorized U.S. aircraft to fly through its airspace.[40] In contrast, Greece, which was concerned about potential retaliatory attacks against its citizens in Egypt and elsewhere, first constrained U.S. permissions by allowing only westbound traffic to stop at Athens Airport and then only with 48 hours of prior notice. Several hours later, the Greek government prohibited all but emergency landings and barred the Navy's squadron of antisubmarine aircraft (P2-Vs) from flying operations.[41] Consequently, the USN aircraft were relocated to either Beirut or Malta, from which they could freely operate.[42] By July 20, the Greek government again modified its access decision by allowing westbound U.S. military cargo to overfly Greece and eastbound traffic to land at any Greek airport, except for Athens after dark.[43]

While the United States remained focused on stabilizing Lebanon, the British military responded to King Hussein of Jordan's July 16 appeal for help by transporting troops from Cyprus to Amman the following day. Before long, however, the landlocked British and Jordanian forces ran short of essential stocks, especially oil, and the United States agreed to help with the resupply.[44] This effort ran into immediate access problems. Initially, the United States and UK wanted to

---

[38] Lemmer, 1963, p. 32.

[39] Dragnich, 1970, p. 66.

[40] Byron R. Fairchild and Walter S. Poole, *History of the Joint chiefs of Staff: The Joint Chiefs of Staff and National Policy, Vol. VII, 1957–1960*, Washington, D.C.: Office of Joint History, Office of the Chairman of the Joint Chiefs of Staff, 2000, p. 158

[41] The Greeks did allow that, if a serious submarine threat materialized, the USN aircraft would be permitted to operate.

[42] Dragnich, 1970, p. 64, 67; Fairchild and Poole, 2000, p. 158.

[43] Dragnich, 1970, p. A-5.

[44] Little and Burch, 1962, pp. 54–55; Dragnich, 1970, pp. 42–43.

Figure 6.3
Changing Access Permissions During Operation Blue Bat

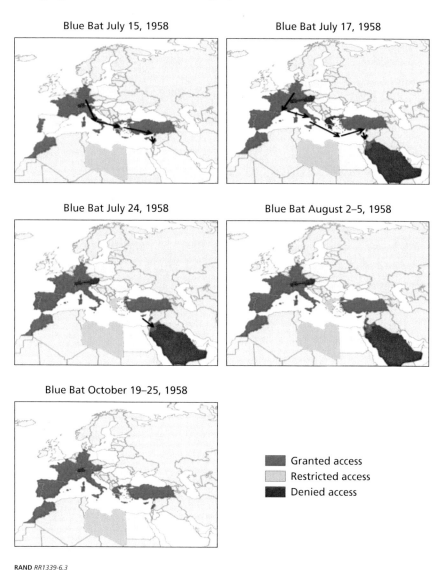

Blue Bat July 15, 1958

Blue Bat July 17, 1958

Blue Bat July 24, 1958

Blue Bat August 2–5, 1958

Blue Bat October 19–25, 1958

Granted access
Restricted access
Denied access

RAND *RR1339-6.3*

transport fuel stored in the British protectorate of Bahrain to Jordan, but Saudi Arabia, which had encouraged the U.S. and British interventions, refused to allow U.S. aircraft to use Dhahran Air Base or to overfly its territory because there were reports in the press that it was providing U.S. aircraft safe passage.[45] Consequently, the United States airlifted fuel from Beirut to Amman, which required overflying Israel. Israeli Prime Minister David Ben Gurion only reluctantly acceded to the U.S. request to pass through Israeli airspace and stipulated that U.S. aircraft remain above 14,500 feet.[46] On August 2, however, a letter of protest from the Soviet Union prompted the Israeli government to abruptly revoke the U.S. clearances and demand that U.S. military aircraft immediately cease transiting through Israeli airspace.[47] After being sharply rebuked by the Eisenhower administration, Ben Gurion reversed his earlier decision on August 5th and again permitted U.S. aircraft to overfly Israel for a limited time.

Shifting access authorizations are not unique to Operation Blue Bat. During the first Gulf War (operations Desert Shield and Desert Storm), several nations modified the basing rights they provided to U.S. forces. For instance, Saudi Arabia, which welcomed hundreds of thousands of U.S. forces on its territory, was initially unwilling to allow USAF B-52 bombers to be stationed in the kingdom. Yet, shortly before the air campaign against Iraq began, the Saudis quietly allowed the bombers to operate from an air base near Jeddah.[48] Similarly, Spain, which was in the midst of negotiating a drawdown of the permanently based U.S. forces on its territory, only gradually relaxed the restrictions that it originally placed on U.S. access for Middle East operations. At the time of the invasion of Kuwait, the Spanish government permitted only five U.S. tanker aircraft on Spanish soil at any one time.

---

[45] "Memorandum of a Conference with the President, White House, Washington, July 20, 1958, 3:45 pm," *FRUS 1958–1960*, Vol. XI, 1992, p. 348.

[46] This altitude threshold affected U.S. operations because it prevented the use of C-119 aircraft, which would have been more efficient for these routes, forcing the United States to use C-124s and C-130s (Little and Birch, 1962, p. 55).

[47] Dragnich, 1970, p. A-7.

[48] Michael R. Gordon, "War in the Gulf: The Bombers Saudis Recapture Ghost Town; Allies Bomb New Iraqi Column, New Bases for U.S.," *New York Times*, February 1, 1991; Jon Lake, *B-52 Stratoforce Units in Operation Desert Storm*, Oxford, UK: Osprey Publishing, 2004, p. 12; Richard L. Olson, *Gulf War Air Power Survey*, Vol. III: *Logistics and Support*, Washington, D.C.: U.S. Government Printing Office, 1993, p. 130.

By August 8, the United States convinced the Spanish government to allow an additional ten tankers to support the rapid deployment of troops to the Persian Gulf. Finally, on August 17, Spain raised the ceiling on tanker aircraft to 30.[49] Madrid also limited the number of transiting A-10 aircraft on the parking ramp at Torrejon Air Base at any one time.[50] Nevertheless, by the time Operation Desert Storm began, Spanish Prime Minister Felipe Gonzalez had consented to basing B-52 bombers at Moron Air Base, as long as the move was not publicized.[51]

Additionally, Turkey's position on basing rights for operations against Iraq evolved over the course of the five months leading up to the war. At the outset, the Turkish government was reluctant to get involved in the buildup against Iraq, preferring instead to maintain its traditional policy of neutrality.[52] Consequently, the United States could not deploy tanker aircraft to Incirlik Air Base, even though it was routinely used as a hub for U.S. aerial refueling operations during peacetime.[53] Although Turkish President Özal was inclined to help the United States, he faced strong opposition within his own party and the influential Turkish military. As a result of disagreements over Turkish support for the war, Turkey's chief of staff, foreign minister, and defense minister all resigned in protest of Özal's desire to support the U.S.-led military operations. Moreover, nearly two-thirds of the Turks polled were against military action against Iraq.[54] Consequently, Özal was initially unwilling to grant access to U.S. forces, which would be costly politically in the event that the United States chose not to go to war against Iraq.[55] Ultimately, Özal forged ahead and incremen-

---

[49] Olson, 1993, p. 80

[50] Project AIR FORCE Desert Shield Assessment Team, *Project AIR FORCE Assessment of Operation Desert Shield: The Buildup of Combat Power*, Santa Monica, Calif.: RAND Corporation, MR-356-AF, 1994, p. 22.

[51] Olson, 1993, p. 130.

[52] Cameron S. Brown, "Turkey in the Gulf Wars of 1991 and 2003," *Turkish Studies*, Vol. 8, No. 1, March 2007, p. 88.

[53] Olson, 1993, p. 193; Project AIR FORCE Desert Shield Assessment Team, 1994, p. 28.

[54] Freedman and Karsh, 1993, p. 353.

[55] Abramowitz, 2000, p. 155.

tally offered the United States increasingly generous access despite the domestic resistance because he believed that supporting the offensive against Iraq presented an opportunity to prove Turkey's value in the post–Cold War world as an ally. A week before the onset of combat operations, Özal succeeded in persuading his cabinet to allow U.S. forces to use Turkish bases for "humanitarian and limited logistics support." Although offensive air operations were still prohibited, additional U.S. combat aircraft were permitted to arrive in Turkey.[56] Furthermore, once the war began, Özal granted a last-minute request from the United States for B-52s flying from Spain to transit through Turkish airspace to bomb Iraq and pushed through the Grand National Assembly a resolution allowing U.S. forces to conduct combat operations from Incirlik Air Base.[57]

As these examples illustrate, access permissions may change quite frequently throughout the course of an operation. Therefore, even if the United States gets a positive answer initially, it should not take this position for granted because access decisions are often revisited. At the same time, there is also the possibility that a negative response will soften over time, particularly if it involves particular restrictions on access. This, in turn, suggests that the United States needs to monitor and continue to work not only to obtain but also to expand and maintain access permissions throughout an operation.

Repeat Offenders

The peacetime and contingency data sets reveal that, in the past, certain countries have proven to be access problems time and time again. We call these nations *repeat offenders*. The past is not a perfect predictor of the future. Nevertheless, the finding that some states seem less inclined to host U.S. forces should be kept in mind when making basing decisions and contingency access requests.

---

[56] Freedman and Karsch, 1993, p. 353; F. Stephen Larrabee and Ian O. Lesser, *Turkish Foreign Policy in an Age of Uncertainty*, Santa Monica, Calif.: RAND Corporation, MR-1612-CMEPP, 2003, p. 165.

[57] Brown, 2007, p. 89. At that time, tankers joined the Joint Task Force Proven Force established at Incirlik (Olson, 1993, p. 193).

As Figure 6.4 illustrates, some countries have contested U.S. peacetime basing rights more than others. In particular, nine states have challenged U.S. peacetime access four or more times. Of these nine nations, four—Turkey, Spain, Portugal, and the Philippines—stand out as the worst offenders, largely in the Cold War transactional era. Ten other nations have initiated two to three challenges, while nine countries have challenged U.S. peacetime basing rights only once. In addition to the aggregate number of challenges, there are temporal differences as well. Many of the challenges occurred during the Cold War and were global in scope, but more recently, the United States has faced peacetime access problems in specific regions. In particular, the realignments of U.S. forces in South Korea and on Okinawa account for six post–Cold War challenges in Northeast Asia. Additionally, there have been several challenges in Central Command's area of responsibility (Central Asia, Persian Gulf, and Horn of Africa).

In contrast, contingency access problems tend to be distributed more evenly. Nonetheless, several states have regularly restricted access or denied the United States permission to use their territories for a particular operation. This is not terribly surprising, especially because the United States has carried out protracted and repeated operations against one country—Iraq—for more than two decades. One would expect that neighboring states have been queried many times for access and that they have enduring interests and/or face persistent constraints that have shaped their responses. Figure 6.5 shows the number of times that a particular country has denied or restricted U.S. contingency access. Most countries have refused U.S. access requests or provided limited access fewer than three times.

Only six countries exceeded that benchmark, with three (Spain, Turkey, and Saudi Arabia) standing out far above the rest.[58] While Spain has refused or provided restricted access a total of six times, all occurred before 1991. In the past several decades, as Spain's democratic institutions have taken root and as it has transitioned away from being

---

[58] Egypt denied U.S. access twice and restricted it three times, but four of those decisions were made about peacekeeping operations in the Sinai peninsula in the aftermath of the 1973 Yom Kippur War.

Figure 6.4
Peacetime Access Challenges, by Country

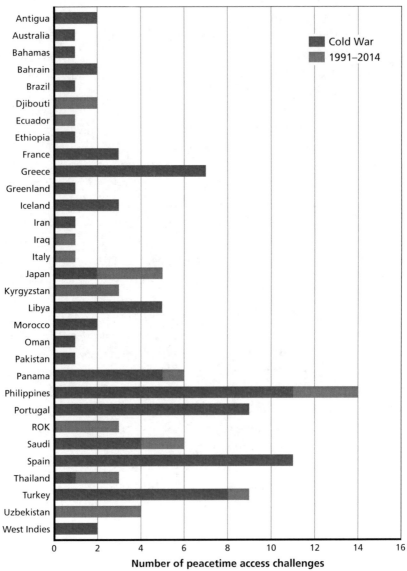

Figure 6.5
Contingency Access Restrictions and Denials, by Country

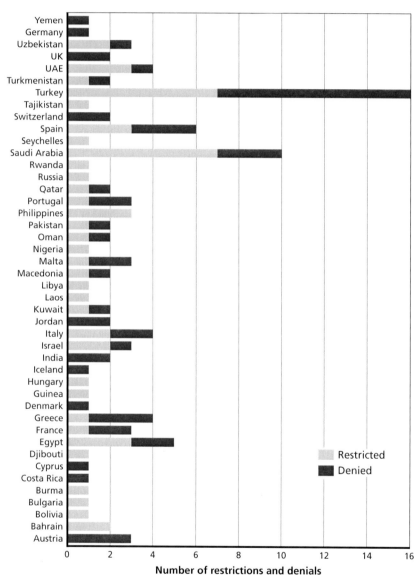

RAND *RR1339-6.5*

a transactional to an enduring partner, contingency access problems have diminished.[59] In contrast, access problems with Turkey and Saudi Arabia have not only persisted but have actually gotten worse in recent years. Only six of Turkey's and three of Saudi Arabia's decisions to restrict or deny U.S. access were during the Cold War. When comparing these two repeat offenders, it is worth noting that Saudi Arabia has tended to restrict U.S. access far more often than deny it. As the case studies reveal, this is largely due to the fact that the Saudis became far less supportive of U.S. sanctions against Iraq and, as a result of domestic opposition and fears of retaliation, were willing to provide access only for noncombat forces. On the other hand, Turkey has denied U.S. access more often (nine times) than restricted it (seven times) but seems evenly disposed toward either course of action. Moreover, the case study analysis indicates that these numbers underrepresent the extent of Turkish restrictions during Operation Northern Watch, the no-fly zone over Iraq. This operation is counted only once in the data set, but over its course, Turkey not only established some of the most restrictive rules of engagement but also habitually cancelled U.S. operations.[60]

Turkey and Saudi Arabia stand out as the least reliable nations for both peacetime and contingency access. Many commentators were shocked when Turkey refused to provide the Bush administration with the full access that it requested for the 2003 invasion of Iraq. This decision was seen as a sign that the relationship between Ankara and Washington had suddenly and perhaps irreparably frayed. Turkey's refusal to allow the United States to launch attacks on the Islamic State in Iraq and Syria from its territory in 2014 elicited similar reactions. Yet Turkey's unwillingness to allow U.S. forces to operate from its territory should come as no surprise. It has exhibited a lack of enthusiasm for non-NATO operations since the mid-1960s. At that time, differences over Cyprus began to seriously erode the shared perception of threat that was the foundation of U.S. access. This ultimately led to a transition to a transactional relationship by 1980. Since 1945, Turkey has

---

[59] For instance, even after deciding to withdraw its forces from Iraq, Spain allowed U.S. forces to continue to use its bases to support operations in Iraq.

[60] Knights, 2005, p. 219.

challenged U.S. peacetime basing rights seven times (including evicting U.S. forces in 1975) and has denied or restricted U.S. requests for contingency access 16 times.

Similarly, the U.S. relationship with Saudi Arabia has been fraught with tension and problems. The kingdom is the only state to have evicted U.S. forces twice (in 1962 and 2003) and has restricted or denied U.S. access ten times. Both Turkey and Saudi Arabia are long-standing U.S. partners but have been very difficult hosts, and there is little reason to expect that to change in the near future.

There is value in understanding previous U.S. experiences with host nations. While the past is not a perfect predictor of future behavior by any stretch, it does provide important context, especially in terms of identifying what a particular nation has tended to be comfortable with in terms of U.S. forces on its territory or what it has been willing to permit for specific types of operations. These factors should be kept in mind when U.S. officials seek to revise basing agreements or determine which countries to ask for what types of access during a crisis. Chapter Seven presents our findings and offers recommendations for policymakers to improve the chances that the United States will obtain and can then maintain the access to foreign territory that it needs in peacetime and during contingencies.

Conclusion

This report has aimed to fill a gap in the existing literature on political access problems by carrying out a comprehensive empirical analysis of the access challenges that the United States must confront. This issue remains vitally important to U.S. national security because the United States depends on access to overseas bases to project military power around the globe. It is therefore incredibly important that the United States distinguish between the nations it can rely on to host a peacetime presence and those that are likely to allow U.S. forces to operate from their territory for particular missions. We employed both qualitative and quantitative methodologies to consider the separate but related problems of peacetime and contingency access risk.

Findings

Political challenges to access have occurred regularly, but the threat has often been overstated. Although there are very real and nontrivial internal and external threats to U.S. access overseas, there is a tendency to inflate the scope and magnitude of these challenges. This misconception about access problems is due in part to the fact that there were no longitudinal data on this issue. Our research shows that peacetime and contingency access challenges have declined since the Cold War. Furthermore, only 10 percent of formal U.S. requests for contingency access have been denied or restricted, while 90 percent have been approved. More important, while contingency access problems have proven to be a hindrance, they have rarely prevented an operation from being executed.

That being said, access to foreign bases cannot be taken for granted, particularly during peacetime. In this day and age, other countries are only willing to enter into much more balanced and circumscribed basing agreements with the United States. By starting with a more-constrained baseline, there is little recourse for the host nation except to ask U.S. forces to leave when access challenges emerge. Additionally, there is less tolerance for U.S. missteps—accidental or not—because they are inevitably publicized. Even enduring partners resent being treated like subordinates or having their sovereign rights infringed on by U.S. forces that overstep their bounds. In short, U.S. policymakers should never assume that access to foreign bases is assured.

The United States faces two distinct access problems, but some partners are likely to be more or less reliable during peacetime and contingencies. Peacetime and contingency access decisions are driven by fundamentally different dynamics. The former are rooted in broader and more-enduring (although not immutable) factors, such as a host nation's domestic political institutions and its access relationship with the United States, while the latter are heavily influenced by context-specific factors. Consequently, the United States may have very secure peacetime access in a nation that denies U.S. forces contingency access because of the particular circumstances. Nevertheless, certain partners tend to be more or less reliable in peacetime and during contingencies. In particular, enduring partner nations—countries with strong elite support for the relationship with the United States—are the least likely to evict or restrict U.S. peacetime basing rights and are also the most likely to allow U.S. forces to operate from their bases during a crisis. In contrast, transactional partners—nations that are primarily motivated by securing compensation—are the most likely to limit or rescind peacetime basing rights and the least likely to permit U.S. forces to use their bases during a contingency. Since 2001, the United States has increasingly relied on bases in transactional partners to combat terrorism. If this practice expands, one should expect peacetime and contingency access problems to grow.

The presence of large permanent bases does not increase the likelihood of securing contingency access. In fact, unstable peacetime access can actually reduce the probability that the United States will ask for permission to use a facility during a crisis. Having a permanent military presence in a nation during peacetime does not guarantee or even increase the probability of being granted permission to use the bases during a contingency. Instead, the type of access relationship is a better predicator of contingency access outcomes. Enduring partners are the only type of host nation more likely to come through with contingency access. Transactional partners are actually less likely to provide access than countries in which the United States has no peacetime basing rights. Unpredictable peacetime access, which is most often associated with transactional partners, can actually reduce the probability that the United States will ask for permission to use bases during an operation for fear of jeopardizing long-term access. That is, if its peacetime basing rights are contested, U.S. officials may not seek contingency access, engaging in an act of self-denial. Dysfunctional peacetime access can therefore reduce the probability of acquiring contingency access.

Certain types of operations—especially limited punitive strikes and MCOs—are associated with access problems. It should come as no surprise that it is easier to obtain access for noncontroversial military operations, such HA/DR, than for those that involve the use of force. What is somewhat surprising is the fact that limited strikes have encountered more difficulty securing access than MCOs. Host nations have more often denied access for the former type of operation but only restricted access for the latter. This outcome seems to be driven by the fact that concerns about retaliation were often greatest with limited strikes. Because these missions do not significantly reduce the military capability of the target, host nations feared that it would be left in power and retain the ability to retaliate. In contrast, while MCOs might be equally if not more provocative, the target should be significantly weakened and therefore less capable of seeking vengeance, even if not removed from power.

Contingency access permissions are dynamic and may change throughout the course of an operation. This may seem obvious, but discussions about contingency access often seem to assume that access decisions are binary and static. In reality, another nation may respond with *yes, no,* or *yes but only under these conditions.* More important, this answer may be amended as time passes, especially for operations that last for several months or even years. Because of the tendency for countries to revisit contingency access decisions, the United States should not take a positive response for granted or assume that a negative or qualified response is absolute. Countries that have provided U.S. forces with restricted access seem most liable to modify a position, although they can grant U.S. forces more latitude or can become more restrictive. Consequently, U.S. officials must endeavor to maintain and expand U.S. access permissions throughout the duration of an operation.

Access permissions are more likely when the host nation has its own reasons for supporting a U.S. operation or when the mission can be credibly presented as legitimate. It is obvious why a nation offered U.S. forces access if its interests were at stake. Even when this was not the case, however, many nations have still been willing to host U.S. forces. The case studies reveal that access permissions were more likely if a government could defend its decision to support a U.S. operation to domestic and international audiences, which largely depended on whether the operation was seen as legitimate. Legitimacy can stem from any number of sources, including responses to overt aggression, an explicit or implicit UNSC resolution authorizing the use of force, or endorsement from a regional international organization.

Access denials were more likely when there was domestic opposition to an operation or the host nation feared that it would be subject to reprisals. In nearly all the cases, these two factors have influenced states' decisions to refuse or restrict contingency access. While domestic opposition is fundamentally an internal threat to access, third parties can help generate or exacerbate both these obstacles. External actors may fan the flames of domestic opposition to a U.S. operation by supporting factions opposed to the United States. More directly, a third party can try to bully potential hosts by threatening to target any nation that provides U.S. forces with access.

Recommendations

These findings suggest that the United States should take the following actions:

Maintain access in enduring partner nations and, whenever possible, avoid transactional partners. The type of access relationship influences the reliability of both peacetime and contingency access, with enduring partners being the most dependable and transactional partners the least dependable. Consequently, the United States should seek to retain bases in enduring partner nations that continue to be useful for future challenges and minimize the number of bases it has in transactional partner nations. And if the United States has no choice but to use bases in transactional nations, try to ensure that there are other comparable options that reduce the bargaining power of the transactional host and can therefore mitigate some of the risks associated with relying on these partners.

Be cognizant of host-nation sensitivities. Although this advice seems obvious, it bears repeating. U.S. officials and forces need to shed any lingering sense of entitlement and recognize that, whether their presence is temporary or permanent, they are visitors in another sovereign nation that has every right to place limits on their activities. Far too often, American officials react with shock and outrage when another country challenges U.S. basing rights or denies U.S. forces access for an operation. An attitude change is not likely to resolve access problems that emerge in high-risk countries (i.e., authoritarian or democratizing transactional partners), but it can help mitigate the irritants and issues that inevitably arise. Most important, deferring to the host nation's wishes and expecting that they will have a say on U.S. military activities can help strengthen relationships with enduring and mutual defense partners, minimizing any internal threats to access that might emerge. It would also help undercut the claims of third parties that seek to delegitimize the U.S. military presence overseas by claiming it is imperialistic.

Be aware of potential host nation's red lines and plan around them. The contingency access analyses reveal that many nations have traditionally been willing to provide certain types of access but not others. While the past is by no means a perfect predictor of future behavior, it is an important guide and something that U.S. military planners should be aware of and consider before requesting access. If U.S. officials are thinking about asking for something unprecedented, they should carefully reflect on a nation's interests and constraints to determine whether the request is likely to be approved. In an ideal world, U.S. forces would have complete freedom of action at their preferred operating locations, but this is simply not practical. It is also not necessary; the U.S. military has proven time and time again that it can find ways to succeed despite operational constraints. Understanding a particular nation's interests in a situation and its history with the United States will help develop mutually acceptable beddowns that are less likely to strain relations with allies and partners. In many instances, it may make sense politically to distribute the U.S. presence instead of asking one partner to host a very large and potentially controversial U.S. force.

If an operation is not in response to overt aggression, the United States should try to enhance perceptions of its legitimacy by securing the explicit or implicit endorsement of international organizations. Although clear cases of self-defense tend to be imbued with inherent legitimacy, many other types of U.S. military activities are not. In these instances, the United States can improve the likelihood of securing and maintaining contingency access by getting international buy-in in the form of an explicit or implicit UNSC mandate or authorization from a regional international organization. Working through institutions can improve the probability of securing access by enhancing the legitimacy of an operation and reassuring host nations that the United States will consult with them and act in a constrained manner.

Try to ensure that host nations are not isolated to reduce their susceptibility to domestic critics and bullying by third parties. In general, the case studies show that nations prefer not to go out on a limb as the only country providing U.S. forces with access. Doing so would make a country the focal point for condemnation at home and abroad—and a potential target for retaliation. Therefore, states seem more comfortable providing U.S. forces with access if there is a formal or informal coalition supporting the operation.

To improve political resiliency, the United States should seek access from multiple countries for any given scenario. In the end, contingency access is very idiosyncratic and remains difficult to predict. Consequently, it is prudent for the United States to hedge against access denials by asking multiple nations that have bases that could be used to support the same operations for access. This reduces the leverage that any one state has in this situation and improves the probability that at least one country will respond positively.

Final Thoughts

A small number of incidents, in particular, Turkey's refusal to allow U.S. ground forces on its territory for the 2003 invasion of Iraq and Kyrgyzstan's decision to expel U.S. forces from Manas Air Base, appear to have had an oversized influence on thinking about access problems. Prominent recent examples have led observers to conclude that the U.S. overseas military presence is politically unsustainable. It is important to put these events in a broader context. Peacetime access challenges have significantly declined since the end of the Cold War. Although access challenges continue to occur periodically, the United States has maintained a global network of overseas bases for nearly 70 years, which is unprecedented in modern times. This network has steadily shrunk from its peak in the late 1950s, but the decision to downsize has often been voluntary. Moreover, many countries welcome the presence of U.S. forces because of the security they offer or because they boost the local economy. Equally important, when the United States has formally asked for access to foreign territory for a particular operation, it has been fully granted an astonishing 90 percent of the time. Like peacetime access challenges, contingency access denials and restrictions have become less common since the end of the Cold War.

In sum, history demonstrates that these threats to access have been overstated. Between 1945 and 2014, both peacetime and contingency access problems were persistent but largely manageable. This conclusion should not, however, create complacency: Access to foreign bases can never be assured.

Moreover, a number of trends suggest that access could become a larger problem in the future. The impressive U.S. track record to date is largely due to the Cold War, American hegemony, and the herculean efforts of American policymakers to build and sustain relationships. Today, there is no longer any single, overriding, and unambiguous global threat akin to the one the Soviet Union presented during the Cold War, which makes securing access more difficult. Additionally, there is often a mismatch between the U.S. desire for flexible basing agreements that can be used for a variety of global operations and the desires of host nations, which involve U.S. assistance with specific and geographically discrete challenges. If America's power were to decline in the future, obtaining and preserving access is likely to become even more challenging because the United States may be seen as a less capable and therefore less desirable security partner and because American policymakers will have fewer carrots to offer to incentivize cooperation. Finally, new information and communication technologies make it even more difficult for the United States and a supportive host government to conceal a U.S. military presence or contain antibase movements. All these factors suggest that access will remain a recurring and perhaps even a growing problem in the coming years.

While it is important not to exaggerate the risks to access, the United States must also be mindful that access is never guaranteed and that changes in the international system are likely to complicate efforts to secure and maintain access in the future. Therefore, U.S. policymakers must be aware of these risks and must also continue to endeavor to create a sustainable posture into the future.

APPENDIX A

Peacetime Access Challenges

Table A.1
Peacetime Access Challenges

| Country | Year | Restrictions | | | | | Eviction | Increased Quid Pro Quo |
		Contraction	Limits on Type	Sovereignty	Duration	Consultation		
France	1954					X		
Libya	1954							X
Panama	1955							X
Portugal	1956							X
Saudi Arabia	1957		X					X
France	1959	X	X					
Morocco	1959	X						
Philippines	1959			X	X	X		
Japan	1960		X	X		X		
Libya	1960							X
Panama	1960			X				
Saudi Arabia	1960	X						
Brazil	1961							X

Table A.1—Continued

| Country | Year | Restrictions | | | | | | Increased Quid Pro Quo |
		Contraction	Limits on Type	Sovereignty	Duration	Consultation	Eviction	
West Indies	1961	X						
Portugal	1962				X			X
Saudi Arabia	1962						X	
Morocco	1963						X	
Spain	1963				X	X		X
Portugal	1964					X		
Libya	1964							X
Panama	1965			X	X			
Philippines	1966				X			
Portugal	1966							X
France	1967						X	
Libya	1967							X
Japan	1969			X		X		
Libya	1969						X	
Pakistan	1969						X	

Table A.1—Continued

Country	Year	Restrictions						Increased Quid Pro Quo
		Contraction	Limits on Type	Sovereignty	Duration	Consultation	Eviction	
Spain	1969				X			X
Turkey	1969					X		
Spain	1970							X
Bahrain	1971							X
Portugal	1971							X
Australia	1974			X				
Iceland	1974	X						
Greece	1974		X					
Portugal	1975					X		
Panama	1975	X						
Thailand	1975						X	
Turkey	1975						X	
Greece	1976	X						X
Spain	1976	X	X					X
Turkey	1976					X		

Table A.1—Continued

Country	Year	Restrictions					Eviction	Increased Quid Pro Quo
		Contraction	Limits on Type	Sovereignty	Duration	Consultation		
Antigua	1977							X
Bahrain	1977	X						
Ethiopia	1977						X	
Panama	1977			X	X			
Turkey	1978			X				
Portugal	1979							X
Barbados	1979						X	
Iran	1979						X	
Philippines	1979	X		X	X			X
Antigua	1980							X
Turkey	1980		X			X		X
Spain	1982					X		X
Greece	1983			X	X			X
Philippines	1983			X		X		X
Portugal	1983			X		X		X

Table A.1—Continued

Country	Year	Contraction	Limits on Type	Sovereignty	Duration	Consultation	Eviction	Increased Quid Pro Quo
				Restrictions				
Bahamas	1984							X
Iceland	1984		X			X		
Oman	1985					X		
Spain	1985	X						
Greenland	1986	X						
Philippines	1987		X					
Turkey	1987							X
Philippines	1988				X			X
Spain	1988	X						
Greece	1990	X						X
Philippines	1991	X						X
Philippines	1992						X	
Italy	1995			X		X		
Japan	1996	X						
Saudi Arabia	1996	X						

Table A.1—Continued

| Country | Year | Restrictions | | | | | | Increased Quid Pro Quo |
		Contraction	Limits on Type	Sovereignty	Duration	Consultation	Eviction	
Panama	1999						X	
ROK	2000			X				
ROK	2002							
Uzbekistan	2002							X
Saudi Arabia	2003						X	
ROK	2004	X						
Turkey	2004		X					
Uzbekistan	2005		X					X
Uzbekistan	2005						X	
Japan	2006	X						
Kyrgyzstan	2009							X
Iraq	2011						X	
Japan	2012	X						
Thailand	2012		X					
Thailand	2012		X					

Table A.1—Continued

Country	Year	Contraction	Limits on Type	Sovereignty	Duration	Consultation	Eviction	Increased Quid Pro Quo
				Restrictions				
Djibouti	2013							X
Djibouti	2014							
Kyrgyzstan	2014						X	

SOURCES: Baker, 2004; Benson, 1981; Emma Chanlett-Avery and Ian E. Rinehart, *The U.S. Military Presence in Okinawa and the Futenma Base Controversy*, Washington, D.C.: Congressional Research Service, August 14, 2014; Sasiwan Chingchit, "After Obama's Visit: the US-Thailand Alliance and China," *Asia-Pacific Bulletin*, No. 189, December 4, 2012; Cooley, 2008; Cooley 2012; Cooley and Spruyt, 2009; Cottrell and Moorer, 1977; Duke, 1989; Zachary A. Goldfarb, "U.S., Djibouti Reach Agreement to Keep Counterterrorism Base in Horn of Africa Nation," *Washington Post*, May 5, 2014; Geoffrey F. Gresh, *Gulf Security and the U.S. Military: Regime Survival and the Politics of Basing*, Palo Alto, Calif.: Stanford University Press, 2015; Grimmett, 1986; Robert E. Harkavy, *Strategic Basing and the Great Powers, 1200–2000*, New York: Routledge, 2007; Linda D. Kozaryn, "U.S. Forces Moving to More Secure Bases in Saudi Arabia," American Forces Press Service, August 1, 1996; Jeffrey A. Lefebvre, *Arms for the Horn: U.S. Security Policy in Ethiopia and Somalia, 1953–1991*, Pittsburgh, Pa.: University of Pittsburgh Press, 1992; Lemmer, 1963; Nash, 1957; Shawn Nickel, "Romania Air Base Replaces Transit Center Manas," press release, U.S. Air Force website, August 22, 2014; Karen Parrish, "Dempsey: U.S.-Thailand Partnership Holds Growth Potential," press release of Defense website, June 5, 2012; Newley Purnell, "U.S. Plans for U-Tapao Airfield Cause Stir," *Wall Street Journal*, June 25, 2012; Randolph, 1986; Sandars, 2000; Sturm, 1969; Craig Whitlock and Greg Miller, "U.S. Moves Drone Fleet from Camp Lemonnier to Ease Djibouti's Saftey Concerns," *Washington Post*, September 24, 2013; and Yeo, 2011.

Contingency Access Methodology and Results

This appendix discusses the methodology and results from the statistical analysis presented in this report in detail. The statistical analysis addressed three interrelated questions: First, what factors affect when unrestricted access is granted? Second, what factors affect the level of access that is granted: unrestricted, restricted, or no access (with a particular focus on the effect of access relationship and operation type)? Third, once the decision to grant access is made, what factors affect the type of access granted?

The appendix will include a discussion of the data we used, followed by a presentation of each of three statistical analyses we conducted: a logit analysis of the correlates associated with unrestricted access, a multinomial logit model to investigate determinants of the level of access granted, and a multinomial logit analysis of factors determining the type of access granted.

Data

The data used in this analysis consisted of an original data set of instances of requests the United States to other nations for contingency access since 1950. The data set includes 1,126 observations. Each access request is coded along a number of dimensions, including the following:

- the start and end date of the associated military operation
- the operation name and operation location

- the operation type (combat, HA, etc.)
- the nation asked for access and the region of that nation
- whether the operation occurred during or after the Cold War
- whether the operation occurred before or after 9/11
- whether the nation asked for access is geographically contiguous with the area of the operation
- whether access was granted or denied
- the type of access granted (combat or nonlethal troops, transit, overflight)
- whether the nation asked for access has permanent U.S. bases
- whether the operation received authorization from an international organization
- the nature of the access relationship between the nation asked for access and the United States (transactional, mutual defense, enduring partnership)
- the Polity IV score of the nation asked for access.[1]

The primary dependent variables of interest for here were whether contingency access was granted and the type of access granted. Other variables included in the data set were used as independent variables to identify important predictors of access request outcomes. Because the majority of variables in the data set are categorical, a full table of descriptive statistics would not be meaningful. Furthermore, many of the relevant cross-tabulations presented earlier in the report highlighted the frequencies of key variables. However, one important note concerns the distribution of the "access granted" variable, which records whether unrestricted, restricted, or no access was granted. As noted in the report, U.S. requests for access have been granted in a large number of cases. Out of 1,126 observations, unrestricted access was granted in 1,014 cases, and restricted access was granted in 57 others. In only 55 cases was access entirely denied. This affects the statistical analysis somewhat; the limited variation in the dependent variable somewhat reduces our confidence in the resulting statistical analysis. That said, as the following discussion will make clear, our statistical analysis does

---

[1]   Polity IV is a data set that assesses the how democratic a nation's political institutions are.

provide insight into some of the factors that appear to make unrestricted access and specific types of access more likely.

Determinants of Unrestricted Access Granted

For the analysis of determinants that affect when the United States
is granted unrestricted access, we used a logit model with a recoded
version of the "access granted" variable as the dependent variable.
We recoded the variable to have only two categories by combining
restricted access cases with the access denied cases. While cases of
restricted access are likely different from complete denials, the advantage of this recoding is that it allowed us to focus solely on factors likely
to encourage unrestricted access, which is the optimal outcome from
the U.S. perspective. The recoding left us with a dichotomous variable
and made a logit regression the most appropriate choice.[2] The results
of a logit model are reported in log odds, so each coefficient provides
information on how much each explanatory variable increases the log
odds of getting a positive outcome (or in this case, the unrestricted
access outcome). The results can also be interpreted in odds ratios,
which report how much more likely a positive outcome is in percentage terms. However, regardless of how they are reported, large positive
coefficients indicate variables that increase the likelihood of the unrestricted access outcome, while negative ones have the opposite effect.[3]
The regression in Table B.1 reports results of the logit analysis in log
odds, but the discussion will emphasize odds ratios, which are easier to
understand intuitively.

Table B.1 highlights the results of the two logit models we used to
asses key determinants of when unrestricted access is granted. Because
of their close correlation, we could not include the variables for perma-

---

[2] Logit models are used with binary response variables that can take on two values, either
"0" or "1." They assume that the conditional mean of the dependent variable follows a Ber-
noulli distribution and then predict the likelihood of a positive, or "1," outcome.

[3] For more on logit models, see William N. Greene, *Econometric Analysis*, 5th ed., Upper
Saddle River, N.J.: Prentice-Hall, 2003.

Table B.1
Determinants of Unrestricted Access Granted

	Unrestricted Access Granted, Logit Models	
Covariate	Model 1 Coeff. (t-stat.)	Model 2 Coeff. (t-stat.)
Proximate	−1.137	−0.976
	(4.30)**	(3.72)**
IOauth	−0.210	−0.170
	(1.22)	(0.99)
Coldwar	−1.168	−0.859
	(3.21)**	(2.21)*
Sep-11	−0.049	0.208
	(0.13)	−0.976
Access Relationship		
Transactional		−0.480
		(1.67)^
Mutual Defense		0.279
		(1.03)
Enduring Partners		1.098
		(1.81)^
Perm. Bases	−0.185	
	(0.75)	
OpType Cat. 2[a]	−1.518	−1.562
	(2.42)*	(2.51)*
OpType Cat. 3	−1.865	−1.833
	(3.09)**	(3.07)**
OpType Cat. 4	−2.310	−2.357
	(4.21)**	(4.32)**
OpType Cat. 5	−3.601	−3.551
	(5.25)**	(5.19)**
Europe[b]	−1.083	−1.120
	(3.26)**	(3.49)**
Southwest Asia (Nation)	−0.867	−0.778
	(2.26)*	(2.17)*

Table B.1—Continued

	Unrestricted Access Granted, Logit Models	
Covariate	Model 1 Coeff. (t-stat.)	Model 2 Coeff. (t-stat.)
Southwest Asia (Operation)	−1.248	−1.190
	(4.67)**	(4.51)**
_cons	7.029	6.513
	(8.36)**	(7.91)**
N	1,123	1,123
Prob > chi2	0.00	0.00

NOTE: ^ $p < 0.10$; * $p < 0.05$; ** $p < 0.01$

[a] Operations Categories: 1: HA/DR, Airlift; 2: Medevac/noncombatant evacuation operation/Rescue; 3: Freedom of Navigation, RAO, PO; 4: Counterterror, counternarcotics, Military Assistance, Show of Force, 5: Combat and Strike

[b] "Nationregion" identifies the region of the nation being asked for access. Controls are included in this regression for Southwest Asia and Europe. 'Opregion' identifies the region where the operation is taking place. A control for Southwest Asia is included in this regression.

nent bases and access relationship in the same model, which is why we chose to run two separate regressions. Note that the statistical results for other covariates are nearly identical in the two specifications. The most noteworthy observation to emerge from these results is that the most important determinants of the decision to grant unrestricted access appear to be the operation type; the access relationship between the United States and the nation asked for access; and, to some extent, the region of the operation and nation being asked for access. The proximate variable and Cold War indicator are also statistically significant. However, the variables for international organization authorization, 9/11, and permanent bases do not appear significant. Also not significant was the Polity IV score, a measure of the level of democracy of the nation asked for access. Several iterations of this variable were explored, but none proved to be significant. Ultimately, we did not include this variable in the final model.

Turning to more detailed discussion of the variables that do affect access decisions,

- Proximity to the operation location appears to have a negative effect. Countries that are contiguous with the country where the operation is occurring are about 40 percent as likely to grant unrestricted access as countries that are not contiguous.
- The granting of unrestricted access is about 40 percent as likely after the Cold War.
- Access relationship is weakly significant but has a sizable effect for transactional relationships and enduring partnerships. Transactional partners are 60 percent as likely to grant unrestricted access as countries with no access relationship, but unrestricted access is about three times as likely among enduring partners as countries with no relationship.
- Operation type does appear to affect the likelihood of access being granted. Access is most likely to be granted for HA/DR operations and less likely for other operation types. Compared with HA/DR operations, medevac, noncombatant evacuation operations, and rescue operations are about 21 percent as likely; freedom of navigation, restricted access operation, and peacekeeping operations are 16 percent as likely; counterterror, counternarcotic, military assistance, and show-of-force operations are 10 percent as likely; and combat and strike operations are 3 percent as likely to receive unrestricted access.
- Finally, including all the regional variables in the model created too much noise in the data to be useful. Furthermore, the majority of the regional variables failed to reach statistical significance. However, there were a few regional variables that we chose to include because of their consistent significance and also to test some additional hypotheses. First, unrestricted access is less likely to be granted when the nation being asked for access is in Southwest Asia (30 percent as likely as other regions) and Europe (about half as likely) and when the operation is in Southwest Asia (30 percent as likely). The fact that access has been less likely to be granted by countries in Southwest Asia and for opera-

tions in this region is not surprising, given the unpopularity of U.S. military operations in the region since the Iraq War. The fact that European countries are less likely to grant access is more surprising. However, a further investigation of the data suggests that this result may be driven by the fact that Europe has, by far, received the greatest number of access requests and granted the greatest number of access requests. It is true that Europe also has made more refusals and a higher percentage of refusals than other regions but has by no means been uncooperative when it comes to granting requests for contingency access.

Determinants of Level of Access Granted: Investigation of Operation Type and Access Relationship

Two of the most significant determinants of the likelihood of unrestricted access being granted, according to our results, are the type of access relationship and the type of operation. To further investigate these results, we conducted additional analysis of these two variables and their effect on the level of access granted. For this analysis, we made two changes. First, we used the full access granted variable, including all three outcomes (unrestricted, restricted, and no access). Second, for the investigation of the effect of operation type, we broke down operation type into a more finely grained set of categories and included the specific categories that were consistent and significant across test specifications.

For this analysis, our dependent variable was a categorical variable with three possible outcomes. This required a different type of model, specifically, a multinomial logit model. The multinomial logit model is similar to the logit model in that it predicts the probability of different outcomes when the dependent variable takes on a set of categorical values. The model takes one of the outcomes as the "base case," and the statistical results provide information on which independent variables make the other outcomes more or less likely than the base outcome.[4] For the purpose of the analysis discussed in this section, "no access granted" is used as the base case, so the results provide information on whether specific covariates make unrestricted access or restricted access more likely than no access being granted. Comparisons between the unrestricted and restricted access categories can also be made, by considering relative effects. Interpreting the results from the regression tables of these models is somewhat difficult. The coefficients are most useful for identifying which covariates are significant and for determining the relative magnitude and direction of the effect of each covariate. To get a better sense of how each covariate affects the likelihood of each outcome, it is useful to compute and compare the predicted probabilities of each outcome at given values of a specific covariate. The following discussion will draw on both the regression table and a table of predicted probabilities.

Access Relationship

Table B.2 shows the regression result using a multinomial logit model to explore the effects of the access relationship on access being granted. These models exclude operation type because the inclusion of operation type and access relationship together in the multinomial model creates significant noise in the data because of the large number of individual categories created. To address this, we focus here on access relationship. It is worth noting that this decision does not affect the size, direction, or significance of the access relationship variable, which is our primary interest in this case. Table B.3 provides the predicted probabilities of each outcome for each type of access relationship.

The regression table shows that the only variables that affect the likelihood of unrestricted or restricted access being granted relative to the base case are the access relationship and several regional controls. However, the access relationship variable is only significant in explaining unrestricted access and when considering enduring partners. The results suggest that enduring partners are more likely to grant unrestricted access and that unrestricted access is less likely with transac-

---

[4] For more information on the details of multinomial logit models, see Greene, 1993, pp. 720–723.

Table B.2
Effect of Access Relationship on Level of Access Granted

	Model 3: Multinomial Logit Model, Restricted and Unrestricted Access Granted *Investigating Access Relationships*	
	Base Case (no access)	**Coeff. (t-stat.)**
Unrestricted access granted	Proximate	−0.632
		(1.73)
	IOauth	−0.323
		(1.40)
	Coldwar	−0.364
		(0.99)
	Sep-11	0.025
		(0.05)
	Access Relatnship	
	Transactional Reltn	−0.515
		(1.40)
	Mutual Defense	0.274
		(0.68)
	Enduring Partners	1.995
		(1.90)^
	Europe[a]	−2.137
		(4.06)**
	Southwest Asia (Nation)	−1.281
		(2.22)*
	Southwest Asia (Operation)	−1.681
		(4.71)**
	_cons	5.730
		(8.08)**
Restricted access	Proximate	−0.012
		(0.02)
	IOauth	0.308
		(1.06)
	Coldwar	−0.604
		(1.23)

Table B.2—Continued

Model 3: Multinomial Logit Model, Restricted and Unrestricted Access Granted
Investigating Access Relationships

	Base Case (no access)	Coeff. (t-stat.)
Sep-11		0.532
		(0.84)
Access Relatnship		0.000
Transactional Reltn		0.290
		(0.62)
Mutual Defense		0.276
		(0.54)
Enduring Partners		1.361
		(1.10)
Europea		−1.935
		(3.11)**
Southwest Asia (Nation)		−0.645
		(0.95)
Southwest Asia (Operation)		−0.351
		(0.76)
_cons		1.362
		(1.60)
Prob > chi2		0.00
N		1,123

^ $p < 0.10$; * $p < 0.05$; ** $p < 0.01$

[a] "Nationregion" identifies the region of the nation being asked for access. Controls are included in this regression for Southwest Asia and Europe. "Opregion" identifies the region where the operation is taking place. A control for Southwest Asia is included in this regression.

Table B.3
Access Relationship and Predicted Probabilities

Access Relationship	Effect	P-value	Probabilities
Transactional relationship	Unrestricted access less likely to be granted than with no access relationship	$p = 0.16$, not significant	Pr(RA) if No Special Relationship: 0.05 Pr(RA) if Transactional Relationship: 0.09 Pr(RA) if Mutual Defense: 0.05 Pr(RA) if Enduring Partnership: 0.03
			Pr(AG) if No Special Relationship: 0.90 Pr(AG) if Transactional Relationship: 0.83 Pr(AG) if Mutual Defense: 0.91 Pr(AG) if Enduring Partnership: 0.9
	Restricted access	Not significant	
Mutual defense	Not significant		
Enduring partnership	Unrestricted access more likely than cases with no relationship	$p = 0.06$	
	Restricted access	Not significant	

tional relationships, although the second relationship is not statistically significant. The results do not suggest a significant link between restricted access and the type of access relationship.

Table B.3 provides some additional insight into the effect of access relationship on each outcome by presenting the predicted probabilities of each outcome (unrestricted and restricted access) at the different values of the access relationship variable (0—no relationship, 1—transactional relationship, 2—mutual defense, 3—enduring partnership). First, the probability of unrestricted access is slightly higher with enduring partnerships than in cases with no relationship and in cases of mutual defense relationships. Unrestricted access is least likely with transactional partners, although it is worth noting that the probabilities with all these variables are very similar, so any observed differences are relatively minor, and the effect of access relationship may, in fact, be substantively small. While the results for restricted access were not statistically significant, the predicted probabilities do show some slight differences. Interestingly, restricted access appears most likely with transactional relationships—almost twice as likely as with no relationship or mutual defense and three times as likely as enduring partnerships, which are least likely to grant restricted access (and which we know are more likely to grant unrestricted access). However, these restricted access results should be interpreted with caution, given the lack of statistical significance in the regression model.

Operation Type

The next set of analyses focuses on the effect of operation type on the level of access granted, either unrestricted, restricted, or no access. For this analysis, we used a more-disaggregated version of the operation type variable that includes more different types of operations. The results from this variable are somewhat less certain and not as "clean" as those using the aggregated broader operation categories because the greater number of categories results in fewer observations per category which, in turn, can make regression results more uncertain or misleading. The greater number of categories can also result in overspecification which further undermines the value of regression results.[5] However, despite these possible limitations, exploring the relationship between the disaggregated operation types and access request outcomes provided some valuable insight into the types of operations for which unrestricted or restricted access is most likely. This led to the following full list of disaggregated operation types:

- airlift
- counternarcotics
- counterterror
- combat
- DR
- foreign internal defense
- freedom of navigation
- HA
- limited strike
- medevac
- military assistance
- noncombat evacuation operations
- peacekeeping operations
- restricted access operations
- rescue
- show of force.

To avoid the problems noted earlier, our analysis included only some of these operation types. First, we excluded all operation types with fewer than 30 observations (airlift, counternarcotics, counterterror, freedom of navigation, medevac, and restricted access operations). Then we explored the effect of the other operation types, including all remaining types as indicator variables, and then eliminating operation types that were not statistically significant (HA/DR, foreign internal defense, noncombat evacuation, peacekeeping, rescue, and show of force operations). Note that eliminating the nonstatistically signifi-

---

[5] For more on overspecification, see Damodar N. Gujarati, and Dawn C. Porter, "Econometric Modeling: Model Specification and Diagnostic Testing," in Damodar N. Gujarati, and Dawn C. Porter, *Basic Econometrics*, 5th ed., New York: McGraw-Hill Irwin, 2009.

cant operation types did not affect the coefficients on the remaining covariates.

Our final model retained three types of operations: combat, limited strike, and military assistance. Even for this smaller number of operation types, the results using the disaggregated operation types had less associated certainty than did the broader operation categories in the previous analyses. Finally, for this analysis, we included the permanent bases variable and not the access relationship variable. As described earlier, this was due to our concerns about overspecification and the effect on the regression results of including too many covariates. Because we saw in the previous set of analyses that the regression results for other covariates were the same whether access relationship or permanent bases was included, this seemed a justifiable substitution.

Table B.4 shows the regression results for the investigation of operation type. Table B.5 compares the predicted probabilities for the specific operation types included in the regression with the baseline probability of each level of access. What we were most interested in was understanding whether a given type of operation increases or decreases the likelihood of each level of access over the baseline.

The regression results suggest that unrestricted access is less likely to be granted for military assistance operations, limited strike, and combat operations than for the base case. We can observe these effects from the predicted probabilities in Table B.5. For example, the predicted probability of unrestricted access for combat operations is 0.75, which is lower than that for all other types of operations, with an average of 0.92. The results for limited strikes are interesting and warrant additional interpretation. Although the likelihood of access being granted for the limited strike operations is lower than for the baseline, it is worth noting that the regression coefficient is positive. This suggests that limited strike operations are more likely to be in the unrestricted access granted category than the no access granted category. However, this is a result of the small number of limited strike operations in the data set (33). Despite this positive coefficient, the most important thing to note is that limited strikes are much less likely than other operation types to be granted unrestricted access. Other variables that are significant predictors of unrestricted access in this regression are similar

Table B.4
Operation Type and Level of Access Granted

	Model 4: Restricted and Unrestricted Access, Multinomial Logit Model *Investigating Operation Type*	
	Base Case (No Access)	**Coeff. (t-stat.)**
Unrestricted access granted	Proximate	−1.346
		(3.36)**
	IOauth	−0.731
		(3.19)**
	Coldwar	−2.608
		(3.39)**
	Sep-11	−1.152
		(1.87)
	Perm Bases	−0.075
		(0.19)
	Combat	−2.214
		(2.66)**
	Military Assistance	−1.904
		(4.73)**
	Limited Strike	0.504
		(5.72)**
	Europe[a]	−2.232
		(4.07)**
	Southwest Asia (Nation)	−1.337
		(2.10)*
	Southwest Asia (Operation)	−1.587
		(4.23)**
	_cons	4.071
		(4.39)**
Restricted access	Proximate	−0.340
		(0.66)
	IOauth	−0.085
		(0.30)
	Coldwar	−2.214
		(2.53)*

Table B.4—Continued

Model 4: Restricted and Unrestricted Access, Multinomial Logit Model _Investigating Operation Type_	
Base Case (No Access)	**Coeff. (t-stat.)**
Sep-11	−0.630
	(0.78)
Perm Bases	0.354
	(0.72)
Combat	−0.884
	(0.94)
Military Assistance	−0.880
	(1.56)
Limited Strike	0.343
	(2.86)**
Europea	−2.160
	(3.30)**
Southwest Asia (Nation)	−0.621
	(0.84)
Southwest Asia (Operation)	−0.356
	(0.69)
_cons	0.303
	(0.23)
Prob > chi2 0.00	
N	1,123

* $p < 0.05$; ** $p < 0.01$

[a] "Nationregion" identifies the region of the nation being asked for access. Controls are included in this regression for Southwest Asia and Europe. "Opregion" identifies the region where the operation is taking place. A control for Southwest Asia is included in this regression.

to those presented in Table B.1 and as discussed earlier. Contiguity decreases the likelihood of unrestricted access. Unrestricted access was

Table B.5
Operation Type and Level of Access Granted

Operation Type	Effect on Access	Predicted Probabilities
Combat	Unrestricted access less likely than base case	Pr(AG) base: 0.90 Pr(AG) combat: 0.75 $p < 0.05$
	Restricted access slightly more likely than base case according to probabilities, but no statistical significance	Pr(RA) base: 0.05 PR(RA) combat: 0.1
Military assistance	Unrestricted access less likely than base case	Pr(AG) base: 0.90 Pr(AG) MA: 0.77 $p < 0.00$
Limited strike	Unrestricted access less likely than base case	Pr(AG) base: 0.9 Pr(AG) strike: 0.47 $p < 0.00$
	Restricted access slightly more likely than base case	Pr(RA) base: 0.05 Pr(RA) strike: 0.06 $p < 0.01$

more likely after the Cold War than during it. Operations in Southwest Asia and requests made to nations in Europe and Southwest Asia are less likely to be granted. The only unique result is the international organization authorization variable, which also appears to decrease the likelihood of unrestricted access.

Turning to the restricted access category, only the limited strike operation retains its statistical significance and appears to increase the likelihood of restricted access being granted very slightly compared with other operation types. Restricted access also appears more likely for combat operations according to the predicted probabilities, but because the combat variable is not significant in the regression, this result should be considered uncertain and interpreted with caution. In terms of other significant predictors of restricted access being granted, restricted access is more likely than an access denial during the Cold War than after it and less likely than an access denial in Europe compared with other regions.

Type of Access Granted

Our final set of analyses focused on identifying the predictors of the type of access granted. We defined four types of access for this analysis: combat forces, nonlethal forces, transit (stop and refuel en route elsewhere), and overflight. These are ranked according to the degree of access, and only the highest level of access is coded (i.e., if a state provides access to combat forces, it may also for nonlethal forces, as well as permit overflight). For this analysis, excluded the very few cases (6) in which nuclear forces were permitted because having a category with so few observations distorted the regression results. This analysis focused only on the observations in which access was granted. The results will, therefore, tell us which specific covariates determine the type of access granted, once the initial decision to grant access (discussed in the preceding two sections) has been made. It is important to note that the statistical results report the effect of each covariate on the likelihood that a given type of access will be granted, in comparison with the base case, defined in this instance as overflight. However, because of the way the variables are coded, it is worth remembering that a specific covariate making it more likely that access for combat troops is provided does not mean that cases with this covariate are likely to provide access for combat troops and not to provide overflight access. It means that cases with this specific characteristic are more likely to provide access for combat troops and also overflight than to provide only overflight access.

For these analyses, we used the same multinomial logit models as in the preceding section. In this case, our dependent variable had four outcome possibilities, and we used the lowest degree of access (overflight) as our base case. Table B.6 shows the regression results from these analyses, and Table B.7 shows the predicted probabilities of each outcome at different values of key covariates. Once again, there are two models, one that includes permanent bases and one that includes

Table B.6
Determinants of Access Type

Multinomial Logit, Predicting Access Type		Model 5	Model 6
Access Type	Covariate	Coeff. (t-statistic)	Coeff. (t-statistic)
Combat troops	Proximate	0.981	0.660
		(2.05)*	(1.30)
	IOauth	−0.404	−0.477
		(1.31)	(1.59)
	Coldwar	−0.200	−0.396
		(0.38)	(0.76)
	Sep-11	−1.018	−1.083
		(2.34)*	(2.51)*
	Access Relatnship	2.136	
		(6.20)**	
	Perm Bases		3.547
			(5.83)**
	Southwest Asia (Operation)[a]	−2.020	−2.261
		(3.95)**	(4.05)**
	Southwest Asia (Nation)	1.308	1.884
		(2.33)*	(3.34)**
	_cons	1.616	1.958
		(3.18)**	(3.62)**
Nonlethal troops	Proximate	0.461	0.110
		(1.01)	(0.23)
	IOauth	−0.955	−1.046
		(3.38)**	(3.80)**
	Coldwar	0.272	0.204
		(0.54)	(0.41)
	Sep-11	−1.632	−1.737
		(3.96)**	(4.24)**
	Access Relatnship	1.784	
		(5.24)**	
	Perm Bases		2.545
			(4.28)**
	Southwest Asia (Operation)a	−2.503	−2.653

Table B.6—Continued

Multinomial Logit, Predicting Access Type		Model 5	Model 6
Access Type	Covariate	Coeff. (t-statistic)	Coeff. (t-statistic)
		(5.04)**	(4.91)**
	Southwest Asia (Nation)	1.089	1.521
		(2.01)*	(2.84)**
	_cons	3.234	3.648
		(6.87)**	(7.26)**
Transit	Proximate	−2.059	−2.422
		(3.83)**	(4.32)**
	IOauth	−0.152	−0.226
		(0.59)	(0.90)
	Coldwar	1.482	1.594
		(2.62)**	(2.80)**
	Sep-11	−1.008	−1.094
		(1.83)	(1.97)*
	Access Relatnship	1.343	
		(3.86)**	
	Perm Bases		1.641
			(2.71)**
	Southwest Asia (Operation)[a]	−2.528	−2.669
		(4.81)**	(4.68)**
	Southwest Asia (Nation)	1.331	1.559
		(2.20)*	(2.57)*
	_cons	1.768	2.061
		(3.34)**	(3.63)**
Overflight	Base Outcome		
N		1,062	1,062

* $p < 0.05$; ** $p < 0.01$

[a] "Nationregion" identifies the region of the nation being asked for access. Controls are included in this regression for Southwest Asia and Europe. "Opregion" identifies the region where the operation is taking place. A control for Southwest Asia is included in this regression.

Table B.7
Predicted Probabilities of Access Type

Variable	Effect or Relationship	Access Type	Direction and Significance	Predicted Probability of Granted Access
Permanent Bases	More-permissive forms of access are more likely for countries that have permanent bases as compared to those without them. Countries with permanent bases are more likely to provide access for combat or nonlethal troops than to simply allow overflight or transit. The effect of permanent bases is especially strong when considering determinants of access for combat troops. Here, countries with permanent bases are twice as likely to grant access as countries without permanent bases. Permanent bases are less decisive when looking at access for nonlethal troops and transit on their own. However, in all cases, having a permanent base increases the likelihood of higher access types. Also note that more-permissive forms of access are generally more likely than less permissive forms of access.	Combat troops	Likelihood increases with PermBase $p < 0.00$	Pr if PermBase=0: 0.17 Pr if PermBase=1: 0.39
		Nonlethal troops	Likelihood increases with PermBase $p < 0.00$	Pr if PermBase=0: 0.56 Pr if PermBase=1: 0.52
		Transit	Likelihood increases with PermBase $p < 0.00$	Pr if PermBase=0: 0.19 Pr if PermBase=1: 0.09
		Overflight	Base	Pr if PermBase=0: 0.08 Pr if PermBase=1: 0.01

Table B.7—Continued

Variable	Effect or Relationship	Access Type	Direction and Significance	Predicted Probability of Granted Access
Access Relationship	Higher levels of access relationship are associated with greater likelihood of higher levels of access. This is especially true of access for combat troops and, to a lesser extent, nonlethal troops. Deeper access relationships are less likely to grant transit or overflight access, likely because they are asked for and grant more extensive access.	Combat troops	Likelihood increases with Accessrel $p < 0.00$	Pr if AccessRel=0: 0.18 Pr if AccessRel=1: 0.26 Pr if AccessRel=2: 0.35 Pr if AccessRel=3: 0.44
		Nonlethal troops	Likelihood increases with Accessrel $p < 0.00$	Pr if AccessRel=0: 0.54 Pr if AccessRel=1: 0.57 Pr if AccessRel=2: 0.55 Pr if AccessRel=3: 0.50
		Transit	Likelihood increases with Accessrel $p < 0.00$	Pr if AccessRel=0: 0.19 Pr if AccessRel=1: 0.15 Pr if AccessRel=2: 0.1 Pr if AccessRel=3: 0.06
		Overflight	Base	Pr if AccessRel=0: 0.09 Pr if AccessRel=1: 0.02 Pr if AccessRel=2: 0.003 Pr if AccessRel=3: 0.001
Proximate (interpreted using model 5)	The regressions suggest that being proximate to the country of the operation increases the likelihood of higher levels of access. Model 5 suggests that proximity is a factor in predicting access for combat troops, making it more likely. On the other hand, proximity makes transit access less likely (e.g., when the country being asked for access is proximate to the country of the operation, higher levels of access are more likely than transit access).	Combat troops	More likely if proximate $p < 0.00$	Pr if Proximate=0: 0.21 Pr if Proximate=1: 0.35

Contingency Access Methodology and Results 181

Table B.7—Continued

Variable	Effect or Relationship	Access Type	Direction and Significance	Predicted Probability of Granted Access
		Nonlethal troops	Not Significant	
		Transit	Less likely when proximate $p < 0.00$	Pr if Proximate=0: 0.24 Pr if Proximate=1: 0.03
		Overflight	Base	Pr if Proximate=0: 0.05 Pr if Proximate=1: 0.04
Cold War (interpreted using model 6)	This variable is most significant for predicting transit access. It has a positive sign, so this suggests that, compared with the base case, transit access was more likely during the Cold War than after. Investigation of other types of access suggests that, overall, higher levels of access are more likely after the Cold War, while lower forms of access are more likely during it.	Combat troops	More likely after $p < 0.00$	Pr if coldwar=0: 0.35 Pr if coldwar=1: 0.21
		Nonlethal troops	Not Significant	
		Transit	More likely during $p < 0.00$	Pr if coldwar=0: 0.06 Pr if coldwar=1: 0.2
		Overflight	Base	Pr if Proximate=0: 0.05 Pr if Proximate=1: 0.04

Table B.7—Continued

Variable	Effect or Relationship	Access Type	Direction and Significance	Predicted Probability of Granted Access
Sept.11 (evaluated using model 6)	Occurring after Sept. 11 appears to have a negative effect on higher levels of access, particularly for combat and nonlethal troops. Results suggest that higher levels of access were less likely after Sept 11. The variable is only weakly significant for predicting the difference between transit and overflight access.	Combat troops	Less likely after, $p < 0.00$	Pr if Sept. 11=0: 0.33 Pr if Sept. 11=1: 0.25
		Nonlethal troops	Less likely after, $p < 0.00$	Pr if Sept. 11=0: 0.59 Pr if Sept. 11=1: 0.42
		Transit	Less likely after, $p < 0.00$	Pr if Sept. 11=0: 0.16 Pr if Sept. 11=1: 0.13
		Overflight	base	Pr if Sept. 11=0: 0.03 Pr if Sept. 11=1: 0.09
IO Auth (interpreted using model 2)	The results are significant only for predicting access for nonlethal troops. The sign is negative, suggesting that compared with the base case IO authorization makes access for nonlethal troops less likely. This may reflect the types of operation where IO authorization is most often sought.	Combat troops	Not Significant	
		Nonlethal troops	Less likely with IO Auth $p < 0.00$	Pr if IOauth=0: 0.6 Pr if IOauth=1: 0.44
		Transit	Not Significant	

Table B.7—Continued

Variable	Effect or Relationship	Access Type	Direction and Significance	Predicted Probability of Granted Access
		Overflight	Base	Pr if IOauth=0: 0.06 Pr if IOauth=1: 0.04

access relationship.[6] Note that we only consider predicted probabilities for covariates that reach traditional levels of statistical significance. The discussion of the results will proceed variable by variable, incorporating both the regressions and the predicted probabilities.

First, it may be useful to discuss the variables that are not in the final model and why. First, operation type did not show a strong, consistent relationship with the type of access granted. Combined with the access granted results, this suggests that, while the type of operation matters a lot for whether or not access is granted, it matters much less for which type of access is granted. As a result of their weak significance and the noise they insert into the overall regression results, we excluded the operation type variables from the final analysis. However, based on our initial specifications, we observed that HA/DR operations are less likely than other types of operations to receive access for combat troops. Trends in the coefficients for the operation type variables also confirmed that combat operations are less likely than other types of operations to receive access overall and less likely to receive access for nonlethal troops or transit purposes. Most likely, this suggests that combat operations are granted higher levels of access, when they are granted access.

We also observed a lot of noise in the regional variables, both those for the nation in which the operation occurs and those for the region of the nation asked for access. The results were typically not statistically significant and highly sensitive to which specific variables were included. We did include a control for Southwest Asia in the final model but chose to exclude the others. We included this variable because it was significant in the specifications described in previous sections and because it was significant in all early specifications of access type. In general, the results for this variable suggest that it has been harder for the United States to get more-permissive types of access for operations in Southwest Asia than elsewhere but easier to get more-

---

[6]   Access relationship is included in this model as a single variable that takes on values from 0 to 3 in ascending level of strength, rather than as a series of dummy variables as before. This limited the number of covariates in the model. Breaking the variable into dummy variables reduced the stability of results and did not affect the substantive interpretation.

permissive forms of access from countries in Southwest Asia (when they grant access, since they are less likely to do so than other regions according to the results above).

Finally, as in the preceding sections, the democracy variable, which used Polity IV data, was never significant and so was dropped from the model.

Turning to a discussion of the variables that were included and significant in the model, permanent bases appear to be associated with more-permissive forms of access. Countries with permanent bases are more likely to provide access for combat or nonlethal troops than to simply provide transit or overflight. The effect of permanent bases is especially strong when considering determinants of the decision to provide access for combat troops. Here, countries with permanent bases are twice as likely to grant access as countries without permanent bases. Permanent bases are less decisive when looking at access for nonlethal troops and transit on their own. It is also worth noting that more-permissive types of access appear more likely overall than less-permissive forms of access. This observation carries through the analysis of access type.

More-established access relationships are also associated with greater likelihood of more-permissive levels of access. This is especially true of access for combat troops and, to a lesser extent, nonlethal troops. Countries with deeper access relationships are less likely to grant transit or overflight access, likely because they are asked for and grant more-extensive access. Looking at the effect of the access relationship on the likelihood of access for combat troops, the predicted probabilities indicate that mutual defense partners are almost twice as likely to grant access as countries with no formal relationship. Enduring partners are about two-and-one-half times as likely to grant this level of access as countries with no relationship.

The regressions suggest that being proximate to the country of the operation increases the likelihood of higher levels of access. Model 5 in Table B.6 suggests that proximity is a factor in predicting access for combat troops, increasing the predicted probability of this type of access by 14 percent, but not for nonlethal troops. On the other hand, proximity makes transit access only less likely. This reflects the fact that, when the country being asked for access is proximate to the country of the operation, higher levels of access are more likely than transit or overflight alone.

Both the Cold War and 9/11 indicators are also significant in the access type models. Overall, higher levels of access are more likely after the Cold War, while lower forms of access are more likely during it. Access for combat troops, for example, is about 14 percent less likely during the Cold War than after it. In contrast, transit access is 14 percent more likely during the Cold War than afterward. The regressions also suggest that occurring after 9/11 appears to have a negative effect on higher levels of access, particularly access for combat and nonlethal troops. The predicted probabilities show that the likelihood of getting access for combat and nonlethal troops and for transit access are lower after 9/11. This is consistent with the results presented earlier, which suggested that the likelihood of unrestricted access being granted overall was less likely after 9/11 than before.

Finally, the international organization authorization variable is significant only for predicting the likelihood of access for nonlethal troops; even in this case, its effect is rather small and surprisingly negative. This suggests that getting authorization from an international organization actually decreases the likelihood of access for nonlethal troops. This may have something to do with the types of operations that receive support from international organizations or the types of access that are asked for in these cases.

Summary

This appendix has summarized the data and methodology used for the statistical analysis in this report. The analysis was intended to assess factors that affect the levels and types of contingency access granted to the United States in using a data set of access requests since 1950. The appendix also presented the detailed statistical results. The results allow us to return to and answer the three questions introduced at the start of the appendix.

First, what factors affect when unrestricted access is granted? The results suggest that the key factors determining when unrestricted access is granted are operation type and access relationship. Unrestricted access is only 60 percent as likely to be granted by transactional partners as by countries with no access relationship, but unrestricted access is about three times as likely among enduring partners as among countries with no relationship. Operation type also appears to matter for the likelihood of access being granted. Access is most likely to be granted for HA/DR operations and less likely for other operation types. Compared with HA/DR operations, medevac, noncombatant evacuation operations, and rescue operations are about 21 percent as likely; freedom of navigation, restricted access, and peacekeeping operation operations are 16 percent as likely; counterterror, counternarcotic, military assistance, and show of force operations are 10 percent as likely; and combat and strike operations are 3 percent as likely to receive unrestricted access.

Second, what factors affect the level of access that is granted: unrestricted, restricted, or no access (with a particular focus on the effect of access relationship and operation type)? Unrestricted access is more likely for enduring partners but less likely where there is a transactional relationship. Access relationship does not affect the granting of restricted access. The more narrowly defined operation types also appear to be associated with the level of access granted. Restricted access is slightly more likely for combat and limited strike operations than for the baseline case. However, in both cases and for military assistance operations, unrestricted access is less likely than for the baseline.

Third, once the decision to grant access is made, what factors affect the type of access granted? More-permissive forms of access are more likely where there is a stronger access relationship (especially for enduring partnerships), where there are permanent bases, after the Cold War, before 9/11, and when the country asked for access is proximate to the country where the operation takes place. Operation type and location, however, appear less directly related to access type.

Contingency Access Codebook

This section details the variables that were included in the contingency access data set and statistical analysis discussed in Chapter Four and Appendix B. In general, we included three different types of explanatory variables: operational characteristics, contextual characteristics, and partner-nation characteristics. The operational characteristics include noting the name and start and end dates of the operation and the following variables:

- *The location of the operation*, or the countries in which the mission took place, may be correlated with access permissions or denials. It is conceivable that the United States has experienced more problems securing access permissions for operations against some countries than others.
- *The geographic region of the operation* could be associated with access outcomes. The United States could plausibly have encountered greater difficulty securing access for operations in some regions, such as the Middle East, where a U.S. military presence is relatively controversial, than in others where it is not.
- Countries may be more willing to allow the United States to use their territories or airspace for some *types of operations* than others. In particular, it seems possible that requests for access for military operations that are generally noncontroversial and relatively benign, such as HA/DR, are likely to be approved. In contrast,

requests for access for combat or strike operations are more likely to encounter resistance.[1]

The contextual characteristics include the following variables:

- The *Cold War* could have affected the ability of the United States to secure access permissions. In particular, some have argued that obtaining access was easier during the Cold War because of the focus on one global threat and strong alliances. Since the end of the Cold War, the United States has relied on less-formal coalitions of the willing, which are thought to be less dependable, to deal with regional adversaries.[2]
- The *9/11 attacks on the United States* could plausibly have increased the willingness of other countries to support U.S. efforts to combat terrorism by allowing U.S. forces to operate from the other countries' territories or airspace.
- Access may be forthcoming if a particular operation is *authorized by an international organization*, such as the UN or NATO.[3] Conversely, operations that have not been sanctioned by an international organization may be viewed as illegitimate, making it more likely that countries will refuse U.S. requests for access.

The partner-nation characteristics captured in the data set include the following:

- The *nation queried* for access rights. It seems plausible that some nations might be more or less inclined to host U.S. forces than

---

[1]   In the data set, we distinguished between HA, DR, airlift, medevac, noncombatant evacuations, rescue, freedom of navigation, no-fly zones, embargoes, shows of force, counterterrorism, peacekeeping, foreign internal defense, military assistance, limited strikes, and combat operations. For some of the statistical analysis, we used the aggregated set of operation types defined in Appendix B.

[2]   Cote, 2001, p. 17.

[3]   Seyom Brown, *Multilateral Constraints on the Use of Force: A Reassessment*, Carlisle, Pa.: Strategic Studies Institute, March 2006, pp. 8–12.

others. There may, therefore, be a group of nations that frequently provided access, while there may be another set of nations that regularly denied or provided only restricted access to U.S. forces.

- The *region of the nation queried* for access. It is possible that the United States may find it more difficult to obtain access in some regions than others. For instance, one might hypothesize that, because of their cultural affinity with the United States, European states may be more willing to host U.S. forces than countries in other regions, such as Africa or the Middle East, where the United States does not have such ties.

- It is commonly asserted that the United States needs to retain its *permanent bases* overseas to obtain access to these facilities during contingencies. We therefore included a variable that captures whether the United States has large permanent garrisons in a country to see whether that was associated with access permissions and whether countries where the United States does not maintain a permanent peacetime military presence were more likely to deny or restrict U.S. access.[4]

- The primary reason that another nation agrees to provide the United States with peacetime access or the *type of access relationship* has been shown to affect the reliability of steady-state basing rights. Although the decision to provide the United States with access is often multifaceted, the primary factor often falls into one of three categories; from most to least dependable, these are a deep security consensus (enduring partnership), a shared perception of threat (mutual defense), and a desire for material benefits (transactional). We included the type of access relationship to see whether this variable also influences contingency access outcomes.

- A number of studies have highlighted the role that domestic political institutions—or a *nation's regime type*—play in a host nation's

---

[4] Permanent bases are considered to be locations at which the U.S. has facilities that are continuously manned (i.e., not cold or warm facilities), by either permanently based or temporarily deployed forces. This variable therefore includes locations in the Middle East, such as Al-Udeid Air Base in Qatar, which is home to the 379th Air Expeditionary Wing.

propensity to contest U.S. peacetime basing rights.[5] Previously, we argued that consolidated democracies offer more-dependable peacetime access than other nations, that authoritarian states are the least reliable host nations, and that democratizing nations are the ones that fall in between. We included this variable to see whether this relationship also held true for contingency access outcomes. To measure regime type, we used Polity IV scores for each country year included in the data set.

- Finally, a *nation's proximity* to a military operation could potentially influence its willingness to support U.S. forces. For proximity, we coded whether a nation queried for access shared a border with the nation(s) that the operation was being carried out in. Countries closer to an operation might be directly affected by the contingency and therefore more willing to allow U.S. forces to operate from their soil. For instance, a nation that shares a border with a country that has experienced a natural disaster might be dealing with a spillover effects, such as refugees. Conversely, countries that are removed from a contingency might prefer to remain uninvolved.[6]

The final set of codes in the data set includes the dependent variables, that is, whether the nation queried granted or denied the U.S. access request and, if that nation provided U.S. forces with access, the type of access. We included two dependent variables:

- *Access granted* captures the basic access decision, that is, whether a nation agreed to allow U.S. forces to operate in its territory with no stipulations, whether a nation provided restricted or conditional access, or whether a nation rebuffed the U.S. request for access altogether. The variable has three outcomes: no access,

---

[5] Calder, 2007, pp. 112–119; Cooley, 2008, pp. 13–18; Pettyjohn and Vick, 2013, pp. 44–50.

[6] Hypothetically, proximity could cut both ways. For instance, a frontline state may not want to provide U.S. forces with access for combat operations for fear that it could be a target for retaliation, while distant nations may be feel at liberty to support U.S. operations without increasing the risk to themselves.

unrestricted access, and restricted access. *Restricted access* means that the host nation put meaningful limits on the type, size, location, or operation of U.S. forces. For instance, many countries are only willing to permit a small contingent of U.S. forces on their soil. Alternatively, some countries have tried to limit the visibility of a U.S. presence by only allowing U.S. forces to use relatively remote bases or to operate during the night. Both examples would be coded as restricted access.

- The *type of access* is a variable that is coded only after a nation has made the decision to provide the United States with access (either unrestricted or restricted). This variable captures the fact that host nations can provide U.S. forces with different degrees of freedom of action. For instance, a nation may allow any type of U.S. forces on its territory, which is coded as combat forces. Conversely, a nation may limit the United States to stationing nonlethal forces at its bases, or it may only allow U.S. forces to transit through its country or airspace. The type of access variable indicates specifically what type(s) of U.S. forces were permitted, which in turn suggests what type(s) of forces were prohibited.

Abbreviations

CND	Campaign for Nuclear Disarmament
DoD	U.S. Department of Defense
DoS	U.S. Department of State
DR	disaster relief
DRC	Democratic Republic of Congo
FRUS	*Foreign Relations of the United States*
FY	fiscal year
GAO	U.S. General Accounting Office (now U.S. Government Accountability Office)
GCC	Gulf Cooperation Council
HA	humanitarian assistance
MCO	major combat operation
NATO	North Atlantic Treaty Organization
NIMBY	not in my backyard
RAF	Royal Air Force
ROK	Republic of Korea
SOFA	status of forces agreement
TASS	Telegraph Agency of the Soviet Union

UAE	United Arab Emirates
UK	United Kingdom
UN	United Nations
UNSC	United Nations Security Council
USAF	U.S. Air Force
USAFE	U.S. Air Forces in Europe
USN	U.S. Navy

References

Abramowitz, Morton, "The Complexities of American Policymaking on Turkey," in Morton Abramowitz, ed., *Turkey's Transformation and American Policy*, New York: Century Foundation, 2000.

Almog, Oma, *Britain, Israel and the United States, 1955–1958: Beyond Suez*, London: Frank Cass Publishers, 2003.

Aloisi, Silvia, "Italy Says Would Consider Libya No-Fly Zone Request," Reuters, February 28, 2011.

"American Bases in Libya Are Illegal," Moscow, March 2, 1948, tr. in Daily Report, Foreign Radio Broadcasts, FBIS-FRB-48-259, March 3, 1948.

Anrig, Christian F., "The Belgian, Danish, Norwegian, and Dutch Experiences," in Mueller, 2015, pp. 267–307.

Arab League, "The Outcome of the Council of the League of Arab States Meeting at the Ministerial Level in Its Extraordinary Session on the Implications of the Current Events in Libya and the Arab Position," Cairo, March 12, 2011.

"Arab States Oppose Plan for War Bases," Moscow Soviet Near Eastern Service, September 17, 1951, tr. in Daily Report, Foreign Radio Broadcasts, FBIS-FRB-51-186, September 18, 1951.

Baker, Anni P., *American Soldiers Overseas: The Global Military Presence*, Westport, Conn.: Praeger Publishers, 2004.

Barnett, Michael N., *Dialogues in Arab Politics*, New York: Columbia University Press, 1998.

Bellucci, Paolo, and Pierangelo Isernia, "Massacring in Front of a Blind Audience? Italian Public Opinion and Bosnia," in Richard Sobel and Eric Shiraev, eds., *International Public Opinion and the Bosnia Crisis*, Lanham, Md.: Lexington Books, 2003.

Benson, Lawrence R., *USAF Aircraft Basing in Europe, North Africa, and the Middle East, 1945–1980*, Ramstein Air Base, Germany: Office of History, Headquarters U.S. Air Forces in Europe, 1981, Declassified July 20, 2011.

Berteau, David J., Michael J. Green, et al., *U.S. Force Posture Strategy in the Asia Pacific Region: An Independent Assessment*, Washington, D.C.: Center for Strategic and International Studies, August 2012.

Binder, David, "Bonn Is Singled Out," *New York Times*, October 27, 1973.

Blaker, James R., *The United States Overseas Basing: An Anatomy of the Dilemma*, New York: Praeger, 1990.

Bloomfield, Jr., Lincoln P., "Politics and Diplomacy of the Global Defense Posture Review," in Carnes Lord, ed., *Reposturing the Force: U.S. Overseas Presence in the Twenty-First Century*, Newport, R.I.: Naval War College Press, 2006.

"Briefing by Shultz and Weinberger on Strikes Against Libya," *New York Times*, April 15, 1986.

Brisay, Thomas D. Des, *Monograph 5: Fourteen Hours at Koh Tang,"* in A. J. C. Lavalle, ed., *USAF Southeast Asia Monograph Series,* Vol. III, Washington, D.C.: Office of Air Force History, U.S. Air Force, 1985.

Bowie, Christopher J., *The Anti-Access Threat and Theater Air Bases*, Washington, D.C.: Center for Strategic and Budgetary Assessments, 2002.

Boyne, Walter J., "El Dorado Canyon," *Air Force Magazine*, Vol. 82, No. 3, March 1999.

Brzezinski, Zbigniew, "National Security Adviser Provides President Jimmy Carter with Information on the Following World Events: An Update on Soviet Disinformation Propaganda Directed at Discrediting U.S.-Spanish Relations; Status of Brazilian-U.S. Relations; Reports of Rhodesian Raids into Mozambique; Investigation into Cuban Corruptionin Angola," memorandum, September 25, 1978, U.S. Declassified Documents Online, July 16, 2016, Declassified on January 31, 2005, DDRS-300095-i1-3.

Bronson, Rachel, *Thicker Than Oil: America's Uneasy Partnership with Saudi Arabia*, New York: Oxford University Press, 2008.

Brown, Cameron S., "Turkey in the Gulf Wars of 1991 and 2003," *Turkish Studies*, Vol. 8, No. 1, March 2007.

Brown, Jonathan N., "Immovable Positions: Public Acknowledgment and Bargaining in Military Basing Negotiations," *Security Studies*, Vol. 23, No. 2, 2014a.

———, "The Sound of Silence: Power, Secrecy, and International Audiences in U.S. Military Basing Negotiations," *Conflict Management and Peace Science*, Vol. 31, No. 4, 2014b.

Brown, Seyom, *Multilateral Constraints on the Use of Force: A Reassessment*, Carlisle, Pa.: Strategic Studies Institute, March 2006.

Burns, William J., *Economic Aid and American Policy Toward Egypt, 1955–1981*, Albany, N.Y.: State University of New York Press, 1985.

Calder, Kent E., *Embattled Garrisons: Competitive Base Politics and American Globalism*, Princeton, N.J.: Princeton University Press, 2007.

Campaign for Nuclear Disarmament, "The History of CND," web page, undated. As of April 6, 2017:
http://www.cnduk.org/about/item/437

Chanlett-Avery, Emma, and Ian E. Rinehart, *The U.S. Military Presence in Okinawa and the Futenma Base Controversy*, Washington, D.C.: Congressional Research Service, August 14, 2014.

Chingchit, Sasiwan, "After Obama's Visit: the US-Thailand Alliance and China," *Asia-Pacific Bulletin*, No. 189, December 4, 2012.

Chipman, John, ed., *NATO's Southern Allies: Internal and External Challenges*, New York: Routledge, 1988.

Chipman, John, "Allies in the Mediterranean: Legacy of Fragmentation," in John Chipman, ed., *NATO's Southern Allies: Internal and External Challenges*, New York: Routledge, 1988, pp. 62–63.

Chivvis, Christopher S., *Toppling Qaddafi: Libya and the Limits of Liberal Intervention*, New York: Cambridge University Press, 2014.

Chun, Clayton K. S., *The Last Boarding Party: The USMC and the SS Mayaguez 1975*, Oxford, UK: Osprey Publishing, 2011.

Church, George J., David Beckwith, Barrett Seaman, and Christopher Ogden, "Hitting the Source: U.S. Bombers Strike at Libya's Author of Terrorism, Dividing Europe and Threatening a Rash of Retaliations," *Time*, Vol. 127, No. 17, April 28, 1986.

Clarke, Duncan L., and Daniel O'Connor, "U.S. Base Rights Payments After the Cold War," *Orbis*, Vol. 37, No. 3, Summer 1993.

Claude, Jr., Inis L., "Collective Legitimization as a Political Function of the United Nations," *International Organization*, Vol. 20, No. 3, Summer 1966.

Cleaves, Yarrow, "U.S. Military Presence in Germany," in Gerson and Birchard, 1991.

Cliff, Roger, Mark Burles, Michael S. Chase, Derek Eaton, and Kevin L. Pollpeter, *Entering the Dragon's Lair: Chinese Antiaccess Strategies and Their Implications for the United States*, Santa Monica, Calif.: RAND Corporation, MG-524-AF, 2007. As of August 27, 2013:
http://www.rand.org/pubs/monographs/MG524.html

Clinton, William J., "The President's News Conference," The American Presidency Project website, October 7, 1994. As of April 6, 2017:
http://www.presidency.ucsb.edu/ws/?pid=49247

Cooley, Alexander, *Base Politics: Democratic Change and the U.S. Military Overseas*, Ithaca, N.Y.: Cornell University Press, 2008.

————, "Manas Hysteria: Why the United States Can't Keep Buying off Kyrgyz Leaders to Keep Its Vital Air Base Open," *Foreign Policy*, April 12, 2010. As of August 27, 2013:
http://foreignpolicy.com/2010/04/12/manas-hysteria/

————, *Great Games, Local Rules: The New Great Power Contest in Central Asia*, Oxford, UK: Oxford University Press, 2012.

Cooley, Alexander, and Daniel Nexon, "'The Empire Will Compensate You': The Structural Dynamics of the U.S. Overseas Basing Network," *Perspectives on Politics*, Vol. 11, No. 4, December 2013.

Cooley, Alexander, and Hendrik Spruyt, *Contracting States: Sovereign Transfers in International Relations*, Princeton, N.J.: Princeton University Press, 2009.

Cordesman, Anthony H., *The Air Defense War Since Desert Fox: A Short History*, Washington, D.C.: Center for Strategic and International Studies, July 1, 1999.

Cordesman, Anthony H., and Abraham R. Wagner, *The Lessons of Modern War*, Vol. II: *The Iran-Iraq War*, Boulder, Colo.: Westview Press, 1990.

Cosmas, Graham A., *The Joint Chiefs of Staff and the War in Vietnam, 1960–1968*, Part 2, Washington, D.C.: Office of Joint History, Office of the Chairman of the Joint Chiefs of Staff, 2012.

Cote, Jr., Owen R., "Assuring Access and Projecting Power: The Navy in the New Security Environment," paper, Cambridge, Mass.: Massachusetts Institute of Technology, April 2001.

————, *The Future of Naval Aviation*, Cambridge, Mass.: Massachusetts Institute of Technology, February 2006.

Cottrell, Alvin J. and Thomas H. Moorer, *U.S. Overseas Bases: Problems of Projecting American Military Power Abroad*, Washington, D.C.: Center for Strategic and International Studies, Georgetown University, 1977.

Criss, Nur Bilge, "U.S. Forces in Turkey," in Duke and Krieger, 1993.

Cruz de Castro, Renato, "Philippine Defense Policy in the 21st Century: Autonomous Defense or Back to the Alliance," *Pacific Affairs*, Vol. 78, No. 3, Fall 2005.

————, "The US-Philippine Alliance: An Evolving Hedge Against an Emerging China Challenge," *Contemporary Southeast Asia*, Vol. 31, No. 3, December 2009.

Daalder, Ivo H., and Michael E. O'Hanlon, *Winning Ugly: NATO's War to Save Kosovo*, Washington, D.C.: Brookings Institution Press, 2000.

Davis, Bradley S., "The Planning Background," in Robert C. Owen, ed., *Deliberate Force: A Case Study in Effective Air Campaigning*, Maxwell Air Force Base, Ala.: Air University Press, 2000.

Davis, Brian Lee, *Qaddafi, Terrorism, and the Origins of the U.S. Attack on Libya*, New York: Praeger, 1990.

Davis, Lynn E., Stacie L. Pettyjohn, Melanie W. Sisson, Stephen M. Worman, and Michael J. McNerney, *U.S. Overseas Military Presence: What Are the Strategic Choices?* Santa Monica, Calif.: RAND Corporation MG-1211-AF, 2012. As of April 8, 2016:
http://www.rand.org/pubs/monographs/MG1211.html

Desch, Michael C., "Bases for the Future: Military Interests in the Post–Cold War Third World," *Security Studies*, Vol. 2, No. 2, Winter 1992.

Dionne, E. J., "Attack on Libya; Reproaches from Far and Wide; West Europe Generally Critical of U.S.," *New York Times*, April 16, 1986.

DoD—*See* U.S. Department of Defense.

Donfried, Karen, ed., *Kosovo: International Reactions to NATO Air Strikes*, Washington, D.C.: Congressional Research Service, April 21, 1999.

Dougherty, Jill, "How the Media Became One of Putin's Most Powerful Weapons," *The Atlantic*, April 21, 2015.

Dragnich, George S., *The Lebanon Operation of 1958: A Study of the Crisis Role of the Sixth Fleet*, Arlington, Va: Center for Naval Analyses, September 1970.

Drezner, Daniel W., "Regime Proliferation and World Order: Is There Viscosity in Global Governance?" paper presented at McGill University, Montreal, November 2007.

Duke, Simon, *United States Military Forces and Installations in Europe*, Oxford, UK: Oxford University Press, 1989.

Duke, Simon, and Wolfgang Krieger, eds., *U.S. Military Forces in Europe: The Early Years, 1945–1970*, Boulder, Colo.: Westview Press, 1993.

Endicott, Judy G., "Raid on Libya: Operation ELDORADO CANYON," in Warnock, 2000.

Facon, Patrick, "U.S. Forces in France, 1945–1948," in Duke and Krieger, 1993.

Fairchild, Byron R., and Walter S. Poole, *History of the Joint Chiefs of Staff: The Joint Chiefs of Staff and National Policy, Vol. VII, 1957–1960*, Washington, D.C.: Office of Joint History, Office of the Chairman of the Joint Chiefs of Staff, 2000.

Fearon, James D., "Selection Effects and Deterrence," *International Interactions*, Vol. 28, No. 5, 2002.

"Filipinos Demand Dismantling of U.S. Bases," Moscow, December 29, 1964, tr. in Daily Report, Foreign Radio Broadcasts, FBIS-FRB-65-002, January 5, 1965.

Finnemore, Martha, *The Purpose of Intervention: Changing Beliefs About the Use of Force*, Ithaca, N.Y.: Cornell University Press, 2003.

Flynn, Robert James, *Preserving the Hub: United States–Thai Relations During the Vietnam War, 1961–1976*, dissertation, Lexington, Ky.: University of Kentucky, 2001.

Freedman, Lawrence, and Efraim Karsh, *The Gulf Conflict 1990–1991: Diplomacy and War in the New World Order*, Princeton, N.J.: Princeton University Press, 1993.

FRUS—*See* the indicated volume of U.S. Department of State, *Foreign Relations of the United States*.

"Further Report on Possible USSR Retaliation," Moscow World Services, November, 30, 1982, tr. in Daily Report, Soviet Union, FBIS-SOV-82-231, December 1, 1982

Gabbatt, Adam, Mark Tran, Haroon Siddique, and Richard Adams, "Libya Military Action—Friday 18 March," news blog, *Guardian*, March 18, 2011.

Gallis, Paul, "Italy," in Donfried, 1999, p. 5.

GAO—*See* U.S. Government Accounting Office (now U.S. Government Accountability Office).

Gerleman, David J., Jennifer E. Stevens, and Steven A. Hildreth, *Operation Enduring Freedom: Foreign Pledges of Military & Intelligence Support*, Washington, D.C.: Congressional Research Service, October 17, 2001.

"Germany's Libya Contribution: Merkel Cabinet Approves AWACs for Afghanistan," *Spiegel Online International*, March 23, 2011. As of April 25, 2016: http://www.spiegel.de/international/world/germany-s-libya-contribution-merkel-cabinet-approves-awacs-for-afghanistan-a-752709.html

Gerson, Joseph, "The Sun Never Sets," in Gerson and Birchard, 1991.

Gerson, Joseph, and Bruce Birchard, eds., *The Sun Never Sets: Confronting the Network of Foreign U.S. Military Bases*, Boston: South End Press, 1991.

Gertler, Jeremiah, *Operation Odyssey Dawn (Libya): Background and Issues for Congress*, Washington, D.C.: Congressional Research Service, March 28, 2011.

Gertler, Jeremiah, Christopher M. Blanchard, Catherine Dale, and Jennifer K. Elsea, *No Fly Zones: Strategic, Operational, and Legal Considerations for Congress*, Washington, D.C.: Congressional Research Service, May 3, 2013.

Gillem, Mark L., *America Town: Building the Outposts of Empire*, Minneapolis: University of Minnesota Press, 2007.

———, "Homeward Bound: Assessing the Geopolitical Ramifications of Sprawl," in L. Rodrigues and S. Glebov, eds., *Military Bases: Historical Perspectives, Contemporary Challenges*, Washington, D.C.: IOS Press, 2009.

Goldfarb, Zachary A., "U.S., Djibouti Reach Agreement to Keep Counterterrorism Base in Horn of Africa Nation," *Washington Post*, May 5, 2014.

Gonzalez, Miguel, "Spain Sets Own Rules of Engagement for Libya Mission," *El Pais* (English), March 24, 2011.

Gordon, Michael R., "War in the Gulf: The Bombers Saudis Recapture Ghost Town; Allies Bomb New Iraqi Column, New Bases for U.S.," *New York Times*, February 1, 1991.

Grant, Rebecca, "The Short Strange Life of PSAB," *Air Force Magazine*, July 2012.

Gray, Christine, "From Unity to Polarization: International Law and the Use of Force Against Iraq," *European Journal of International Law*, Vol. 13, No. 1, 2002.

"Greece to Let Bases Be Used for NATO Operations in Libya," *Kathimerini* (English), March 18, 2011. As of April 13, 2016: http://www.ekathimerini.com/132594/article/ekathimerini/news/greece-to-let-bases-be-used-for-nato-operations-in-libya

"Greeks March in Protest of U.S. bases," Moscow TASS, July 16, 1985, tr. in Daily Report, Soviet Union, FBIS-SOV-85-137, July 17, 1985.

Greene, William N., *Econometric Analysis*, 5th ed., Upper Saddle River, N.J.: Prentice-Hall, 2003.

Gresh, Geoffrey F., *Gulf Security and the U.S. Military: Regime Survival and the Politics of Basing*, Palo Alto, Calif.: Stanford University Press, 2015.

Grimmett, Richard F., *U.S. Military Installations in NATO's Southern Region*, Washington, D.C.: U.S. Government Printing Office, 1986.

Gujarati, Damodar N., and Dawn C. Porter, "Econometric Modeling: Model Specification and Diagnostic Testing," in Damodar N. Gujarati, and Dawn C. Porter, *Basic Econometrics*, 5th ed., New York: McGraw-Hill Irwin, 2009, pp. 467–522.

Harkavy, Robert E., *Bases Abroad: The Global Foreign Military Presence*, New York: Oxford University Press, 1989.

———, *Strategic Basing and the Great Powers, 1200–2000*, New York: Routledge, 2007.

Havens, Thomas R. H., *Fire Across the Sea: The Vietnam War and Japan, 1965–1975*, Princeton, N.J.: Princeton University Press, 1987.

Haulman, Daniel L., *United States Air Force and Humanitarian Airlift Operations, 1947–1994*, Maxwell Air Force Base, Ala.: Air Force Historical Research Agency, 1998.

———, "Rebellion in the Congo: Operation DRAGON ROUGE," in Warnock, 2000.

———, "Crisis in Southeast Asia: Mayaguez Rescue," in Warnock, 2000, pp. 105–114.

Head, William P., *War from Above the Clouds: B-52 Operations During the Second Indochina War and the Effects of the Air War on Theory and Doctrine*, Maxwell Air Force Base, Ala.: Air University Press, 2002.

Headquarters U.S. Military Assistance Command Vietnam, *B-52 Study*, December 1, 1966.

Heginbotham, Eric, Michael Nixon, Forrest E. Morgan, Jacob Heim, Jeff Hagen, Sheng Li, Jeffrey Engstrom, Martin C. Libicki, Paul DeLuca, David A. Shlapak, David R. Frelinger, Burgess Laird, Kyle Brady, and Lyle J. Morris, *The U.S.-China Military Scorecard: Forces, Geography, and the Evolving Balance of Power, 1996–2017*, Santa Monica, Calif.: RAND Corporation, RR-392-AF, 2015. As of April 6, 2016:
http://www.rand.org/pubs/research_reports/RR392.html

Hensel, Howard M., "Soviet Media Perspectives on the Crisis in Panama, 1987–1990: A Case Study of the Application of Propaganda Techniques," in Howard M. Hensel and Nelson Michaud, eds., *Global Media Perspectives on the Crisis in Panama*, Burlington, Vt.: Ashgate, 2011

Herr, W. Eric, *Operation Vigilant Warrior: Conventional Deterrence Theory, Doctrine, and Practice*, Maxwell Air Force Base, Ala.: School of Advanced Airpower Studies, June 1996.

Horton, Scott, "The Mess at Manas," *Harper's Magazine*, February, 4, 2009.

Hurd, Ian, "Legitimacy, Power, and the Symbolic Life of the UN Security Council," *Global Governance*, Vol. 8, No. 1, January 2002.

"Indian Popular Protests Against Diego Garcia Base Reported," *Moscow TASS*, February 23, 1974tr. in Daily Report, Soviet Union, FBIS-SOV-74-040, February 27, 1974.

"Iranian Shah Tool of U.S. Imperialists," Moscow Soviet Near Eastern Service, June 5, 1960, tr. in Daily Report, Foreign Radio Broadcasts, FBIS-FRB-60-109, June 6, 1960.

"The Iron Lady Stands Alone," *Time*, April 28, 1986, Vol. 127, No. 17.

Iverson, Paul A., "No Peace or Justice: America's Plans to Expand a US Military Base in Vicenza, Italy," *No DalMolin*, March 20, 2007. As of October 24, 2014:
http://www.nodalmolin.it/No-Peace-or-Justice-America-s#.UyH7ZtxL1G4

"Japanese CP Calls for Abolition of U.S. Bases in Japan," Moscow Domestic Service, May 12, 1975, tr. in Daily Report, Soviet Union, FBIS-SOV-75-093, May 13, 1975.

Johnstone, Diana, and Ben Cramer, "The Burdens and the Glory: U.S. Bases in Europe," in Gerson and Birchard, 1991.

Kapsis, James E., "From Desert Storm to *Metal Storm*: How Iraq Has Spoiled US-Turkish Relations," *Current History*, Vol. 104, No. 685, November 2005.

Katzenstein, Peter J., ed., *The Culture of National Security: Norms and Identity in World Politics*, New York: Columbia University Press, 1996.

Keaney, Thomas A., and Eliot A. Cohen, *Revolution in Warfare? Air Power in the Persian Gulf*, Annapolis, Md.: Naval Institute Press, 1995.

Knights, Michael, *Cradle of Conflict: Iraq and the Birth of the Modern U.S. Military,* Annapolis, Md.: Naval Institute Press, 2005.

Kowert, Paul, and Jeffery Legro, "Norms, Identity, and Their Limits: A Theoretical Reprise," in Katzenstein, 1996.

Kozaryn, Linda D., "U.S. Forces Moving to More Secure Bases in Saudi Arabia," American Forces Press Service, August 1, 1996. April 7, 2016: http://archive.defense.gov/news/newsarticle.aspx?id=40755

Krepinevich, Andrew, Barry Watts, and Robert Work, *Meeting the Anti-Access and Area Denial Challenge*, Washington, D.C.: Center for Strategic and Budgetary Assessments, 2003.

Krepinevich, Andrew, and Robert O. Work, *A New Global Defense Posture for the Transoceanic Era*, Washington, D.C.: Center for Strategic and Budgetary Assessments, 2007.

Kreps, Sarah E., "Multilateral Military Interventions: Theory and Practice," *Political Science Quarterly*, Vol. 123, No. 4, Winter 2008.

———, "Elite Consensus as a Determinant of Alliance Cohesion: Why Public Opinion Hardly Matters for NATO-led Operations in Afghanistan," *Foreign Policy Analysis*, Vol. 6, No. 3, July 2010.

Kissinger, Henry, *Years of Upheaval*, Boston: Little, Brown and Company, 1982.

Lake, Jon, *B-52 Stratoforce Units in Operation Desert* Storm, Oxford, UK: Osprey Publishing, 2004.

Lambeth, Benjamin S., *Air Power Against Terror: America's Conduct of Operation Enduring Freedom*, Santa Monica, Calif.: RAND Corporation, MG-166-1-CENTAF, 2005. As of August 27, 2013: http://www.rand.org/pubs/monographs/MG166-1.html

———, *NATO's Air War for Kosovo: A Strategic and Operational Assessment*, Santa Monica, Calif.: RAND Corporation, MR-1365-AF, 2001. As of April 6, 2016: http://www.rand.org/pubs/monograph_reports/MR1365.html

Larrabee, F. Stephen, *Troubled Partnership: U.S.-Turkish Relations in an Era of Global Geopolitical Change,* Santa Monica, Calif.: RAND Corporation, MG-899-AF, 2010. As of April 6, 2016: http://www.rand.org/pubs/monographs/MG899.html

Larrabee, F. Stephen, and Ian O. Lesser, *Turkish Foreign Policy in an Age of Uncertainty*, Santa Monica, Calif.: RAND Corporation, MR-1612-CMEPP, 2003. As of April 6, 2016:
http://www.rand.org/pubs/monograph_reports/MR1612.html

Lefebvre, Jeffrey A., *Arms for the Horn: U.S. Security Policy in Ethiopia and Somalia, 1953–1991*, Pittsburgh, Pa.: University of Pittsburgh Press, 1992.

Leffler, Melvyn P., "The American Conception of National Security and the Beginnings of the Cold War, 1945–48," *American Historical Review*, Vol. 89, No. 2, April 1984.

———, *A Preponderance of Power: National Security, the Truman Administration, and the Cold War*, Palo Alto, Calif.: Stanford University Press, 1993.

Lemmer, George F., *USAF Oversea Bases 1957–1961*, Washington, D.C.: USAF Historical Division Liaison Office, April 1963.

Lesser, Ian O., "Turkey, the United States and the Delusion of Geopolitics," *Survival*, Vol. 48, No. 3, Autumn 2006.

Lewis, Paul, "In Malta, Ties to the West at Issue Again," *New York Times*, May 11, 1987.

Linz, Juan J., and Alfred Stepan, "Toward Consolidated Democracies," *Journal of Democracy*, Vol. 7, No. 2, 1996.

Lipson, Charles, *Reliable Partners: How Democracies Have Made a Separate Peace*, Princeton, N.J.: Princeton University Press, 2003.

Little, Douglas, *American Orientalism: The United States and the Middle East Since 1945*, Chapel Hill, N.C.: University of North Carolina Press, 2008.

Little, Robert D., and Wilhelmine Burch, *Air Operations in the Lebanon Crisis of 1958*, USAF Historical Division Liaison Office, October 1962, declassified February 23, 1982.

Lostumbo, Michael, Michael J. McNerney, Eric Peltz, Derek Eaton, David R. Frelinger, Victoria A. Greenfield, John Halliday, Patrick Mills, Bruce R. Nardulli, Stacie L. Pettyjohn, Jerry M. Sollinger, and Stephen M. Worman, *Overseas Basing of U.S. Military Forces: An Assessment of Relative Costs and Strategic Benefits*, Santa Monica, Calif.: RAND Corporation, RR-201-OSD, 2013. As of August 27, 2013:
http://www.rand.org/pubs/research_reports/RR201.html

Luck, Edward C., "The United States, International Organizations, and the Quest for Legitimacy," in Stewart Patrick and Shepard Forman, eds., *Multilateralism and U.S. Foreign Policy*, Boulder, Colo.: Lynne Rienner Publishers, 2002.

Lundestad, Geir, *The United States and Western Europe Since 1945*, Oxford: Oxford University Press, 2003.

Lutz, Catherine, ed., *The Bases of Empire: The Global Struggle Against U.S. Military Outposts*, London: Pluto Press, 2009.

Lynch, Marc, *Voices of the New Arab Public: Iraq, Al-Jazeera, and Middle East Politics Today*, New York: Columbia University Press, 2006.

Maccauley, Thurston, *History of the 322nd Air Division (MATS): 1 July–December 1964*, Military Air Transport Service, undated.

Marshall, Monty G., *Polity IV Project: Political Regime Characteristics and Transitions, 1800–2013*, Center for Systemic Peace and Societal Systems Research, July 16, 2016.

Martin, David C., and John Walcott, *Best Laid Plans: The Inside Story of America's War Against Terrorism*, New York: Harper and Row Publishers, 1988.

Martin, Lisa L., *Democratic Commitments: Legislatures and International Cooperation*, Princeton, N.J.: Princeton University Press, 2000.

Mason, R. Chuck, *Status of Forces Agreement (SOFA): What Is It, and How Has It Been Utilized?* Washington, D.C.: Congressional Research Service, January 5, 2011.

Migdalovitz, Carol, "Greece," in Donfried, 1999, p. 4.

———, *Iraq: Turkey, the Deployment of U.S. Forces, and Related Issues*, Washington, D.C.: Congressional Research Service, May 2, 2003.

Mills, Patrick, Adam R. Grissom, Jennifer Kavanagh, Leila Mahnad, and Stephen M. Worman, *A Cost Analysis of the U.S. Air Force Overseas Posture: Informing Strategic Choices*, Santa Monica, Calif.: RAND Corporation, RR-150-AF, 2013. As of April 8, 2016:
http://www.rand.org/pubs/research_reports/RR150.html

"Minutes of National Security Council Meeting, Washington, May 13–14, 1975, 10:40 pm–12:25 am," *1969–1976 ebook*, Vol. X, Washington, D.C.: United States Government Printing Office, 2013, document 295.

Molotov, V. M., "Results of the Berlin Conference: Statement by V.M. Molotov, Minister of Foreign Affairs to the U.S.S.R.," *New Supplement*, No. 6, March 16, 1954, Memorial University Libraries Digital Archives Initiative. As of July 16, 2016:
http://collections.mun.ca/PDFs/radical/ResultsOfTheBerlinConference.pdf

Monteleone, Carla, "The Evolution of the Euro-Atlantic Pluralistic Security Community: Impact and Perspectives of the Presence of American Bases in Italy," *Journal of Transatlantic Studies*, Vol. 5, No. 1, 2007.

Montgomery, Evan Braden, "Counterfeit Diplomacy and Mobilization in Democracies," *Security Studies*, Vol. 22, No. 1, 2013.

———, "Contested Primacy in the Western Pacific: China's Rise and the Future of U.S. Power Projection," *International Security*, Vol. 38, No. 4, Spring 2014.

Morgan, Dan, "Western Europe Keeping Out of Middle East Crisis Moves," *Washington Post*, October 26, 1973.

Moroney, Jennifer D. P., Patrick Mills, David T. Orletsky, and David E. Thaler, *Working with Allies and Partners: A Cost-Based Analysis of U.S. Air Force Bases in Europe*, Santa Monica, Calif.: RAND Corporation, TR-1241-AF, 2012. As of April 8, 2016:
http://www.rand.org/pubs/technical_reports/TR1241.html

Morrow, James, D., "Capabilities, Uncertainty, and Resolve: A Limited Information Model of Crisis Bargaining," *American Journal of Political Science*, Vol. 33, No. 4, November 1989.

Mueller, Karl P., ed., *Precision and Purpose: Airpower in the Libyan Civil War*, Santa Monica, Calif.: RAND, RR-676-AF, 2015. As of April 6, 2016:
http://www.rand.org/pubs/research_reports/RR676.html

Nardulli, Bruce R., "The Arab States' Experiences," in Mueller, 2013, p. 313.

Nardulli, Bruce, Walter L. Perry, Bruce R. Pirni, John Gordon, and John G. McGinn, *Disjointed War: Military Operations in Kosovo*, Santa Monica, Calif.: RAND Corporation, MR-1406-A, 2002. As of April 6, 2016:
http://www.rand.org/pubs/monograph_reports/MR1406.html

Nash, Frank, "United States Overseas Military Bases: A Report to the President," December 1957, declassified December 13, 1996.

"NATO Bases in Europe Threaten Peace, Liquidation Demands," Moscow Krasnaya Avezda, March 31, 1974, tr. in Daily Report, Soviet Union, FBIS-SOV74-066, April 4, 1974.

Nickel, Shawn, "Romania Air Base Replaces Transit Center Manas," press release, U.S. Air Force website, August 22, 2014. As of April 7, 2016:
http://www.af.mil/News/ArticleDisplay/tabid/223/Article/494562/romania-air-base-replaces-transit-center-manas.aspx

Odom, Thomas P., *Dragon Operations: Hostage Rescues in the Congo, 1964–1965*, Fort Leavenworth, Kan.: Combat Studies Institute, U.S. Army Command and General Staff College, Leavenworth Papers 14, 1988.

O'Donnell, Guillermo, and Philippe Schmitter, *"Transitions from Authoritarian Rule: Tentative Conclusions About Uncertain Democracies*, Baltimore, Md.: Johns Hopkins University Press, 1986.

"OIC Chief Backs No-Fly Zone Over Libya," Emirates 24/7 News website, March 8, 2011. As of April 6, 2016:
http://www.emirates247.com/news/world/
oic-chief-backs-no-fly-zone-over-libya-2011-03-08-1.365480

Olson, Richard L., *Gulf War Air Power Survey*, Vol. III: *Logistics and Support*, Washington, D.C.: U.S. Government Printing Office, 1993.

"Opposition to Euromissile Deployment Very Serious," Moscow Novoye Vremya, April 10, 1981, tr. in Daily Report, Soviet Union, FBIS-SOV-81-074, April 17, 1981.

Pape, Robert A., "Soft Balancing Against the United States," *International Security*, Vol. 30, No. 1, Summer 2005.

"Paper Questions U.S. Plans for Island Near Oman," Moscow, March 28, 1977, tr. in Daily Report, Soviet Union, FBIS-SOV-77-060, March 29, 1977.

Pargeter, Alison, *Libya the Rise and Fall of Qaddafi*, New Haven, Conn: Yale University Press, 2012.

Parrish, Karen, "Dempsey: U.S.-Thailand Partnership Holds Growth Potential," press release, U.S. Department of Defense website, June 5, 2012. As of April 7, 2016:
http://archive.defense.gov/news/newsarticle.aspx?id=116620

Patchin, Kenneth L., *Flight to Israel: A Historical Documentary of Strategic Airlift to Israel, 14 October–14 November 1973*, Scott Air Force Base, Ill.: Military Airlift Command, April 30, 1974, declassified November 18, 1993.

Pedlow, Gregory W., and Donald E. Welzenbach, *The Central Intelligence Agency and Overhead Reconnaissance: The U-2 and Oxcart Programs*, Washington, D.C.: Central Intelligence Agency, 1992. As of April 7, 2015:
http://www2.gwu.edu/~nsarchiv/NSAEBB/NSAEBB434/

Peters, John E., Stuart Johnson, Nora Bensahel, Timothy Liston, and Traci Williams, *European Contributions to Operation Allied Force*, Santa Monica, Calif.: RAND Corporation, MR-1391-AF, 2001. As of April 6, 2016:
http://www.rand.org/pubs/monograph_reports/MR1391.html

Pettyjohn, Stacie L., *U.S. Global Defense Posture, 1783–2011*, Santa Monica, Calif.: RAND Corporation, MG-1244-AF, 2012. As of August 27, 2013:
http://www.rand.org/pubs/monographs/MG1244.html

———, *The Posture Triangle: A New Framework for U.S. Air Force Presence*, Santa Monica, Calif.: RAND Corporation, RR-402-AF, 2013. As of April 6, 2016:
http://www.rand.org/pubs/research_reports/RR402.html

Pierre, Andrew J., *Coalitions: Building and Maintenance: Gulf War, Kosovo, Afghanistan, War on Terrorism*, Washington, D.C.: Institute for the Study of Diplomacy, Edmund A. Walsh School of Foreign Service, Georgetown University, 2002.

Pollack, Kenneth, *The Threatening Storm: What Every American Needs to Know Before an Invasion in Iraq*, New York: Random House, 2002.

Pomerantsev, Peter, "Russia and the Menace of Unreality," *The Atlantic,* September 9, 2014.

Posen, Barry, "Command of the Commons: The Military Foundations of U.S. Hegemony," *International Security*, Vol. 28, No. 1, Summer 2003.

Prados, Alfred B., *Iraq Challenges and US Responses: March 1991 Through October 2002*, Washington, D.C.: Congressional Research Service, November 20, 2002.

————, *Middle East: Attitudes Toward the United States*, Washington, D.C.: Congressional Research Service, December 31, 2011.

Project AIR FORCE Desert Shield Assessment Team, *Project AIR FORCE Assessment of Operation Desert Shield: The Buildup of Combat Power*, Santa Monica, Calif.: RAND Corporation, MR-356-AF, 1994. As of April 6, 2016: http://www.rand.org/pubs/monograph_reports/MR356.html

Puddington, Arch, *Freedom in the World 2013: Democratic Breakthroughs in the Balance*, Washington, D.C.: Freedom House, 2013.

Purnell, Newley, "U.S. Plans for U-Tapao Airfield Cause Stir," *Wall Street Journal*, June 25, 2012.

Putnam, Robert D., "Diplomacy and Domestic Politics: The Logic of Two-Level Games," *International Organization*, Vol. 42, No. 3, Summer 1988.

"Questions and Answers," Moscow, TASS Radioteletype, May 11, 1960, tr. in Daily Report, Foreign Radio Broadcasts, FBIS-FRB-60-093, May 12, 1960

Randolph, R. Sean, *The United States and Thailand: Alliance Dynamics, 1950–1985*, Berkley, Calif.: Institute of East Asian Studies, University of California, 1986.

"Report on Conditions in Europe Given," July 10, 1950, tr. in Daily Report, Foreign Radio Broadcasts, FBIS-FRB-5-132, July 10, 1950.

Risse-Kappen, Thomas, "Collective Identity in a Democratic Community: The Case of NATO," in Katzenstein, 1996

Robinson, Eugene, "U.S. Halts Attacks on Iraq After Four Days," *Washington Post*, December 20, 1998.

Sandars, Christopher, *America's Overseas Garrisons: The Leasehold Empire*, New York: Oxford University Press, 2000.

Satter, David, *The Last Gasp of Empire: Russia's Attempts to Control the Media in the Former Soviet Republics*, Washington, D.C.: Center for International Media Assistance, National Endowment for Democracy, January 8, 2014.

Schaller, Michael, *Altered States: The United States and Japan Since the Occupation*, New York: Oxford University Press, 1997.

Segawa, Makiko, "Japan Conservatives See China's Hand in Okinawa Anti-Base Movement," Shingetsu News Agency, January 21, 2011.

Shaheen, Kareem, "GCC Wants No-Fly Zone Over Libya," *National UAE*, March 8, 2011.

Shlaim, Avi, "Israel, the Great Powers and the Middle East Crisis of 1958," *Journal of Imperial and Commonwealth History*, Vol. 2, No. 2, May 1999.

Shlapak, David A., John Stillion, Olga Oliker, and Tanya Charlick-Paley, *A Global Access Strategy for the U.S. Air Force*, Santa Monica, Calif.: RAND Corporation, MR-1216-AF, 2002. As of August 27, 2013:
http://www.rand.org/pubs/monograph_reports/MR1216.html

Shulimson, Jack, *Marines in Lebanon 1958*, Washington, D.C.: Historical Branch, G-3 Division, Headquarters, U.S. Marine Corps, 1966.

Shuster, Alvin, "Alert Puzzles Europeans," *New York Times*, October 27, 1973.

Siegel, Adam B., *Basing and Other Constraints on Ground-Based Aviation Contributions to U.S. Contingency Operations*, Arlington, Va.: Center for Naval Analyses, March 1995.

Simich, Laura, "The Corruption of a Community's Economic and Political Life: The Cruise Missile Base in Comiso," in Gerson and Birchard, 1991.

Simma, Bruno, "NATO, the UN and the Use of Force: Legal Aspects," *European Journal of International Law*, Vol. 10, No. 1, 1999.

Solovyov, Dmitry, "U.S. Spies on China from Kyrgyz Base: Russian TV," Reuters, April 5, 2009.

"Soviet Responses to Strengthening West European Defense Noted," Beijing Renmin Ribao, September 13, 1979, tr. in Daily Report, People's Republic of China, FBIS-CHI-79-187, September 25, 1979.

Spiller, Roger J., *"Not War But Like War": The American Intervention in Lebanon*, Fort Leavenworth, Kan.: Combat Studies Institute, U.S. Army Command and General Staff College, Leavenworth Papers 3, 1981.

Stanik, Joseph T., *El Dorado Canyon: Reagan's Undeclared War with Qaddafi*, Annapolis, Md.: Naval Institute Press, 2003.

Stillion, John, and David T. Orletsky, *Airbase Vulnerability to Conventional Cruise-Missile and Ballistic-Missile Attacks: Technology, Scenarios, and U.S. Air Force Responses*, Santa Monica, Calif.: RAND Corporation, MR-1028-AF, 1999. As of April 6, 2016:
http://www.rand.org/pubs/monograph_reports/MR1028.html

St. John, Ronald Bruce, *Libya and the United States, Two Centuries of Strife*, Philadelphia, Pa.: University of Pennsylvania Press, 2002.

Sturm, Thomas, *USAF Overseas Forces and Bases: 1947–1967*, Washington, D.C.: Office of Air Force History, March 1969.

Tanji, Miyume, *Myth, Protest and Struggle in Okinawa*, New York: Routledge, 2006.

Thompson, Alexander, "Coercion Through IOs: The Security Council and the Logic of Information Transmission," *International Organization*, Vol. 60, No. 1, January 2006.

Torres, Stefanie, "General Ham Visits Air Operations Center Responsible for Operation Odyssey Dawn Air Campaign," U.S. Air Forces in Europe, Air Forces Africa website, March 23, 2011. As of Auguts 8, 2016:
http://www.usafe.af.mil/News/Article-Display/Article/254150/general-ham-visits-air-operations-center-responsible-for-operation-odyssey-dawn/

United Nations, Charter of the United Nations, June 26, 1945. As of April 7, 2016:
http://www.un.org/en/documents/charter/

United Nations Security Council, Resolution 1973, 2011. As of Auguts 8, 2016:
http://www.un.org/en/ga/search/view_doc.asp?symbol=S/RES/1973(2011)

U.S. Arms Delivers to Israel Continue, FRG Objects," Moscow TASS, October 25, 1973, tr. in Daily Report, White Book, FBIS-FRB-73-207, October 26, 1973.

"U.S. Bases Abroad Vulnerable to Attack," Moscow, Soviet Home Service, October 14, 1953, tr. in Daily Report, Foreign Radio Broadcasts, FBIS-FRB-53-202, October 15, 1953.

U.S. Department of Defense, *Report of the Quadrennial Defense Review*, Washington, D.C.: U.S. Department of Defense, May 1997.

———, *Kosovo/Operation Allied Force After-Action Report*, Washington, D.C., January 31, 2000.

———, *Quadrennial Defense Review Report*, Washington, D.C., September 30, 2001.

———, *Quadrennial Defense Review Report*, Washington, D.C., February 6, 2006.

———, *Sustaining U.S. Global Leadership: Priorities for 21st Century Defense*, Washington, D.C., January 2012, pp. 4–5

U.S. Department of State, *Foreign Relations of the United States 1958–1960*, Vol. XI: *Lebanon and Jordan*, Washington, D.C.: U.S. Government Printing Office, 1992.

———, *Foreign Relations of the United States 1958–1960*, Vol. XII: *Near East Region; Iraq; Iran; Arabian Peninsula*, Washington, D.C.: U.S. Government Printing Office, 1992.

———, *Foreign Relations of the United States 1958–1960*, Vol. XIII: *Arab-Israeli Dispute; United Arab Republic; North Africa*, Washington, D.C.: U.S. Government Printing Office, 1992.

———, *Foreign Relations of the United States 1961–1963*, Vol. XVII: *Near East*, Washington, D.C.: U.S. Government Printing Office, 1994.

———, *Foreign Relations of the United States 1964–1968*, Vol. XXVI: *Indonesia; Malaysia-Singapore, Phillippines*, Washington, D.C.: U.S. Government Printing Office, 2000.

————, *Foreign Relations of the United States 1964–1968*, Vol. XXIX, Part 2: *Japan*, Washington, D.C.: U.S. Government Printing Office, 2006.

————, *Foreign Relations of the United States 1969–1976* Vol. X: *Vietnam, January 1973–July 1975*, ebook, Washington, D.C.: United States Government Printing Office, 2010.

U.S. General Accounting Office, *Military Damage Claims in Germany: A Growing Burden*, Washington, D.C., October 9, 1980.

————, *Kosovo Air Operations: Combat Aircraft Basing Plans Are Needed in Advance of Future Conflicts*, Washington, D.C., May 2001.

"U.S. Military Subjugates W. Europeans," Moscow Soviet Home Service, December 11, 1951, tr. in Daily Report, Foreign Radio Broadcasts, FBIS-FRB-51-245, December 12, 1951.

"U.S. Policy Built on Foreign Bases," Moscow Soviet European Service, July 9, 1957, tr. in Daily Report, Foreign Radio Broadcasts, FBIS-FRB-57-132, July 10, 1957.

Vallentiny, Edward, *USAF Posture in Thailand, January–December 1967*, Project CHECO Report, HQ PACAF, Directorate, Tactical Evaluation Checo Division, March 25, 1969.

Van Tol, Jan, with Mark Gunzinger, Andrew Krepinevich, and Jim Thomas, *AirSea Battle: A Point-of-Departure Operational Concept*, Washington, D.C.: Center for Strategic and Budgetary Assessments, 2010.

Vick, Alan J., *Air Base Attacks and Defensive Counters: Historical Lessons and Future Challenges*, Santa Monica, Calif.: RAND Corporation, RR-968-AF, 2015. As of April 6, 2016:
http://www.rand.org/pubs/research_reports/RR968.html

Voeten, Erik, "The Political Origins of the UN Security Council's Ability Legitimize the Use of Force," *International Organization*, Vol. 59, No. 3, Summer 2005.

Wagoner, Fred E., *Dragon Rouge: The Rescue of Hostages in the Congo,* Washington, D.C.: National Defense University, 1980.

Walt, Stephen, *The Origins of Alliances*, Ithaca, N.Y.: Cornell University Press, 1987.

————, "Why Alliances Endure or Collapse," *Survival*, Vol. 39, No. 1, 1997.

Walt, Stephen A., *Taming American Power: The Global Response to U.S. Primacy*, New York: W.W. Norton and Company, 2005.

Warnock, Timothy, ed., *Short of War: Major USAF Contingency Operations, 1947–1997*, Washington, D.C.: Air Force History and Museums Program, 2000.

Watson, Jr., George M., "The Mayaguez Rescue," *Air Force Magazine*, July 2009, pp. 68–72.

Weitsman, Patricia A., *Waging War: Alliances, Coalition, and Institutions of Interstate Violence*, Palo Alto, Calif.: Stanford University Press, 2014.

Wetterhan, Ralph, *The Last Battle: The Mayaguez Incident and the End of the Vietnam War*, New York: Plume Group, 2002.

White, Paul K., *Crises After the Storm: An Appraisal of U.S. Air Operations in Iraq Since the Persian Gulf War*, Washington, D.C.: Washington Institute for Near East Policy, 1999.

Whitlock, Craig, "U.S. Considering Ankara's Request to Base Predators in Turkey to Fight a Kurdish Group in Northern Iraq," *Washington Post*, September 10, 2011.

Whitlock, Craig, and Greg Miller, "U.S. Moves Drone Fleet from Camp Lemonnier to Ease Djibouti's Saftey Concerns," *Washington Post*, September 24, 2013.

Wittner, Lawrence S., *The Struggle Against the Bomb*, Vol. 3, Palo Alto, Calif.: Stanford University Press, 2003.

"The Women's Peace Camp," BBC, November 10, 1999.

Woodward, Bob, *Bush at War*, New York: Simon and Schuster, 2003.

"World-Wide U.S. Bases Threaten Peace," Moscow, Soviet Home Service, March 20, 1949, tr. in Daily Report, Foreign Radio Broadcasts, FBIS-FRB-49-053, March 21, 1949.

Yaqub, Salim, *Containing Arab Nationalism: The Eisenhower Doctrine and the Middle East*, Chapel Hill, N.C.: University of North Carolina Press, 2004.

Yeo, Andrew, "Local-National Dynamics and Framing in South Korean Anti-Base Movements," *Kasarinlan: Philippine Journal of Third World* Studies, Vol. 21, No. 2, 2006.

———, "Not in Anyone's Backyard: The Emergence and Identity of a Transnational Anti-Base Network," *International Studies Quarterly*, Vol. 53, 2009.

———, "Anti-Base Movements in South Korea: Comparative Perspective on the Asia Pacific," *The Asia-Pacific Journal: Japan Focus*, June 2010.

———, *Activists, Alliances, and Anti-U.S. Base Protests*, Cambridge, UK: Cambridge University Press, 2011.

Yergin, Daniel, *The Prize: The Epic Quest for Oil, Money and Power*, New York: Free Press, 1991.

Zenko, Micah, *Between Threats and War: U.S. Discrete Military Operations in the Post–Cold War World*, Palo Alto, Calif.: Stanford University Press, 2010.